OWN YOUR FUTURE
AI FOR ALL

ANTARA & WINNIE

Own Your Future - AI for All

http://humanitydrivestechnology.com/

Printed in the United States of America.
ISBN-13: 979-8-9918904-5-8 (Paperback)
            979-8-9918904-7-2 (Hardcover)

CONTENTS

ACKNOWLEDGMENTS

WE ARE PART of a community and ecosystem, to which we acknowledge our thanks.

Antara

To my husband, for your unwavering support and encouragement as I navigate new paths and pursue different journeys. To my parents, who planted the seeds of curiosity and creativity in my childhood and showed me, by example, how to live boldly. And to my sister and dear friends, for always being a sounding board throughout my many endeavors. Thank you all for being a constant source of strength and inspiration.

Winnie

To my husband, Michael, for your unwavering support and endless patience as I embarked on this journey of learning and writing. To my children, Winnie, Michael, and Rosie, for your enthusiasm, curiosity, and constant encouragement throughout the process. And to our beloved goldendoodle, Giuseppe, whose calming presence was a true comfort during the many hours spent at my desk.

Winnie and Antara

With deep gratitude for the friendship that has blossomed into this shared source of inspiration, both for us and, we hope, for many others.

Thank you, Karen Stocz Oemler, for helping us discover our collective voice, and Patricia Rivera, for igniting the spark that set our aspirational butterfly aflame.

INTRODUCTION

WELCOME TO AI FOR ALL—WHERE HUMANITY DRIVES TECHNOLOGY

CONGRATULATIONS! YOU TOOK the first step in staying ahead of the game and surviving and thriving in the world of artificial intelligence (AI). You are choosing to drive the bus rather than being a passenger. You are in it to win it.

AI as a change driver is so radical that it is like looking into a kaleidoscope. The image is confusing, the path to the end is disjointed and, frankly, hard to follow. On the plus side, the image is colorful and has a sense of wonder and fun with a splash of the unknown. And to us, that is what AI is. Like the kaleidoscope, we will need to dissect the complexities of the image to reveal the underlying meaning and help you find a clear pathway between points. There are two ways to look at the unknowns with AI—either with fear or excitement. In this book, we are choosing excitement.

If we were to sum up one lesson that keeps us connected and pushing forward, it is that, when looking ahead, the evolution of technology has always had more unknowns than knowns. If you can replace reluctance with curiosity and resistance with creativity, you take the fear of the unknown and replace it with enthusiasm, eagerness, and zeal!

Figure 0.1. Replace fear of the unknown with
enthusiasm, eagerness, and zeal.

AI is staring us all in the face. It is literally everywhere. And it feels like it came out of nowhere. Well, not really *nowhere*. Of course, since the COVID-19 pandemic, AI has become a hot topic, and it is ubiquitous—on every site, in commercials, talked about in the media, news shows, and beyond. There are predictions that by 2030, about 300 million jobs will be impacted by AI in some way.[1] In addition, it will rock the stock market and create real opportunities.[2]

---

[1] Michelle Toh, "300 Million Jobs Could Be Affected by Latest Wave of AI," CNN, March 29, 2023, https://www.cnn.com/2023/03/29/tech/chatgpt-ai-automation-jobs-impact-intl-hnk/index.html.

[2] Kweilin Ellingrud, Saurabh Sanghvi, Gurneet Singh Dandona, Anu Madgavcar, Michael Chui, Olivia White, and Paige Hasebe, "Generative AI and the Future of Work in America," McKinsey Global Institute, July 26, 2023, https://www.mckinsey.com/mgi/our-research/generative-ai-and-the-future-of-work-in-america.

Get to Know Us

So who are we, and why should you give anything we say credence?

We are Antara and Winnie, two colleagues-turned-friends—probably closer than family now—who basically grew up in corporate America together. Luckily, and sometimes with much sweat and tears, we had a front-row seat to some of the wildest disruptions in the last two decades in society and within some of the biggest companies in the world.

We started our careers at a point in digital history when all companies were scrambling to get online. That meant stable architecture, clean data, and enterprise-wide functional software to feed and enable digital consumer experiences. While retailers were trying to build shopping carts and telephone companies were trying to introduce electronic billing, banks were getting online with access to observing, tracking, and managing money.

Collectively, our roles focused on designing products, managing programs, and creating frameworks to scale innovation globally. To give some examples, we built digital shopping carts, changed how consumers were authenticated online, and supported mergers and acquisitions for Fortune 100 companies. We helped banks manage through the 2008 banking crisis and sunset the businesses that were unable to maintain the fast past of change. We helped banks build their first mobile apps, innovated peer-to-peer payments, and had the opportunity to build our own brands in our own businesses.

Some familiar household names we have worked for or with include Citi, Chase, Capital One, Procter & Gamble, Campbell Soup, PECO, Con-Ed Simon Malls, JCPenney, GE, Motorola, GlaxoSmithKline, Shell Exploration and Production, Avon Products, Burger King, PayPal, Venmo, Apple Pay, Google Pay, and on and on and on.

Basically, we have been around the proverbial block.

What was the show like? We tend to work with a couple of hundred people every year who design and build systems that count money, move money, deposit money, lend money . . . well, you get the point. We have been at it for twenty-five years. So, if an average human year of work in hours is two thousand hours when we add up all the work we were lucky to participate in, which includes the hundred-plus folks we work with year over year, then it adds up to . . . wait for it . . . 10 million hours of collective learning, which in turn equates to 1,141 years of continuous learning. That is the show we have been watching and participating in. We had our eyes open and paid attention. We learned how to quickly adapt, grow, and course-correct when needed. We learned not to be afraid when things become dicey or challenging. The challenges gave us the most memorable lessons as well as opportunities to build some of the best products and platforms in the marketplace. This is what we bring to the table.

So now you know a little bit about us. But why are we writing a book on AI?

As the world was waking up to AI while coming out of the COVID-19 pandemic, we were too. We have been friends for a long time and often discuss what is happening in the world, our jobs, and so forth, and what we should do about it. The pace at which AI is evolving made it impossible to ignore, and we knew it was time to get in the driver's seat. We also recognize that there is a learning curve to this type of change, which is promising to be larger than all other transformative, disruptive changes we have experienced together or separately.

So we started researching, reading, writing, and sharing, and this is where our combined curiosity and creative genes came into play.

Our research led to three "Aha" moments that got us to this book.

- Aha moment # 1—AI is a mystery to many, but it really isn't that hard.
- Aha moment # 2—by 2030, around 300 million jobs may change, and we know we are in the impact zone.
- Aha moment # 3—This isn't about tech. AI is about how humanity drives technology.

The Aha moments triggered a set of actions and reactions in both of us. First, we knew we needed to get enlightened and educated. We recognized that we needed to assess our own thinking when it comes to transformation change and understand where a pivot in thinking may be required. The more we learned, the more we knew we needed to share our knowledge with others.

Book Structure

We know we can self-solve, and if we can solve a problem, we can scale the solution for others. So we wrote a book. The book evolved into four parts that are designed to help you learn and plot your path forward.

- Part 1 (chapters 1, 2, and 3) is all about building your foundation. *Axis* represents all of the surrounding points of reference we need to internalize and build on to embark on an AI journey. We cover the history of AI, introduce new terminology, talk about lessons from the past, discuss how we will iterate to move into the future, and how we will use a North Star to plot the future.
- Part 2 (chapters 4 and 5) is about *Accountability*. It tells you why you need skin in the game and will help you figure out what drives you, what your touchstone is, and what types of choices you can make to pivot in a world being transformed by AI. In chapters 4 and 5, we focus on what you need to personally assess to be successful in driving your own personal and professional outcomes.
- Part 3 (chapters 6, 7, and 8) elaborates on pathways to learn, do, and change. *Approach* highlights what we believe are the AI pillars of choice—play, grow, and disrupt.
- Part 4 (chapters 9 and 10) tells you how to bring it home. *Amplify* encourages you to assess how to move forward, pacing how to embrace the change and how to do so within your own location in an organization or personal sphere.

You will get a mix of history, lessons learned, and self-solving tactics. We also structured each chapter consistently with a purpose in mind. Each chapter starts with an introduction with embedded objectives that help make each concept consumable. Then it moves into the meat of the chapter, which articulates each objective in detail. We summarize each chapter with a "So What?" and then a "Now What?" section. The "So What?" section reinforces the significance of the chapter's content. It drives home each chapter's ideas and articulates why this information matters. The "Now What?" section serves to direct readers toward immediate action after reading the chapter, urging them to apply the knowledge gained. Complimenting the "Now What?" is a series of questions we encourage you to answer. These questions become your personal action plan to apply what you have learned. It acts as a decisive guide, bridging theory with practice by presenting practical exercises, thought-provoking questions, suggested readings, and engaging activities aimed at reinforcing understanding and promoting deeper learning.

Overarching Concepts

Here are a few concepts we will rely on later on in the book:

- **North Star:** The North Star in a company is like a bright guiding light that shows where the company wants to go. It's the main goal that an organization aims for, guiding its mission, vision, and long-term goals. The North Star helps everyone in the company understand what they're working toward and ensures everyone is moving in the same direction. Every chapter is meticulously aligned with the North Star, ensuring that the focus on planning, learning, transforming, and measuring progress all revolves around the central goal of an organization and each individual.
- **Touchstone:** AI touchstones serve as guideposts in our personal learning and growth journey, illuminating key moments where we can scale our understanding and influence. They remind us of the importance of accountability and responsible decision-making as we navigate the evolving landscape of AI in our roles and organizations. By embracing these touchstones, we empower ourselves to grow and adapt, ensuring that our actions contribute positively to the transformation of our workplaces and the wider world.
- **Coordinates:** The concept of organizational coordinates of altitude, latitude, and longitude to anchor *AI for All* in roles and people represents a framework for situating individuals within an organization's ecosystem based on their proficiency, breadth of knowledge, and depth of expertise, as well as their curiosity, creativity, and cadence to lead or embrace change.

Complemented by Axis, the core reference point of today and potential movement for tomorrow, this framework provides a comprehensive roadmap for navigating the evolving landscape of AI and ensuring that everyone finds their place and purpose within it.

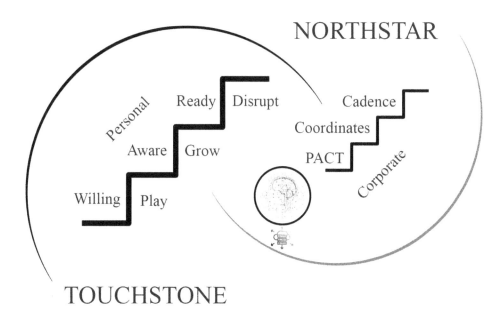

Figure 0.2. Overarching concepts.

- **PACT:** PACT is a method for making AI accessible to everyone, focusing on four key areas: pivot, align, culture, and transform.
  - o **Pivot:** In *AI for All*, a pivot means changing perspectives and strategies to ensure fairness and accessibility. It involves being flexible and open to change so that organizations and individuals can adapt to new challenges and opportunities in the AI world.
  - o **Align:** Alignment is about bringing together different parts of the AI world—like people, technology, and policies—to work toward common goals. It's about breaking

down barriers and building trust to ensure everyone is on the same page.

o **Culture:** Culture is all about the values and behaviors that shape how organizations work. In *AI for All*, it's important to create a culture of inclusivity and transparency where everyone feels empowered and accountable for their actions.

o **Transform:** Finally, transform is about using AI to change the world for the better. It's about using technology to solve problems and make a positive impact on society.

Summary

A key priority is to encourage our readers to take action, learn and do. So, before we jump into the heart of the book, let's level set and take stock of where you are in your AI journey. Take a minute and write down answers to three questions:

1. Do I know about AI?
2. Do I know how AI will impact my life?
3. Do I know how to turn AI into an opportunity?

My "ahas" about AI

Figure 0.3. You can write your answer above in the book so you can keep this as your guide as you move forward in your AI journey.

We will circle back to these questions throughout the book, and we hope your answers shape a positive future for you as you come with us on this journey. At the end of the book, we will ask you these questions again, with the same instructions. The goal is to have a clear line of sight to how you will harness the power of AI.

AXIS

PART 1

ESTABLISHING THE FOUNDATION FOR AI SUCCESS

WELCOME TO AXIS, a section dedicated to unraveling the essential components and far-reaching implications of artificial intelligence (AI). Just as an axis provides stability and direction, these chapters serve as a foundation for understanding and harnessing the power of AI in today's rapidly evolving landscape. The Axis section comprises three chapters aimed at providing readers with a comprehensive understanding of artificial intelligence (AI), its strategic implications for organizations, and gives insights necessary for navigating the AI landscape effectively.

The first chapter, *Unveiling Intelligence: Journeying into the Core of AI*, sets the stage by demystifying AI and exploring its historical evolution. By defining AI and elucidating its fundamental components—algorithms, models, and data—the chapter equips readers with the technical understanding needed to grasp the essence of AI. It also offers a glimpse into the vast opportunities in AI, preparing readers for practical applications discussed in subsequent chapters. By exploring its historical evolution and dissecting its fundamental components—algorithms, models, and data—we lay the groundwork for a deeper understanding of AI's capabilities and potential applications. Through this exploration, readers will gain invaluable insights into the building blocks of AI and the pivotal role they play in reshaping industries and driving innovation.

In chapter 2, *The Value of the North Star in AI Transformation*, the focus shifts to strategic alignment and the pivotal role of the North Star in guiding organizational direction. This chapter emphasizes the transformative potential of integrating AI into strategic planning, urging leaders to reassess their North Star strategy through an AI lens. By aligning AI transformation goals with the core mission, organizations can drive innovation, foster customer-centricity, and achieve resilience in today's competitive landscape.

Chapter 3, *Measuring what Matters*, delves into the intricacies of evaluating AI investments and measuring success. It highlights the importance of prioritization, learning from past experiences, and understanding evolving consumer behaviors in targeting AI investments effectively. By differentiating AI from traditional technology automation and exploring metrics for success, organizations can identify high-impact areas for AI implementation, drive value generation, and ensure sustainable growth.

In the digital age, understanding the impact of AI is paramount for organizational success. This chapter explores the societal and economic implications of AI across diverse domains, from finance to commerce. By delving into key metrics and measurements, readers will learn how to assess AI's influence and leverage its transformative potential to drive efficiency, profitability, and competitiveness.

Through the Axis section, readers will embark on a journey to navigate the intricate landscape of AI, gaining invaluable insights and practical knowledge to unlock its transformative potential and drive innovation in their organizations. Together, these chapters provide readers with a baseline understanding of AI, its historical context, and its strategic implications for organizations. By equipping readers with the necessary knowledge and insights, the Axis section prepares them to navigate the complexities of AI integration, drive innovation, and harness the transformative power of AI for organizational success.

1

UNVEILING INTELLIGENCE

JOURNEYING INTO THE CORE OF AI

Introduction

OUR PATH TO understanding begins with a retrospective glance at history, tracing the emergence of modern AI. What fuels the anticipation of its profound impact on the future? And, crucially, what comprises AI's essence, destined to catalyze transformative change in the long run?

Knowledge of AI grants us the power to articulate its intricacies. Through dialogue, we not only comprehend but also shape the narrative. In this collective endeavor, humanity drives technology, creating a fusion of familial, communal, and professional realms.

In this chapter, we have a handful of goals. We want to make sure you, as a reader, get up to speed on the history of AI. Where did it start? How has it progressed over the years? We also think it is critical to have an understanding of the language of AI. Shared language allows us to communicate with one another, bridges gaps in our collective understanding, and fuels collaboration. To that end, we also have taken key concepts and described them in a way that is consumable for all of our readers. Our objectives for this chapter are as follows:

1. We will explore the history of AI and the important developments of the twentieth and twenty-first centuries.

2. You'll learn the basic language and concepts of AI for better understanding.
3. We will review some of the hardware and software basics and terminology.

We want this to be so simple that once you read it, you will immediately say, "I get it."

You may feel behind in AI now, but once you are familiar with the concepts and are having fun, you will believe that tomorrow offers boundless potential.

History: How Did the World of AI Evolve?

In order to understand where we are going with AI, we need to understand where we have been. Like many concepts, AI had humble beginnings that grew from a few curious individuals who had ideas that they wanted to expand upon. Those ideas were shared and challenged and then embraced by others who were curious and creative and looking for ways to improve humanity.

So, What Is AI?

Artificial intelligence (AI) refers to the "ability of a digital computer or computer-controlled robot to perform tasks commonly associated with intelligent beings."[3] These tasks include reasoning, discovering meaning, generalizing, and learning from past experiences. In essence, AI enables computers to simulate human intelligence and problem-solving capabilities, either independently or in conjunction with other technologies.

To simplify, "AI is technology that enables computers and machines to simulate human intelligence and problem-solving capabilities."[4] With

---

[3] B. J. Copeland, "Artificial Intelligence," Britannica, last updated March 25, 2024, https://www.britannica.com/technology/artificial-intelligence.

[4] "What is AI?," IBM, accessed March 27, 2024, https://www.ibm.com/topics/artificial-intelligence.

generative AI, computers can interact with humans using natural language via text or speech.

The exact birth date and time of AI is debated. However, we know it was born at the intersection of computer science and mathematics. It is inherently multidisciplinary. We also know AI has been in existence for over seventy years and has evolved with each decade. AI now permeates various fields, from academia to space exploration and the military, showcasing its versatility and impact. Universities push AI's boundaries; while in space, it aids navigation and data processing. In the military, AI enhances intelligence analysis and strategic planning. Commercially, AI drives innovation, optimizing processes and enriching consumer experiences. Today, AI is more than a concept; it's an integral part of our technological landscape, shaping our present and future endeavors.

The 1950s

The journey of computing began eons ago with rudimentary tools like the abacus and evolved through Charles Babbage's analytical engine and the advent of electronic computers. We believe the concept of AI emerged in the 1950s, with early research focusing on problem-solving and symbolic methods. In fact, there are references to a maze-solving mouse named Theseus, which was part of an early experiment by Claude Shannon, a pioneer in the field of information theory. In 1950, this robotic mouse, designed to navigate through a maze, reflected the integration of basic computing concepts and rudimentary robotics. The mouse was designed to "remember" its path through the maze using telephone relay switches. Researchers applied algorithmic thinking and logic to create a system that could process information and make decisions even in a constrained environment such as the maze. While primitive compared to contemporary AI, this[5] early experiment showcased the potential of utilizing computing principles to enable machines to perform tasks that required problem-solving capabilities, laying the groundwork for the future evolution of artificial intelligence.

Most, however, say that the true birth of AI started at a Dartmouth conference in 1956, where the term *artificial intelligence* was first coined

---

[5]   Daniel Klein, "Mighty Mouse," MIT Technology Review," December 19, 2018, https://www.technologyreview.com/2018/12/19/138508/mighty-mouse/.

by John McCarty. This was actually a summer-long conference focused on investigating "thinking machines."[6] This period saw alternating phases of optimism and reduced interest, known as "AI winters." Yet, today, AI experiences renewed vigor, driven by advances in machine learning and computing power.

The 1960s

Meet Eliza, who, by the way, is older than both of this book's authors by a decade—a groundbreaking chatbot from the 1960s. Created by Joseph Weizenbaum at MIT, Eliza captivated audiences with her ability to engage in natural language conversations. People flocked to interact with her, amazed by her seemingly human-like responses. PCs were in their infancy, so the people who did interact with Eliza were scientists and academics—essentially the "Sheldons of the world" (for *Big Bang Theory* fans).

Eliza's impact extended beyond academia, sparking widespread interest in AI and even inspiring references in popular culture, including the iconic film *2001: A Space Odyssey*. While Eliza's original incarnation may no longer be in use, her legacy continues to inspire innovation in artificial intelligence today, with modern chatbots and virtual assistants owing a debt to her pioneering spirit.

The 1970s

In the vibrant landscape of the 1970s, AI continued its ascent, brimming with remarkable events and characters that shaped its trajectory. At the forefront stood the establishment of the Stanford Artificial Intelligence Laboratory (SAIL) in 1970, helmed by luminaries John McCarthy and Donald Knuth. SAIL swiftly became a melting pot of innovation, drawing brilliant minds and fostering collaborative breakthroughs that pushed the boundaries of AI research.

Meanwhile, across the Atlantic, Alain Colmerauer and Philippe Roussel made waves with the creation of the PROLOG programming

---

6   Coursera staff, "The History of AI: A Timeline of Artificial Intelligence," Coursera, May 16, 2024, https://www.coursera.org/articles/history-of-ai.

language in 1972 at the University of Aix-Marseille. This milestone sparked advancements in symbolic reasoning and logic programming, propelling AI into new realms of exploration.

The era also witnessed the dawn of expert systems, exemplified by MYCIN, crafted by Edward Shortliffe at Stanford. MYCIN's prowess in medical diagnosis showcased AI's potential in specialized domains, laying the groundwork for future applications.

However, not all was smooth sailing. The publication of the Lighthill report in 1973 cast a brief shadow, leading to what is now known as an AI winter—periods when interest in AI research dwindled and funding was reduced.[7] Undeterred, researchers pressed on, delving into rule-based systems and knowledge representation techniques. These methodologies aimed to imbue machines with the ability to comprehend and organize information, setting the stage for monumental strides in the years to come.

Amid this whirlwind of innovation, luminaries like Terry Winograd and Marvin Minsky left indelible marks, with Winograd focusing on natural language understanding and Minsky shaping AI research at MIT. Their contributions, alongside countless others, laid the bedrock for future breakthroughs, paving the way for AI's continued evolution and impact on our world.

The 1980s

AI surged ahead with remarkable progress and the dawn of commercial ventures. Universities remained hotbeds of innovation, highlighted by a captivating moment at Carnegie Mellon where Hans Moravec and his team wowed spectators by guiding a vehicle through a challenging course, showcasing AI's potential in robotics. Meanwhile, MIT's Danny Hillis shook up the scene with the groundbreaking Connection Machine, revolutionizing parallel processing. Not to be outdone, expert systems like R1/XCON from Carnegie Mellon demonstrated AI's knack for complex decision-making. Symbolist and IBM's Deep Thought entered the fray, signaling AI's commercial dawn.

---

[7]   Radhika Wijendra, "AI Winter: Past, Present and Future," Medium, August 11, 2021, https://medium.com/@radhika_wijendra/ai-winter-955874b1f18c.

The 1990s

The 1990s are brimming with pivotal moments that propelled AI into the spotlight. In 1997, IBM's Deep Blue chess computer made history by defeating world chess champion Garry Kasparov, showcasing AI's prowess in strategic decision-making. This event marked a milestone in AI's journey, especially in the realm of gaming.[8]

During this decade, another breakthrough emerged with reinforcement learning algorithms. Led by researchers like Gerald Tesauro at IBM, reinforcement learning revolutionized neural network training methods, pushing AI forward significantly. Neural networks are complex computational models inspired by the human brain's structure. These networks, composed of interconnected artificial neurons organized into layers, excel in tasks like pattern recognition and decision-making. Their impact on AI technology is profound, revolutionizing applications from natural language processing to autonomous vehicles. This innovation paved the way for the evolution of artificial intelligence, introducing techniques that transformed the entire field.

Expert systems continued to evolve, finding increasing integration in industries like healthcare and finance. Systems like MYCIN and CADIAG-IV advanced in capabilities, aiding medical professionals in diagnoses and supporting financial decision-making, respectively.

Amid these transformations, visionary entrepreneurs like Jeff Bezos, Larry Page, Sergey Brin, and Pierre Omidyar reshaped the tech landscape. Bezos revolutionized e-commerce with Amazon, while Page and Brin transformed information retrieval through Google. Omidyar's eBay envisioned a global online marketplace. These innovators not only founded industry giants but also pioneered AI integration, leveraging it to enhance user experiences and drive groundbreaking advancements in recommendation systems and search algorithms. Their collective impact remains a driving force in shaping e-commerce and internet services.

---

[8] Deborah Yao, "25 Years Ago Today: How Deep Blue vs. Kasparov Changed AI Forever," AI Business, May 11, 2022, https://aibusiness.com/ml/25-years-ago-today-how-deep-blue-vs-kasparov-changed-ai-forever

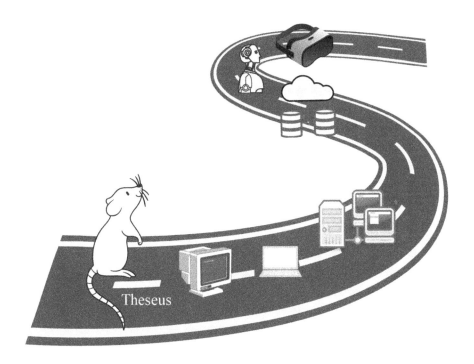

Figure 1.1. The history of AI is a winding path
marked by many important milestones.

The Turn of the Century and Where We Are Today

The 2000s marked a transformative era for AI as it transitioned from a research topic to an integral part of daily life, particularly with the exponential expansion of AI in various corporations. Tech giants like Google, Amazon, and Facebook played pivotal roles, seamlessly integrating AI into their services.

Machine learning (ML) and data analytics took center stage, driving advancements in personalized recommendations and content moderation. These technologies will be defined in the next section. Google refined its search algorithms and introduced groundbreaking features like personalized search results and the knowledge graph. Amazon's recommendation engine evolved significantly, employing deep learning techniques to offer nuanced product suggestions. Facebook employed AI for content moderation, continuously advancing its capabilities to address user safety concerns. In the 2010s, AI became even more deeply integrated into our lives with the emergence of virtual assistants like Siri, Alexa, and Google Assistant. These assistants transformed human interaction with technology, providing convenience and efficiency across various tasks and routines. Additionally, AI made significant strides in areas like healthcare diagnostics, autonomous vehicles, and gaming, showcasing its versatility and potential for societal transformation.

Today, AI showcases sophisticated capabilities in symbolic reasoning, expert systems, and machine learning, overcoming challenges with resilience and continuous innovation. It seamlessly integrates into daily life, influencing interactions and decision-making, while growing ethical awareness emphasizes responsible AI practices. Innovations like OpenAI's GPT-4, IBM Watson's healthcare applications, and advancements in adversarial training techniques demonstrate AI's evolution. The machine learning landscape, driven by models like BERT (Bidirectional Encoder Representations from Transformers), showcases the transformative power of data in applications like predictive analytics in healthcare. BERT is a type of model developed by Google for understanding natural language. It's good at discovering the meanings of words based on the words around them. BERT has been trained on a lot of text data to learn about language, and it can be adjusted to work on different tasks. It's widely used in various language-related tasks because it's very effective.[9]

A common use of algorithms we interact with every day is predictive texting. Predictive text is when you start typing in your messaging application, and words will pop up based on letters you type or words you say. The technology helps suggest words or phrases as you type based on what you've written before and on common language patterns. They learn from how you type and correct mistakes, making it easier and faster to write messages.

---

[9]   Javier Canales Luna, "What Is BERT? An Introduction to BERT Models," DataCamp, Radar AI Edition, November 2023, https://www.datacamp.com/blog/what-is-bert-an-intro-to-bert-models.

AI's ability to understand and interpret visual and auditory data revolutionizes perception, while everyday integration through virtual assistants like Siri and Alexa enhances convenience. Ethical awareness and societal transformation are crucial considerations, ensuring AI's positive impact while addressing challenges. Proactive measures are essential as AI continues to shape a connected, intelligent world with ethical considerations at its core.

Two examples of AI features that are widely used today include voice assistants and search algorithms. Amazon (with Alexa), Apple (with Siri), and Google (with Google Assistant) utilize AI-powered voice assistants. These assistants can perform tasks like answering questions, setting reminders, playing music, controlling smart home devices, and more, all through natural language commands. They make it easier for users to interact with their devices and access information hands-free.

When you use Google to search for information or products, AI algorithms work behind the scenes to deliver relevant and accurate search results. These algorithms consider factors like the relevance of web pages, your location, and the context of your search to provide the most helpful results quickly.

Before we go further, let's define a few key things and name a few more to understand the sum of the parts and the whole.

The Basics

Think of AI as learning a foreign language. For example, when a child learns a language, they hear it from their parents from birth. They are surrounded by it, so it becomes second nature. Now, you have entered grade school or high school, and you are tasked with learning a foreign language. It is not as easy or intuitive because you constantly flex back to your native language and add the step of translation rather than internalization. Learning to use AI is the same, and there are a few concepts we will repeat to help you internalize them.

Here is an example of why the correct terminology matters: Antara was on vacation in the Caribbean islands. She really loves spicy food, and she loves trying new dishes when she's traveling. Not knowing the difference between *caliente* and *picante*, she asked the waitress to make sure her food was caliente. Pleased with herself for flexing her Spanish, she smiled broadly when she received her food. But the food wasn't spicy, so she sent it back, asking the waitstaff to make it more "caliente." A few minutes later, she received scalding hot food.

You see, in Spanish, *picante* and *caliente* can both be translated as "hot," but they are used in different contexts: *Picante* specifically refers to something spicy or hot in terms of flavor, like spicy food. *Caliente* generally means hot in terms of temperature, such as hot water or hot weather. So, while both words can convey the idea of heat, *picante* is more associated with spicy flavor, whereas *caliente* is used for physical temperature. As such, how language is used to frame and describe AI has significant implications on a person's ability to understand the concept, and that is why the language of AI matters.

In AI, there are a few basic terms and functions that, when you invest the time to understand them, help everything become easier. We are not suggesting you become a technologist. What we are suggesting is that when you understand that algorithms, models, and data are not interchangeable and you know the differences between hardware and software, you get what you want when you place your order.

The core components in modern AI encompass algorithms, models, and data, forming the foundational framework for artificial intelligence systems to operate effectively and make informed decisions. After you have finished this section, we want you to have an understanding of algorithms and models and how they use data as a collective.

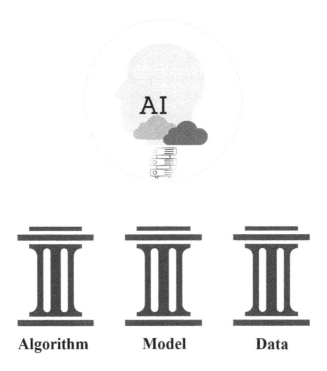

| Algorithm | Model | Data |

Figure 1.2. Algorithms, models, and data all have different functions that contribute to forming the foundational framework for artificial intelligence systems.

Algorithms

In AI, algorithms are like recipes or roadmaps that guide the computer's decision-making processes. They're sets of mathematical instructions that help computers learn and solve problems. They use these mathematical instructions to process data, which is the raw information that AI learns from. Models are the frameworks that organize how algorithms interact with data. They help AI make sense of the data by recognizing patterns, making predictions, and learning from experiences. So, algorithms use models to analyze data, helping AI make informed decisions and predictions.

There are a multitude of types of algorithms used in AI. Take the example of a recommendation algorithm used by streaming platforms like Netflix or Spotify. This algorithm analyzes your past viewing or listening history and the behavior of other users with similar tastes. Based on this data, it suggests new movies, TV shows, or songs that you might enjoy. The same happens with Spotify or Pandora when it comes to music. If you play one artist, similar artists will follow based on what the algorithm thinks you like. If you don't like a suggested song, you can train the model by stopping the song or giving it a thumbs-down. It is unlikely the model will suggest that artist or song in the future.

The way you use an algorithm can be compared to using an elevator button—see figure 1.3. Basically, the algorithm works by identifying patterns in your preferences and predicting what you might like next. This helps personalize your experience, and it keeps you engaged with the platform. The example below illustrates what an algorithm does, which is similar to executing a step-by-step procedure. In the diagram, there is an input, which is when you press the call button. It kicks off a set of instructions to process a series of steps to move the elevator to the right floor and open the doors. This is a simple example of how an algorithm works.

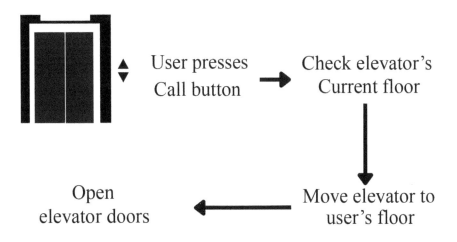

Figure 1.3. An elevator call button is a simple algorithm.

Here are some examples of algorithms:

- Decision trees—act like a flow chart and break a problem into smaller steps with decision points
- Random forests— use many decision trees as opposed to one for improved accuracy
- Support vector machines (SVMs)— help classify data
- Neural networks—imitate the brain's learning
- Clustering algorithms like K-means and hierarchical clustering—group similar data
- Natural language processing (NLP) algorithms —understand, interpret, and generate human language, enhancing AI's human-like interactions and understanding

Models

Models are the blueprints behind AI's decision-making and control mechanisms, defining how AI processes information and makes predictions. Models are like the plans AI uses to make decisions and control its actions. They show how AI thinks about information—just like how humans process data. The models will then train the algorithm so that the algorithm can evolve. This intelligence (model, data, and algorithm) is constantly evolving like an ecosystem, and it doesn't require human intervention.

Let's take a large language model (LLM) as an example of a model used in AI. An LLM is like a giant library filled with books about language rules and patterns. When you ask it a question or give it a task, it searches through these books to find the best answer or solution. It's like having a super-smart librarian who can quickly find the information you need from a vast collection of books.

Here is an example: GPT-3 (Generative Pre-Trained Transformer 3) is the third iteration of OpenAI's language model series. It is massive, with 175 billion parameters and is considered a powerful general-purpose language model. ChatGPT is a variant of GPT-3 and focuses on conversational interactions.[10]

To simplify, imagine a chef who knows every recipe in the world. When you tell the chef what you want to cook, they instantly come up with a recipe using their vast knowledge. Similarly, an LLM like GPT is like that chef but for writing—it knows a ton about language and can generate text on almost any topic you give it. When you give parameters like allergies or taste preference, or constraints like calories (hopefully, we don't have to count calories), then the model will give an optimal choice/decision.

There are many types of models—not just supermodels. Here are a few examples:

- Regression models—analyze relationships between variables to predict outcomes

---

[10]   Sydney Butler, "ChatGPT vs. GPT-3: What's the Difference?" How-to Geek, July 10, 2023, https://www.howtogeek.com/897570/chatgpt-vs.-gpt-3-whats-the-difference/.

- Classification models—categorize data into groups based on specific characteristics
- Neural network models—simulate the brain's structure to process complex data and include feedforward, convolutional, and recurrent networks
- Generative models—create new data that resembles existing examples like generative adversarial networks (GANs)
- Reinforcement learning models—learn through trial and error, receiving rewards for successful actions

Understanding these models sheds light on AI's decision-making processes and its ability to learn, predict, and create.

Data

Data is the backbone of AI, influencing every aspect of its operations. Data are the ingredients in our AI recipe. There are also a number of actions that transpire with data.

Imagine a bustling factory floor where precision machinery hums with activity, producing high-quality automotive parts. These machines are critical assets in the manufacturing process, ensuring seamless production and meeting strict quality standards. However, any unexpected downtime due to machine failure can disrupt the entire production line, leading to costly delays and missed deadlines.

To prevent such disruptions, the factory implements a predictive maintenance system powered by AI. Sensors meticulously placed on each machine continuously gather a wealth of data, including temperature fluctuations, vibration levels, and performance metrics. This data serves as the lifeblood of the AI system, providing valuable insights into the health and condition of the machinery.

As the machines operate, the AI system diligently analyzes the incoming data in real-time, sifting through vast streams of information to detect subtle patterns and anomalies. By leveraging advanced algorithms and machine learning techniques, the AI system can predict with remarkable accuracy when a machine is likely to experience a breakdown or require maintenance.

For example, if the data reveals a slight deviation in vibration patterns or a gradual increase in temperature beyond normal thresholds, the AI system flags these anomalies as potential warning signs of impending issues. This early detection allows maintenance teams to proactively intervene, scheduling repairs or adjustments before the machine malfunctions or grinds to a halt.

In essence, the predictive maintenance system acts as a guardian angel for the factory's machinery, ensuring optimal performance, minimizing downtime, and maximizing productivity. By harnessing the power of AI and data-driven insights, the manufacturing facility can operate with greater efficiency, reliability, and cost-effectiveness, ultimately delivering superior quality products to consumers on time, every time.

When we think of data, there are processes that happen:

- Data collection involves gathering relevant information from various sources.
- Data cleaning and preprocessing refine raw data to ensure accuracy and consistency.
- Feature engineering extracts useful patterns and insights from data for AI algorithms to process effectively.
- Data storage involves organizing and storing data in databases and data warehouses for easy access and retrieval.

Big data technologies like Hadoop and Spark enable the processing of vast amounts of data efficiently. Understanding the role of data in AI is crucial, as it directly impacts decision-making, driving insights, predictions, and actions.

Imagine you are streaming ads in the elevator we discussed in the previous section. The model itself needs the algorithm to tell it what to do. It also needs data to actually create or present output. See figure 1.4.

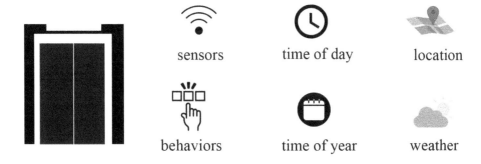

The AI elevator ad system collects data to understand patterns and then trains on this to stream ads to users

Figure 1.4. An advertisement system in the elevator collects data to understand patterns that may appeal to viewers. It is continuously trained on the data to stream relevant ads to elevator riders.

More Explanations that Relate to AI Technology

Not understanding the basics of AI lingo is like being at a party where everyone is speaking a secret language, and you're left feeling like the odd one out who didn't get the memo! It's that sinking feeling when folks start tossing technical terms around, and you're nodding along like you're in on the joke, but secretly, you're Googling acronyms under the table. It's the struggle of trying to decode conversations about AI without feeling like you accidentally stumbled into a sci-fi convention. So, let's ditch the secret handshake of jargon and bring everyone to the cool kids' table of understanding!

At this point, if you feel good about algorithms, models, and data—mission accomplished. That being said, that isn't everything. There is more about the technology that will be helpful either now or in the future. As a point of reference, think back to your own learning path. You may have had a reference that you kept with you as you progressed through your educational journey. In Antara's case, it was *Advanced Level Physics* by Michael Nelkon and Philip Parker. She carried around this book from high school into her college career as a reference book to help build her engineering muscle.

In her early days as project manager, Winnie carried around *The Project Management Body of Knowledge* (PMBOK) guide like it was a bible. Winnie also carried around *Earned Value Project Management* because she needed the constant reference to make sure she was using the content correctly. The point is that as you read the below content, feel free to read it twice or come back to it when you need it, as it may be the best way to internalize the concepts.

AI Hardware

AI hardware refers to specialized components designed for AI tasks. These components, such as graphics processing units (GPUs), tensor processing units (TPUs), and field-programmable gate arrays (FPGAs), are optimized to perform complex computations efficiently.

GPUs excel at handling parallel processing tasks commonly found in deep learning algorithms. TPUs are developed by Google to accelerate machine learning workloads, particularly those related to neural networks. They are specialized in executing matrix operations quickly, which is crucial for many AI algorithms. For example, you likely have a smartphone with a camera. When you take a photo, the AI software inside your phone uses AI-specific hardware, like a GPU, to quickly analyze the image. It can recognize faces, adjust the lighting, and even suggest filters based on what's in the picture. This process happens almost instantly, allowing you to capture better photos without needing to manually edit them. So, the AI hardware helps make your phone's camera smarter and more capable of producing great photos without you having to do much work.

FPGAs offer flexibility in AI hardware design. They allow developers to customize their processing capabilities according to specific AI tasks. This adaptability makes FPGAs suitable for various AI applications, especially those requiring specialized optimizations. Let's say you're in charge of organizing a big event, like a concert or a festival. You have a huge space to set up, and you need different areas for food, entertainment, and seating. Instead of using fixed structures such as traditional buildings, you decide to use tents that can be easily moved and rearranged based on the needs of each event. These tents are like FPGAs in AI hardware—they offer flexibility and can be customized to fit different purposes. So, just as you can adjust the layout of the tents to suit different events, developers can customize FPGAs to optimize AI tasks, making them ideal for various applications.

AI Software

The AI software space is growing fast. AI software refers to computer programs, libraries, frameworks, and algorithms designed to enable AI capabilities. These tools are used to develop, train, deploy, and manage AI models and applications.

Frameworks like TensorFlow and PyTorch provide comprehensive platforms for building and training deep learning models. They offer high-level application programming interfaces (APIs) and abstraction layers that simplify the development process. Additionally, AI software includes natural language processing (NLP) libraries such as NLTK and spaCy, which enable the processing and understanding of human language.

Other AI software tools focus on specific tasks, such as computer vision libraries like OpenCV for image and video analysis or reinforcement learning frameworks like OpenAI Gym for developing AI agents that learn through interaction with environments. Overall, AI hardware and software work together to drive innovation, enabling the development, training, and deployment of cutting-edge AI models across diverse domains.

Pulling It All Together

Let's bake some cookies. Your oven (hardware) provides the heat needed to bake them. You use a recipe (algorithm) to mix ingredients (data) like flour, sugar, and eggs, creating cookie dough (model). To follow the recipe accurately, you might use a kitchen timer (software) to keep track of baking time. When the cookies are done, you can enjoy delicious treats. In this example, the oven, recipe, ingredients, timer, and finished cookies represent the hardware, algorithms, data, software, and models, respectively, forming an ecosystem for cookie baking, just like in AI. Maybe you're not an expert baker, so you need some extra help understanding certain cooking terms or techniques. That's where NLP libraries like NLTK and spaCy come in handy. They're like having a dictionary or cooking encyclopedia right at your fingertips, helping you process and understand the language used in the recipe, making it easier to follow along and create a delicious cookie.

Understanding AI Tech

Scary but true—there is even more about AI tech that bears discussion. It is probably one of the reasons people feel intimidated by the topic. But never fear, we are going to make it easy to understand. If you feel like you drank from the firehose, don't despair; you can skip ahead. If you get to chapter 8, *Disrupt*, pop back and read as you need. If you can power through the next bit, we promise you will get some bragging rights at happy hours and dinners.

AI DevOps is all about streamlining the process of developing and deploying AI and machine learning applications. It uses specialized hardware like GPUs, TPUs, and FPGAs to handle complex computations efficiently. Imagine you're a student preparing for a big exam, and you need to study different subjects efficiently. AI DevOps is like having a customized study plan tailored to learn effectively and excel in your exams.

Continuous integration (CI) ensures that AI code is regularly updated and tested, similar to checking a recipe before baking a cake. Continuous delivery (CD) then makes it easy to send the tested code to different places, like sending a recipe to various kitchens. CI is like having a team of assistants who regularly check your recipe to make sure it's perfect. They review the ingredients, measurements, and instructions to catch any mistakes or improvements needed—just like CI regularly updates and tests AI code. Once your recipe passes the checks, CD steps in to make sure it gets to where it needs to be. It's like having a system in place to send your perfected recipe to different sections of the kitchen in your restaurant. Whether it's the main kitchen, the pastry section, or the catering department, CD ensures that your recipe is delivered accurately and efficiently, ready to be used to bake delicious cakes in various settings.

Version control keeps track of changes in AI code, just like different versions of a recipe. Infrastructure as code (IaC) sets up and manages all the tools and resources needed for AI work, similar to setting up a kitchen with ingredients and utensils. Think of version control as a way to keep track of changes in AI code, kind of like how you keep track of different versions of a recipe— like when you tweak the ingredients or adjust the instructions to make the recipe better. Now, IaC is like setting up and managing everything you need to work on AI projects but in a virtual kitchen. It's like organizing all your ingredients, utensils, and cooking tools neatly in your kitchen before you start baking. With IaC, you can easily set up and manage all the tools and resources required for your AI work, just like setting up a kitchen for cooking.

Automated testing checks the AI code to make sure it works correctly. Monitoring and logging track how the AI system is working, similar to keeping an eye on a baking cake. Imagine automated testing as a way to check if the AI code is working correctly, just like when you taste-test cake batter to make sure it's delicious before baking. And then, monitoring and logging are like keeping an eye on the cake while it's in the oven. You're watching to see how it's baking and making sure it's turning out just right.

Platforms for AI deployment enable developers to implement and execute AI models in real-world environments, ensuring scalability and reliability. They are like having a catering service that takes care of delivering and serving food at events, ensuring everything runs smoothly.

If we look ahead, some emerging technology patterns are as follows:

- Automated machine learning (AutoML) tools: They are like magic helpers who do the heavy lifting by automatically selecting the best algorithms, tweaking settings, and even handling boring tasks like data preprocessing. It's like having a super-smart assistant that takes care of all the complicated stuff so you can focus on the fun parts of AI.

- Reinforcement learning frameworks: Reinforcement learning frameworks are like training programs for AI to learn from its experiences, similar to how you might teach a pet new tricks. These frameworks provide a structure for AI to make decisions and take actions based on feedback it receives.

- Explainability and interpretability tools: These tools help us understand why AI makes certain decisions, much like a teacher explaining why a math problem is solved a certain way. They have insights into how AI algorithms work and why they produce specific outcomes. It's like having a clear explanation for why a weather forecast predicts rain based on factors like temperature and humidity.

For humanity to drive technology forward, it must grasp algorithms, models, data, hardware, software, and the ongoing evolution of intelligence augmentation.

So What?

We have described what AI means. We have also given you the history of how it evolved over the decades to remind you that it isn't new. Understanding where AI has been makes it easier to understand what AI is and what you need to know to harness the power of AI in the future.

Understanding the fundamental components of AI, including algorithms, models, and data, illuminates the intricate processes underlying artificial intelligence systems. Algorithms serve as the guiding principles, akin to recipes, steering the decision-making processes of AI by processing data through mathematical instructions. Models provide the organizational frameworks that allow algorithms to analyze data, recognize patterns, and make predictions, ultimately facilitating informed decision-making. Data, as the raw material, fuels the entire AI ecosystem, influencing every aspect of its operations and driving insights, predictions, and actions. Together, these components form the bedrock of AI technology, reshaping industries, revolutionizing human-computer interactions, and heralding a new era of innovation and progress.

Now What?

As we go deeper into the chapters ahead, a vast landscape of opportunities in AI will unfold. Each chapter offers insights into practical applications. We are setting the stage for you to move forward into this book and gain valuable knowledge that will enable you to leverage AI in your personal and professional life.

For the intrepid leaders, there are pivotal roles waiting to be embraced: lead the charge as a strategy architect, crafting visionary plans to utilize AI for organizational success; spearhead technological innovation as a chief technology officer, driving the development of cutting-edge AI solutions; ensure operational excellence as a chief operations officer, overseeing the seamless integration of AI into business operations.

For passionate technologists, explore the ranks of data scientists who unravel the secrets hidden within vast datasets; embrace the challenge of machine learning engineers who craft predictive algorithms to tackle real-world problems; explore the frontiers of AI research as scientists, pushing the boundaries of innovation; master the intricacies of language as NLP specialists, unlocking the power of human communication; navigate the visual realm as computer vision engineers, interpreting the world through the lens of AI.

For language and experience enthusiasts, explore a role such as AI business analysts who uncover market trends using AI-powered tools; become a UX/UI designer and create intuitive interfaces for AI applications; take on the role of AI trainer and develop training methodologies to improve AI performance; oversee the operations of AI systems as an operations manager, ensuring smooth sailing in the digital realm; dive into data extracting to augment decision-making.

As you build your AI muscle, you will determine how you want to play and grow with AI. So, if you need to, as you read forward, reference back to this chapter to reinforce the basics related to AI. Before you move to chapter 2, let's jot down what you have learned.

Top 3 learnings

Figure 1.5. What are three things you learned in this chapter?

DEFINING THE AI
NORTH STAR

THE VALUE OF ALIGNED TRANSFORMATION

Introduction

A SHARED PURPOSE. A clear goal. That is our vision of the North Star. Every organization needs a shared purpose or goal to anchor its constituents. And to that extent, we believe individuals also need a clear purpose or goal to help them ensure that they are working on the right things. We all know how easy it is to lose sight of our goals. How many times have you had a goal or a priority you wanted to complete and then suddenly found yourself working on something else—something less important?

In this chapter, we focus on an organization's North Star strategy in the context of the AI paradigm shift. We explore the overall concept of the North Star, its origins, and why it has shown promise as a strategy driver, giving examples of market leaders who have embraced the strategy concept of North Star and who have had tangible outcomes. We also narrow in on the North Star concept in the context of AI. After all, how we embed and embrace AI is our focus.

Readers and leaders will walk away with the ability to stress test their North Star, asking the following questions:

- Is my North Star still valid with the emergence of AI?

- Is the path to the North Star accelerated with the integration of AI?
- Does my organization need to shift and evolve the North Star with the emergence of AI?
- What is my role as it relates to AI and the North Star?

Our objectives in the chapter are as follows:

1. We define the North Star strategy and its components to establish a foundational understanding of the North Star concepts.
2. We will delve into the assessment of your North Star with an AI mindset. Recognizing the aspirational direction is crucial in comprehending the impact of emerging technologies, especially with AI. This will allow you to see how AI can impact or influence your North Star.
3. We showcase a real-world example of a company that has successfully employed a North Star strategy before and during the emergence of AI. This example provides practical insights into the application of the North Star concept, offering a perspective for readers to learn some practical lessons.

Defining the North Star Strategy

When we talk about the North Star strategy, it is easy to get lost in nomenclature. Language can either bring people a common understanding or it can create confusion when people bring their own interpretations to the table. For example, some may hear the term *North Star* and equate it to the metaphor of the North Star, a fixed point in the night sky that has been used for centuries as a navigational aid, providing a reference for travelers to find their way. Others may quickly interpret the North Star as a business strategy. Even in the business sense, there are different interpretations of what the North Star is and how it is used. The first time Winnie heard a reference to the North Star was during a digital transformation for a Fortune 100 company. The transformation executive used the term *North Star* to represent an end state for a process, not an organizational mission. In this example, Winnie and her team pushed back on the possibility of process nirvana, suggesting that it is an impossible state. Many years later, through our combined experiences, we now embrace the benefits of a clear North Star, especially as AI integrates into organizations.

Candidly, thinking back at the Fortune 100 companies we have worked for, the North Star hasn't always been clear. Organizations typically publish a mission or vision, but the people doing the work don't always know what the mission or vision is, and they certainly don't make sure their work aligns with it. In addition, companies may have a North Star but call it a "mission" or "goal" . . . which leads to future confusion.

The use of the North Star Strategy actually originated as a product-based strategy designed to help businesses maximize product delivery by determining an overall shared organizational goal, usually a metric. It was created to rally teams around a single goal with a metric to measure progress. For our purposes, a solid North Star strategy has a few components, including a clear and consistent goal that aligns the entire organization and a single North Star metric that all teams can rally around. The North Star strategy with a North Star metric is not just about setting a destination but also about understanding the journey. Design thinking infuses this strategy with a human-centered approach, ensuring that the chosen metric aligns with the needs and desires of the target audience.

There are characteristics or attributes related to the North Star goal and mission, and metric. The consistent goal should be the focal point around which design thinking principles revolve and should foster a deep understanding of consumer needs and drive innovative solutions. The North Star metric is how we measure progress against the North Star and should be the primary measure of consumer value.

The North Star Metric (NSM), is a concept made popular by a start-up founder and investor named Sean Ellis. The NSM is a singular measure that both converges a company's focus on its core mission and reflects the value provided to customers.[11]

The North Star metric should also represent your current product strategy and align business objectives across the organization. If identified correctly, the North Star metric is not a lagging indicator; it is a leading indicator of future business outcomes. This means that, ideally, it will help direct your activities and tell you when to course-correct proactively. And,

---

[11]   Stuart Brameld, "The North Star Metric & Framework," Grow the Method, February 2023, https://growthmethod.com/the-north-star-metric/.

to go a step further, any other key indicator you use should align with the North Star metric. The North Star metric, when approached with design thinking principles, becomes a dynamic tool for innovation and adaptation. It is not a static goal but rather a fluid marker that evolves as consumer preferences and market dynamics change. What it comes down to is that, as a concept, the North Star should not be overly complex.

While many large-scale organizations now have a (public) North Star, it isn't just a tool for the behemoth company only. All organizations have the opportunity to rally around a shared North Star, regardless of their size or scale. Small and midsized organizations can better understand their consumers, drive innovation, and ultimately achieve greater success when they identify their North Star goal and metric.

In summary, the North Star strategy aligns teams and people within an organization with a clear goal and a way to measure progress toward that goal. It helps organizations stay focused and make sure everyone is working toward the same thing. Ultimately, it is consumer-focused and flexible to evolving consumer needs. Whether big or small, organizations benefit from having a North Star to guide them to success.

Evaluating the North Star in an AI World

Years ago, Winnie taught project management as part of a partnership between the Project Management Institute, Delaware Valley Chapter (PMI-DVC), Villanova University, and a handful of other universities. In that class, she used a slide that had a picture of the organization's strategic mission and showed how the projects and programs should align with that mission (see figure 2.1). The goal of the slide was to remind students, mostly project managers, that if they weren't working on those projects and programs deemed strategic, then it was time to reassess and look for another project or job. Realistically speaking, the first projects and teams that get cut are those working on non value-add work. It was a tough but ultimately truthful message, one we use to evaluate everything we work on.

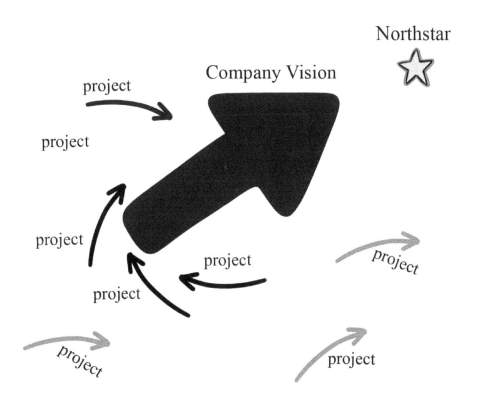

Figure 2.1. All of an organization's projects and
programs should align with its North Star.

Using the same mindset, we are asking our readers to look at the strategic mission, goal, or North Star of your organization and do a gut check. Is your organization's North Star, goal, or mission valid with the emergence of AI? From our perspective, all layers of leadership within the organization should question their North Star in the presence of their AI strategy.

If you don't have an AI strategy, don't worry. Different organizations are on different journeys when it comes to AI. You just need to establish where you are on that journey. If there is no approach to AI in sight, you are in a great place to assess the longevity of your relationship and role with your organization—but more about that when we talk about personal transformation in chapter 4.

The emergence of AI will, should, and can influence, change, or evolve the stated North Star. The objective in this section is to learn how to look at the North Star through the lens of the AI paradigm shift. The North Star needs to fuel the AI agenda, and the AI paradigm shift needs to validate or influence the evolution of the organization's North Star. AI is changing the finish line and the aspirational direction for many, if not all, of us.

An easy way to understand if your North Star will hold up in an AI world is to look at real-life use cases against technology change in specific industries.

Use Case: Broadcast Media

Let's take a look at what has been happening in the broadcast media world. First, we will set the stage and look at what has happened in the industry over time. Then we will assess different applications of AI strategies and then determine how to use the North Star metrics to help propel an organization that is willing to embrace change forward.

Setting the Stage and Looking to the Past

Fifteen years ago, broadcast media companies were focused on solving the last mile, laying fiber, and gaining entrance into households using hardware. Over the course of the last decade, there have been material changes in the landscape of broadcast media and technology, and content has been decoupled from hardware. Think about it. In the last fifteen years, mobile usage has grown exponentially, giving users the ability to view content from anywhere on any device. The use of technology, both internet and satellite, has increased the availability of broadcast content, the speed of downloads, and the overall user experience. The consumption of mobile media has shifted with the introduction of digital video recorders and streaming platforms. Fifteen years ago, you needed a recording device to record, stop, and pause content. (Remember the DVR?) Now that is all available as part of your streaming service—not to mention the availability of on-demand content when you want it how you want it.

These advances in technology have led to drastic changes in consumer behavior. In 2022, the average time spent on mobile devices increased 2.5 percent year-over-year to over 4.5 hours per day. In 2021, overall media consumption among U.S. adults was estimated to be around 666 minutes per day, or 11.1 hours—a 20.2 percent increase from 2011.[12]

Assessing the Approach to the Future

We are at a stage where leveraging AI will change the game for broadcast media/cable companies who are willing to embrace the trends. There are a number of strategies to be examined when considering your path in integrating AI capabilities. For example, AI can enhance and possibly influence consumer choices when it comes to programming. AI can analyze consumer behavior to personalize content recommendations. It can also take personalization one step further and be used to curate specific content, such as creating trailers or summaries for shows or movies that are tailored to a specific viewer profile. AI can also analyze data to predict trends and viewer behavior. This can help in making strategic decisions about content acquisition and scheduling. Using AI in this way can ultimately increase consumer engagement, satisfaction, and profitability.

Another strategic way to use AI technology is to focus on improvements that simplify the user experience. For example, one AI strategy is the use of AI-powered voice recognition to select viewing based on voice commands. With the right technology, you can simplify the search experience, allowing the user to move from typing to search to using voice commands. AI can also enhance the user experience by improving consumer service, giving answers to questions using chatbots or virtual assistants, which improves overall consumer response times.

The strategic applications of AI are increasing exponentially. As such, it will be critical to remember when selecting an approach to be mindful of your goals and the overall consumer strategy. It would be too easy to over-engineer the consumer experience by electing to do too much. Therefore, it is crucial to comprehend your North Star strategy and ensure that your North Star metric effectively reinforces the strategy, harnessing the full power that AI can offer.

---

[12] Petroc Taylor, "Annual Mobile Data Usage Worldwide from 2020 to 2027, By Device," Statista, April 27, 2023, https://www.statista.com/statistics/1370201/global-mobile-data-usage/; Kateryna Hanko, "35+ Must-Know Phone Usage Statistics for 2022," Clario, April 8, 2022, https://clario.co/blog/phone-usage-statistics/.

Evolving the North Star Metric to Drive Success with AI

We have already defined the North Star metric. Let's explore how we use the metric to measure the success of your North Star strategy as it evolves with AI. For context, your North Star, measured by your North Star metric, needs to be optimized for your shareholders against your budgets to show success in the markets,

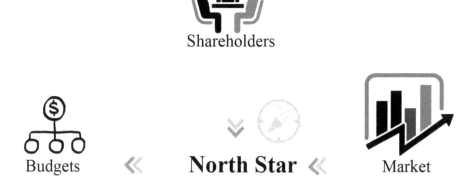

Figure 2.2. Optimizing your North Star for shareholders
and the market, against your budget.

First, it is critical to understand your overarching strategic mission. If your mission is consumer engagement, you can measure changes in engagement via personalization tactics using a metric related to active users or watch time per user. If you want to measure personalization success and engagement using personalized content, you can measure the number of personalized trailers watched from beginning to end or a percentage of users who watched AI-curated content.

If the mission is ease of access and voice recognition is the pillar you plan to leverage, you can measure the number of successful voice commands or percentage of users using voice capabilities. If the metric is consumer satisfaction, you can measure average response time in call centers.

The point is that the North Star metric should align with your company's mission and long-term goals. It should be a leading indicator of success and something that your entire team can rally around. The metric will need to evolve as your business grows with market change and as new technology emerges.

Netflix

To wrap up our broadcast media example, let's look at Netflix. Netflix's mission statement is "to entertain the world."[13] They aim to provide access to best-in-class TV series, documentaries, feature films, and games, regardless of where you live. Their members have control over what they want to watch, all within a simple subscription model.

As for their vision statement, Netflix aspires to become the best global entertainment distribution service. This vision drives their commitment to delivering high-quality content to audiences worldwide. Netflix's mission revolves around entertainment while their vision focuses on global excellence in content distribution. The Netflix North Star metric is "watch time" and reflects their focus on depth of engagement.

Netflix uses a combination of AI, data science, and machine learning to create a product-based, consumer-focused approach. Their North Star has been enhanced with the application of technology over time. In fact, their first pivot was when they moved away from the DVD market. Netflix established their North Star metric when they were transitioning from a DVD rental service to a streaming platform. This was around the time when they went public in 2002. The original North Star metric for Netflix was the percentage of consumers who put three or more DVDs in their queue.[14]

---

[13]   Daniel Pereira, "Netflix Mission and Vision Statement," Business Model Analyst, June 22, 2023, https://businessmodelanalyst.com/netflix-mission-and-vision-statement/.

[14]   "Netflix History: From DVD Rentals to Streaming Success," BBC, January 23, 2018, https://businessmodelanalyst.com/netflix-mission-and-vision-statement/; Roland Wijnen, "Netflix: How a DVD Rental Company Changed the Way We Spend Our Free Time," Business Models Inc. (blog post), accessed March 22, 2024, https://www.businessmodelsinc.com/en/inspiration/blogs/netflix-how-a-dvd-rental-company-changed-the-way-we-spend-our-free-time.

They focused on increasing this metric as it indicated a more engaged user who was less likely to unsubscribe. Over time, Netflix increased this North Star metric from 60 percent to 90 percent, where 90 percent of consumers had at least three DVDs in their queue. This directly influenced first-month retention and had a significant influence on Netflix's business results and profitability.[15]

The Netflix strategic mission has remained consistent and über-focused on their primary goal—entertaining the world. The North Star metric, however, has evolved with the emergence of technology and changed from DVDs in queue to watch time.

This tells us the following about Netflix and their strategic mission:

1. Netflix was able to maintain their North Star strategy focus on entertaining the world throughout their evolution and growth.
2. Netflix evolved its North Star metric to align with technological advancement and to measure the depth of engagement.
3. The North Star strategy and metric clearly focus the organization on the consumer, consumer preference, and personalization, which drive engagement.
4. The North Star strategy and metric are enhanced and fueled by AI. AI has been a game-changer in the context of scale for Netflix.

Netflix's strategy has proven successful, evident in the substantial growth across various key indicators. As the adage goes, "numbers don't lie," and Netflix has experienced significant expansion in its consumer base. Starting with 24 million subscribers in 2011, the streaming giant has remarkably increased its reach to an impressive 260 million subscribers by 2023.[16] Additionally, the company's workforce has undergone substantial growth, with employee numbers rising from 2,045 in 2012 to 12,800 in

---

[15]   Shruti Mishra, "Metric That Fueled Netflix's Ability to Become a Media Giant of 150 Billion USD," Medium, November 19, 2022. https://medium.com/@hey-shrutimishra/metric-that-fueled-netflixs-ability-to-become-a-media-giant-of-150-billion-usd-7c719755ab65.

[16]   Brian Dean, "Netflix Subscriber and Growth Statistics: How Many People Watch Netflix in 2023," Blacklinko, March 27, 2023, https://backlinko.com/netflix-users.

2022, marking a more than six-fold increase.[17] This surge in personnel reflects the company's expansion and increasing operational demands.

The financial success of Netflix is underscored by its revenue figures, showcasing a remarkable upward trajectory. In 2012, the company's revenue stood at $3.609 billion, and by 2022, it had surged to an impressive $31.616 billion, representing a nearly nine-fold increase.[18] This financial prosperity can be attributed to strategic decisions made by Netflix over the past decade. Notable among these decisions include the pivotal shift from DVD rentals to streaming services, the strategic creation of original content, and the integration of AI and machine learning technologies to enhance user experience. These factors collectively underscore the effectiveness of Netflix's strategic initiatives, contributing to the remarkable growth observed across consumer base, employment, and revenue.

What If I Don't Have a North Star?

The answer is simple—you build one with AI as a key component.

Creating a North Star holds significant value, particularly when AI plays a pivotal role. The reality is that not every organization has adopted the North Star vision, which is a strategy that originated in Silicon Valley and was reportedly embraced over time by tech giants like Facebook and Google. Some small and midsize businesses may not feel the need for a North Star, and even some larger, well-established organizations don't see the necessity for it. There is a perspective that the North Star concept initially started as a product-centric go-to-market strategy. Wherever it started, companies have embraced it because it is effective when used properly.

We propose that having a North Star is a valuable tool to unify stakeholders and team members. In the era of AI, we strongly believe that incorporating an AI lens into your North Star can be a game-changer in today's competitive marketplace. AI serves as a natural accelerant, making

---

17   Julia Stoll, "Quarterly Netflix Subscribers Count Worldwide 2013–2023," Statista, January 31, 2024, https://www.statista.com/statistics/250934/quarterly-number-of-netflix-streaming-subscribers-worldwide/.

18   "Netflix Revenue 2010–2024 NFLX," Macrotrends, accessed June 7, 2024, https://www.macrotrends.net/stocks/charts/NFLX/netflix/revenue.

it even more crucial to have a guiding metric. Therefore, if your organization currently lacks a North Star metric, consider developing one that leverages AI as a powerful accelerant for success.

How to Build a North Star

Constructing a North Star for your business involves a strategic process. Start by defining the fundamental purpose of your business, looking beyond mere profit, and identifying the value it aims to bring to consumers and society. Establish the core values that represent your business's principles, guiding the behavior and decisions of everyone involved. Envision the future state you want your business to achieve, creating a long-term vision that will serve as a guiding light.

Break down this vision into specific, measurable goals and objectives, ensuring they are realistic milestones contributing to the realization of your overarching vision. Emphasize a consumer-centric focus by clearly defining how your business aims to provide value to your consumers and understanding their needs. Engage your team in the process, gathering input to ensure that the North Star reflects a collective vision and commitment.

Craft a concise and inspiring mission statement that encapsulates your business's purpose, values, and goals, making it memorable and easy to communicate. Clearly communicate your North Star to all stakeholders, including employees, consumers, and partners, using various channels to share your mission and vision. Integrate your North Star into the decision-making processes of the business, referring back to your guiding principles whenever faced with choices or challenges.

Regularly revisit your North Star to assess its relevance, considering the evolving nature of businesses, and be open to refining your mission and vision as needed. Celebrate successes aligned with your North Star, recognizing efforts that contribute to the realization of your vision. Seek continuous feedback from consumers, employees, and other stakeholders to gauge how well your business is adhering to its guiding principles. This systematic approach ensures the development and sustainability of a meaningful North Star for your business.

By following these steps, a small business can create a North Star that not only guides its current operations but also inspires and directs its future growth and development.

Fictional Use Case

Let's consider a fictional tech startup, TechVision Innovations, which aims to develop cutting-edge solutions for sustainable energy. Here's how TechVision could apply the process outlined in building a North Star:

1. Define your purpose.

TechVision's fundamental purpose is to revolutionize the energy sector by creating innovative and sustainable technology solutions that reduce reliance on traditional energy sources and mitigate environmental impact.

2. Understand your values.

The core values of TechVision include a commitment to environmental sustainability, technological excellence, and collaboration. These values guide every decision made within the company.

3. Identify a vision for the future.

TechVision envisions a future where renewable energy sources power communities globally, reducing carbon footprints and fostering a cleaner, sustainable planet.

4. Clarify goals and objectives.

The company breaks down its vision into specific goals, such as developing a solar-powered smart grid system and achieving a 30 percent reduction in carbon emissions within the next five years.

5. Define a consumer-centric focus.

TechVision engages with communities to understand their energy needs and tailors its solutions to address those specific requirements, ensuring a consumer-centric approach.

6. Involve your team.

The development team, engineers, and business strategists at TechVision collaboratively contribute to shaping the North Star, aligning their efforts with the shared vision of sustainable energy innovation.

7. Craft a mission statement.

TechVision's mission statement succinctly communicates its purpose, values, and goals: "TechVision Innovations is dedicated to pioneering sustainable energy solutions, driven by a commitment to environmental stewardship and technological advancement."

8. Communicate clearly.

The mission and vision are communicated through internal meetings, external presentations, and the company website, ensuring that all stakeholders are aware of TechVision's overarching objectives.

9. Integrate it into decision-making.

When faced with decisions, TechVision refers back to its North Star, ensuring that choices align with the commitment to sustainability and technological excellence.

10. Monitor and adapt.

TechVision regularly assesses the relevance of its goals and objectives, adapting to emerging technologies and market trends to stay at the forefront of sustainable energy innovation.

11. Celebrate successes.

When milestones are achieved, such as the successful implementation of a solar-powered smart grid in a pilot community, TechVision celebrates these successes, recognizing the team's efforts.

12. Seek feedback.

Continuous feedback loops are established with consumers, environmental experts, and internal teams to understand how well TechVision is living up to its guiding principles and making necessary adjustments.

In this use case, the systematic approach to building a North Star has helped TechVision Innovations align its entire organization toward a shared vision, fostering innovation and commitment to sustainable energy solutions.

Relationships to the North Star (Roles)

Every one of us is involved in the North Star journey. Whether defining, communicating, managing, reporting, or promoting it, we all have a stake in the game.

North Star Owners

Creating a North Star strategy and metric is a collaborative effort that involves multiple stakeholders within an organization. The executive leadership team, led by the CEO and top-level executives, often takes a leading role in defining the overarching vision and mission that form the foundation of the North Star strategy. Strategy and planning teams work closely with executive leadership to translate this vision into actionable strategies and goals, conducting market analysis and defining key performance indicators that contribute to the North Star metric. Product teams, marketing teams, consumer insights and experience teams, and data and analytics teams all play critical roles in shaping and executing the strategy. Employee engagement teams facilitate workshops and gather feedback to ensure alignment with the entire workforce. The process often involves cross-functional collaboration to consider different perspectives. While responsibilities are shared among these stakeholders, having a clear leader or sponsor overseeing the process is essential to ensure alignment with the organization's overall objectives. The creation of a North Star strategy is an ongoing, iterative process that requires continuous monitoring, adaptation, and engagement from all relevant parties.

North Star Monitoring and Reporting

Monitoring and reporting on the North Star metric is a multifaceted effort that involves several key teams within an organization. The data and analytics teams play a pivotal role by setting up systems for data collection, analysis, and reporting to ensure that the organization has accurate and up-to-date information related to the metric. Performance management teams collaborate closely with data and analytics to develop dashboards and metrics that provide insights into the organization's overall performance. The strategy and planning teams are responsible for aligning the organization's goals with the North Star metric, monitoring progress, and providing insights into the effectiveness of current strategies. Executive leadership, including the CEO and top executives, holds the ultimate responsibility for overseeing performance and ensuring alignment with the North Star metric. Cross-functional teams may be formed to collaborate on monitoring activities, providing a holistic view of the organization's performance. Communications teams convey progress and achievements to both internal and external stakeholders, while technology teams ensure the necessary infrastructure is in place for accurate monitoring. Employee engagement teams facilitate internal communication, ensuring that employees are aware of their contributions to the organization's goals. Regular reporting cycles, such as monthly or quarterly reviews, help assess progress and inform strategic decisions, making the collaborative effort of these teams crucial for the sustained success of the North Star metric.

Using AI to Influence North Star Creation and Monitoring and Reporting

AI serves as a transformative force in the creation and monitoring of a North Star strategy. In the creation phase, AI's advanced analytics capabilities enable the analysis of extensive datasets, unveiling patterns and trends crucial for understanding consumer behavior and market dynamics. It aids in predictive modeling, simulating scenarios to inform strategic decisions and set goals effectively. AI-driven personalization enhances consumer-centricity, aligning the North Star metric with individualized needs. Additionally, automation in decision-making expedites strategy formulation, leveraging algorithms to recommend aligned approaches. In the monitoring phase, AI's continuous analytics provide real-time insights, detecting deviations from expected patterns and offering predictive analytics to anticipate market changes. Natural language processing extracts valuable insights from qualitative data, shaping the North Star based on consumer sentiments. Furthermore, AI's machine learning capabilities enable continuous adaptation, ensuring the North Star remains relevant as it learns from evolving data. Overall, AI significantly enhances the precision, adaptability, and data-driven nature of both North Star creation and monitoring processes.

AI's ability to process vast amounts of data, identify patterns, and provide predictive insights enhances both the creation and monitoring phases of a North Star strategy. It empowers organizations to make data-driven decisions, adapt to changing conditions, and achieve greater precision in reaching their strategic objectives.

So What?

The North Star serves as the anchor for all activities within an organization. Without it, priorities can become misaligned, and the overall purpose of the organization may become disjointed and siloed. The integration of AI into the North Star strategy fundamentally changes the game for organizations across industries. It prompts a crucial question: Does your North Star hold up in the age of AI? With the emergence of AI capabilities, organizations have the opportunity to reassess their strategic direction and leverage technology to drive innovation and consumer-centricity. By stress-testing the North Star with an AI mindset, leaders can ensure that their goals align with the transformative potential of AI, ultimately propelling their organizations forward in today's competitive landscape.

Aligning the core mission with AI transformation goals yields several strategic advantages. This alignment ensures strategic focus and clarity, preventing the dilution of efforts by guaranteeing that every AI initiative, decision, and investment resonates with the overarching purpose. Innovation is guided by a clear purpose, making AI initiatives purpose-driven and directly contributing to the fulfillment of the company's core mission. Stakeholders, including employees, consumers, and partners, benefit from a unified narrative that fosters a sense of purpose and direction, enhancing engagement and commitment. Decision-making becomes more coherent and strategic, guided by the alignment as a compass when faced with choices related to AI implementation. Aligning the North Star with AI transformation goals provides resilience during the transformation journey, allowing companies to weather uncertainties and changes more effectively. This alignment also positions companies uniquely in the market, giving them a competitive advantage by leveraging AI to directly address core challenges or opportunities outlined in their North Star. It contributes to a cohesive organizational culture, as employees understand how their work connects to the broader mission, fostering a sense of purpose and motivation in their contributions to AI initiatives. The alignment facilitates the measurement of impact, allowing companies to assess the success of AI initiatives based on their contribution to the core mission and establishing accountability for the transformative journey. Furthermore, companies become more adaptable to change, as the alignment provides a stable foundation amid evolving market dynamics, enabling flexibility in AI strategies while staying true to the enduring mission. External stakeholders perceive the company as purpose-driven, making consumers and partners more likely to resonate with and support companies that align AI transformation goals with a meaningful and enduring core mission.

Now What?

Moving forward, organizations must actively evolve their North Star strategies to harness the full power of AI. This involves incorporating AI-driven insights into goal-setting, monitoring, and reporting processes. Leaders should engage cross-functional teams to collaboratively define and refine the North Star metric, ensuring alignment with overarching strategic objectives and consumer needs. Moreover, organizations must invest in AI technologies and data analytics capabilities to drive informed decision-making and adaptability in the face of evolving market dynamics.

If you have gotten this far, you now understand that in an organization, we all need to follow the same guiding light, adhere to the same mission, and measure your progress collectively—if we don't, people, teams, and silos will lose their way, hurting the organization's overall success and the downstream consumer.

You have the baseline knowledge of the technology behind AI and how to use it to enhance the North Star. In the next chapter, let's talk about how to measure your progress.

Northstar Alignment

Organization
Northstar

My
Northstar

Connected?   Yes / No

Figure 2.3. Does your personal North Star align
with your organization's North Star?

MEASURING WHAT MATTERS

FOCUS ON IMPACT

Introduction

HOW DO WE assess the value of AI investments to determine where to start? Integrating AI into a business requires careful consideration due to limited time and resources. Prioritization is crucial for success, even if it means stepping out of our comfort zone. By focusing on tasks that truly matter, we can achieve our goals and move forward effectively. To find the right tasks to work on, we first need to know what to measure. This chapter explains what to analyze to target potential investment that will generate the most value. Our focus in this chapter will be in the context of the organization because AI is a collective change that will manifest in the organization first.

This chapter also helps the reader learn from the past to help plan for the future. Reflecting on consumer behavior, we'll observe the profound changes spurred by digital advancements like the internet, mobile phones, and cloud computing. As technology has progressed, consumers increasingly seek convenient and cost-effective options. This retrospective delves into how digital transformation has reshaped consumer preferences and decision-making processes, emphasizing the delicate balance between convenience and affordability. By understanding these shifts, individuals and leaders can better adapt AI innovation to the evolution of consumption patterns. In the end, we want to learn from the past through the lens of the consumer to drive our plans for the future.

The objectives of this chapter are to understand the following concepts and the metrics that measure them including:

1. How technology automates something to remove inefficiencies.
2. How automation can actually delight consumers and have a positive impact on satisfaction and engagement scores.
3. When to integrate AI converging the experiential and monetization path.

This is the goal (see figure 3.1): The ability to automate with technology that focuses on a consumer-centric outcome—not just because of the technical wow factor but because it gives the consumer something they want to pay for. We will show how the final measurement exceeds the cost of development in net new revenues while satisfying the consumer—again, giving the consumer something they want to pay for over and over again and knowing how to measure that before, during, and after.

Below are two brief examples of situations in our careers where both of us learned that beyond using metrics to forecast and invest, it is critical to test and learn and validate each metric. We also learned the importance of cadence and coordinates that inform decisions and make them timely. Meaning, as Kenny Rogers says, "You got to know when to hold 'em, know when to fold 'em, know when to walk away, and know when to run."

Personal Journey 1

As her family was growing in the early 2000s, Winnie was looking for alternatives to achieve faster financial growth to create financial security. In addition to her full-time job, she started to look at other ways to augment her bank account, knowing that she could potentially have three kids in college at once if she got lucky. As she began to research opportunities, she stumbled across the concept of owning a franchise.

A franchise is a business model where a company (the franchisor) grants individuals or other businesses (franchisees) the right to operate a business using its brand, products, services, and operating systems. In exchange, the franchisee typically pays an initial franchise fee and ongoing royalties to the franchisor. Most franchises have something called an FDD (financial disclosure document). This is a legal document that provides prospective franchisees with essential information about the franchisor, the franchise system, and the terms and conditions of the franchise agreement. The purpose of the FDD is to ensure transparency and to help potential franchisees make informed decisions before entering into a franchise agreement. The FDD has traditionally been a great tool to predict monetary outcomes for someone who wants to do more of the same. When it comes to a disruptive product or service, however, you need other data points to help predict outcomes based on the unknowns.

Back to Winnie's story. When Winnie reviewed the FDD of a specific franchise, she was astounded by return on investment (ROI) in the FDD. She did some additional research, interviewed other franchises, but in the end, she selected the franchise based primarily on the ROI listed in the FDD. She also was looking for an opportunity that would disrupt and that aligned well with the potential returns. So then what happened? Long story short, she stood up the franchise, and then closed it down within two years and had to endure the experience of losing a ton of money. While she took the actions recommended by the franchisor, the ROI never came to fruition. Why?

Well, it wasn't the happiest of outcomes, but her experience was an immensely valuable teaching moment and an exercise in self-awareness. There are some key lessons as they relate to metrics, measures, and knowing your consumer. The first is truly knowing everything that goes into a strong ROI metric, including understanding the consumer metrics, the market, and audience for the product and the monetization connection. In Winnie's case, she didn't truly embrace our second and third objectives, which are focused on the delight of the consumer and the path to monetize.

The experience was offered in a retail location that was not suitable for the service—wrong place, wrong time, wrong consumers. Winnie was offering an experience that did not delight consumers in this market. Just because you build it doesn't mean the consumer will come, and if you offer a product where the consumer does not exist, you will have a hard time selling it. As such, there wasn't a positive impact on consumer satisfaction or engagement, which means the ROI didn't pan out. In addition, more prework was needed to understand and predict who would purchase the service in this market. Basically, the path to monetize didn't exist. Obviously, these are things that would have been good to know before she embarked on this journey. That being said, they are worth their weight in gold as lessons learned and should absolutely be considered by anyone embarking on any business venture.

Personal Journey 2

Antara has experienced a plethora of chronic health issues from her childhood that have impeded growth in her personal and professional life. They have required her to walk away from opportunities she could have otherwise taken. In connecting with others with similar challenges, she learned she was not alone and there was a pattern of a lack of care coordination for people with chronic symptoms. People in this category were basically on their own to find a solution that was financially sustainable and conveniently accessible. Researching the issue, Antara recognized that symptom management though alternative medicine and wellness practices along with traditional medical and pharmaceutical was not only a huge opportunity but also a solution for those who were left behind. She did the research and learned that 70 percent of the population live with at least one chronic illness, 30 percent of those with two or more conditions. So what did she do?

Antara built a business from the ground up. The business brought a diverse set of alternate care provided under one roof along with primary care and specialty care. The idea was to manage a diverse set of symptoms in a convenient location, with the right providers, both alternative and traditional, and get insurance to play in this sandbox, making it financially available and sustainable. It was a great idea, altruistic with the potential for great returns. So what happened?

She stood up the business and operated for four years before she shut her doors. Why?

When we reminisce, we still think this is a great idea. But why didn't it succeed?

Let's answer using an example: You have a patient with asthma who smokes. The patient knows they need to quit but simply can't. In this scenario, the business model required that a doctor refer the patient for acupuncture and hypnotherapy and provide a script so that insurance would pay for the service. Both the patient and the doctor were consumers of this product. The challenge was in getting the doctor to promote and support the alternative path. While the patient could be delighted, the doctor wasn't always delighted or invested in this alternative path. Both consumers (patient and doctor) needed to be on board for Antara to monetize the outcomes long-term. What it comes down to is that Antara was unable to remove inefficiencies from the ground up. The inefficiencies were at the top of the medical system. The second issue was really understanding the full consumer base and the metrics they adhere to. Her consumers were patients, doctors, and insurance companies, and they all aligned to different metrics and measures. At the time, she didn't really understand the measure or have the capacity to create the metrics. I mean really how do you delight all three groups? The third issue was the path to monetization. The path was heavily dependent on insurance, which is in itself a flawed system. Antara also had the hard lesson of draining her life savings. These lessons, while hard, came at a price, but again, worth their weight in gold on how to assess, align, and promote disruptive change for success.

We need to be mindful of disruptive changes like AI. We have learned that you must ground yourself in objective criteria. Hence, this chapter on metrics. We share these personal stories because we learned valuable lessons about measuring what matters. There is no one-size-fits-all when determining what to measure.

AI vs. Traditional Technology Automation

To understand what metrics are worth measuring, led and driven by AI, let's first untangle how AI is different from traditional technology automation or any other disruptive change. This will help us understand how measurements for AI will evolve differently from common practices in measuring cost and return on investment for IT.

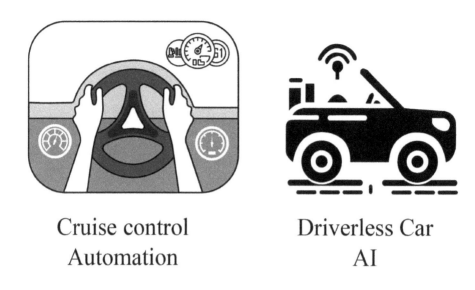

Cruise control   Driverless Car
Automation   AI

Figure 3.1. Example of traditional automation vs. AI.

In traditional paradigms of technology automation, the primary focus is on identifying repetitive, rules-based tasks that are time-consuming and resource-intensive. Key metrics used for prioritizing these tasks include their frequency, complexity, volume, error rates, resource usage, cost implications, and alignment with organizational objectives.

Tasks that are performed frequently, have low complexity, involve large volumes of work, exhibit high error rates, and require significant resource utilization are typically earmarked for automation. This strategic approach aims to enhance efficiency and accuracy while reducing operational costs. Moreover, ensuring that automation initiatives align with strategic goals ensures that investments contribute effectively to overall organizational success.

However, the approach to prioritizing AI implementation shifts the focus from merely automating repetitive tasks to identifying processes that traditionally rely on human cognitive abilities. This shift involves recognizing tasks and processes where AI technology can either replace human intelligence or complement it to enhance efficiency and effectiveness. In essence, while traditional automation prioritizes tasks based on their repetitive nature and resource consumption, prioritizing AI candidates involves identifying tasks that require human cognition and determining how AI can either automate or augment those tasks. Tasks characterized by high complexity become focal points for AI integration to streamline operations and enhance accuracy. The metrics of frequency, volume, and error rates remain similar to IT automation.

We start by measuring what needs transformation. The complexity of a task and its dependence on human cognitive capabilities are the key metrics unique to determining where AI can be integrated.

Let's take a look at the top four cognitive capabilities that play key roles in most employees' day-to-day work and how well-suited they are to AI integration: natural language understanding, decision-making and problem-solving, image and object recognition, and predictive analytics and forecasting.

Natural Language Understanding

Natural language understanding (NLU) is about teaching computers to understand human language better. It involves breaking down sentences to figure out what they mean, including understanding the words used, the context they're in, and what the person is trying to say. This helps computers interact with people more like humans do. NLU uses techniques like recognizing different parts of speech, understanding the meanings behind words, and learning from examples to improve over time. It's used in things like virtual assistants, translation apps, and analyzing how people feel in online reviews.

Decision-Making and Problem-Solving

Analyzing complex datasets, identifying patterns, and making strategic decisions based on incomplete or ambiguous information are tasks essential for executives, analysts, and decision-makers across various industries. Decision-making is choosing what to do from a set of options, while problem-solving is finding a solution to a challenge or obstacle. In simple terms, decision-making is picking the best path forward and problem-solving is figuring out how to overcome hurdles to reach a goal. Both involve thinking through options and making choices based on what's known.

Image and Object Recognition

Image and object recognition is a function of computer vision that focuses on identifying objects, faces, patterns, and anomalies in images or videos. Image recognition is when computers learn to understand what's in pictures, like identifying objects or scenes. Object recognition is a specific type of image recognition that focuses on identifying individual objects, like people or animals, within images. Both are used in various areas—from security and autonomous vehicles to healthcare and retail—to help computers "see" and understand the world around them.

Predictive Analytics and Forecasting

Predicting future trends, outcomes, and behaviors based on historical data and current variables requires advanced statistical analysis, machine learning models, and predictive algorithms.

Predictive analytics and forecasting are ways to guess what might happen in the future based on what's happened in the past. Predictive analytics uses data to make educated guesses about future events, while forecasting specifically predicts future trends or values based on past patterns. They're both helpful for planning and decision-making in business, finance, and other areas.

Now, let's take the four areas—natural language understanding, decision-making and problem-solving, image and object recognition, and predictive analytics and forecasting—and identify and measure where we can eliminate inefficiencies with an example.

Business Example to Remove Inefficiencies: MBRs and QBRs

Let's consider a key leadership activity in many businesses: monthly business reviews (MBRs) and quarterly business reviews (QBRs). These are essential for evaluating performance and aligning strategies.

MBRs focus on assessing key performance indicators and addressing deviations from targets, promoting collaboration and data-driven decisions. QBRs provide deeper insights into business performance and goals, informing strategic decision-making.

Despite their importance, these reviews rely heavily on manual processes and human intellect, which can slow decision-making and degrade its quality over time. Efforts have been made to leverage data tools and technologies, but challenges persist in translating data into actionable insights.

Introducing AI into these processes can augment human intelligence. AI can help scale decision-making abilities, especially in tasks requiring complex analysis or predictions. By combining AI's efficiency with human cognition, we can enhance the effectiveness of strategic meetings, unlocking new opportunities for growth and informed decision-making.

	With AI	**Manual/Labor-intensive**
Efficiency	AI can automate data collection and analysis, reducing time spent on these tasks. This can be measured by the decrease in hours spent on data preparation.	Time investment is significant in manual processes. Calculate the number of hours spent by each team member in preparing for, participating in, and following up on MBRs and QBRs.
Accuracy	AI algorithms can process large amounts of data with high precision, reducing the likelihood of human error. This can be measured by the decrease in errors found in reports.	Manual data collection and analysis can lead to errors, impacting decision-making. While difficult to measure directly, the cost of these errors can be inferred from the impact of decisions made based on inaccurate data.
Insightfulness	AI can uncover insights from complex data that humans might overlook. This can be measured by the increase in actionable insights derived from business data.	Manual processes may not be able to uncover all insights due to human limitations, potentially leading to missed opportunities.
Predictive Power	AI can use historical data to make accurate predictions about future trends. This can be measured by the accuracy of these predictions compared to actual outcomes.	Manual processes lack the predictive power of AI, potentially leading to less accurate forecasts.

	With AI	**Manual/Labor-intensive**
Decision-Making	AI can provide data-driven recommendations, leading to more informed decision-making. This can be measured by the increase in decisions backed by data.	Manual decision-making processes may not always be data-driven, potentially leading to less optimal decisions.
Cost Savings	By automating data analysis, AI can reduce the need for additional resources, leading to cost savings. This can be measured by the decrease in operational costs related to data analysis.	Manual processes require resource allocation, such as meeting spaces, equipment, and any software or tools used for data analysis and presentation.
Revenue Growth	With more accurate and insightful data analysis, businesses can make better decisions that drive revenue growth. This can be measured by the increase in revenue after implementing AI-driven MBRs and QBRs.	Manual processes may have opportunity costs. Evaluate what other tasks or projects could have been accomplished in the time spent on MBRs and QBRs. This can be harder to quantify but is an important factor to consider.

Table 3.1.

Decision-making metrics play a pivotal role in evaluating the outcomes of MBRs and QBRs, serving as key indicators of organizational performance and strategic alignment. By quantifying various elements such as human labor, delays, missed opportunities, errors, and failures, these metrics provide valuable insights into the effectiveness of decision-making processes and their impact on business outcomes.

Today

200+ Hours
with 20+ people

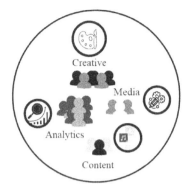

Tomorrow 50x Improvement in Productivity

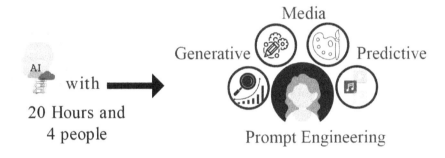

Figure 3.2. With AI, the MBR process is optimized and a
material improvement in productivity will be realized.

This example demonstrates how we measure the opportunity and measure the outcome. By leveraging these metrics, organizations can make informed decisions, mitigate risks, and capitalize on opportunities identified during their business reviews, ultimately enhancing their ability to navigate and succeed in today's dynamic business landscape.

- Human labor: Decision-making entails the expenditure of human labor across different organizational levels, quantified by the total labor costs associated with meetings, discussions, and analysis, measured in dollars.

- Delays: Delays in decision-making can be measured by the estimated financial impact of the time elapsed between recognizing the need for a decision and its actual implementation, calculated in terms of lost revenue or opportunities, resulting in potential monetary losses.
- Missed opportunities: The cost of missed opportunities can be evaluated by estimating the potential revenue or market share lost due to delayed or suboptimal decisions, expressed in dollars through metrics such as unrealized sales targets or foregone growth opportunities.
- Errors: Errors in decision-making can be quantified by assessing the financial impact of mistakes, including the cost of rectification, potential loss of consumers, or damage to reputation, measured in dollars through metrics such as error-related expenses or consumer compensation.
- Failures: The cost of failures resulting from poor decisions or indecision can be assessed by calculating the financial losses incurred, including project failures, revenue decline, or market share loss, quantified in dollars to gauge the overall impact on the organization's financial performance.

To summarize, we measured a number of different components that are required to make the MBR/QBR process happen. We assessed where AI could be leveraged, looking at the four categories of cognitive capabilities to create a streamlined process and remove inefficiencies. We validated our outcomes by using metrics that measured the outcome (saving time and money).

Measuring Delight

The basics of what can be measured tell a story and help us to make decisions clearly. Let's take a page from the past. As technology has evolved, consumer behaviors have changed. As the behaviors changed, demand patterns evolved, and this created new patterns of financial ebb and flow.

Metrics and measurements play a pivotal role in quantifying the best investment sequence for AI transformation by optimizing outcomes in both monetization and experiential improvements. Through carefully selected metrics, organizations can gauge the effectiveness of various AI initiatives in generating revenue and enhancing user experiences. Metrics related to revenue growth, cost reduction, consumer satisfaction, and operational efficiency provide valuable insights into the impact of AI investments. By analyzing these metrics over time, organizations can identify the most impactful AI projects and prioritize their implementation to achieve the highest return on investment and the most significant experiential improvements.

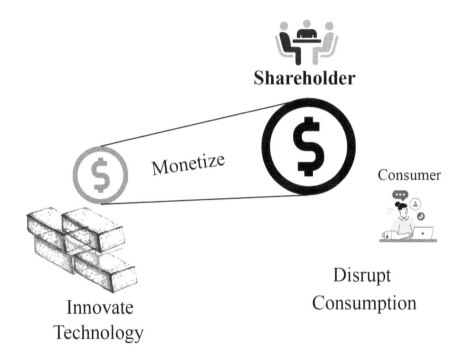

Figure 3.3. Ideally, the final measurement will exceed the cost of development in net new revenues.

Successfully Measured

Let's examine how technology has influenced consumer behavior and reshaped supply-and-demand dynamics through various metrics of success we have assessed as users and consumers in the digital age.

LinkedIn, known for professional networking, likely measures success through its user engagement metrics, such as the number of connections made, job applications submitted, and content interactions within its platform. These metrics reflect the platform's effectiveness in facilitating meaningful professional connections and career advancement opportunities.

Instagram, a visual-centric platform, probably gauges success through metrics like user engagement rates, follower growth, and the number of impressions generated by sponsored content. These metrics showcase Instagram's impact on brand awareness, consumer engagement, and influencer marketing effectiveness.

eBay, an online marketplace, on the other hand, tends to evaluate success based on metrics such as gross merchandise volume, average selling price, and seller feedback ratings. These metrics indicate eBay's ability to facilitate transactions, drive sales volume, and maintain trust and satisfaction among its user base.

Amazon, a leading e-commerce platform, may measure success through metrics like conversion rate, consumer acquisition cost, and consumer lifetime value. These metrics demonstrate Amazon's effectiveness in converting website visitors into consumers, acquiring new consumers cost-effectively, and maximizing long-term consumer value.

PayPal, a digital payment platform, can assess success using metrics such as transaction volume, payment volume growth, and net new active accounts. These metrics illustrate PayPal's role in facilitating secure and seamless transactions, driving payment volume growth and expanding its user base globally.

Netflix, a subscription-based streaming service, has been known to evaluate success through metrics like subscriber growth rate, churn rate, and average revenue per user. These metrics reflect Netflix's ability to attract and retain subscribers, minimize churn, and maximize revenue from its subscriber base.

Apple, a technology company, has evolved over the years and in the past decade seems to have been measuring success through metrics like product sales revenue, consumer satisfaction scores, and app store downloads. These metrics showcase Apple's performance in driving product sales, delivering exceptional user experiences, and fostering developer ecosystem growth.

Across these examples, the chosen metrics serve as key indicators of success, reflecting each platform's effectiveness in achieving its goals, driving user engagement, and delivering value to consumers and stakeholders alike.

Notable Attempts to Delight

Let's explore digital disruptors that struggled to gain traction and adoption, with the metaverse being one notable example:

Metaverse, envisioned as a virtual reality space where users could interact and engage in immersive experiences, faced challenges in gaining widespread adoption due to technical limitations, high entry barriers, and a lack of compelling content. Metrics such as user engagement, monthly active users, and revenue generation fell short of expectations, indicating the metaverse's struggle to attract and retain users in a competitive landscape.

Google Glass, once hailed as a groundbreaking wearable technology, failed to gain widespread adoption due to concerns over privacy, usability issues, and limited practical applications. Metrics such as user engagement rate, app downloads, and active user growth stagnated, indicating a lack of interest and enthusiasm among consumers and developers alike.

Juicero, a startup aiming to revolutionize juicing with its high-tech juicer, faced significant challenges in gaining traction due to its high price point, cumbersome design, and the availability of more affordable alternatives. Metrics such as sales revenue, consumer acquisition cost, and consumer retention rate fell short of expectations, highlighting Juicero's struggle to attract and retain consumers in a competitive market.

Quibi, a short-form mobile video platform backed by prominent Hollywood executives, failed to capture audiences' attention despite its star-studded content lineup and innovative technology. Metrics such as daily active users, user retention rate, and advertising revenue failed to meet projections, signaling Quibi's inability to sustain user engagement and monetize its platform effectively.

Segway, hailed as a game-changing personal transportation device, faced challenges in mainstream adoption due to its high price, niche appeal, and regulatory restrictions. Metrics, such as sales volume, market share, and consumer satisfaction scores remained below expectations, indicating

Segway's failure to penetrate mass markets and achieve widespread consumer acceptance.

Despite their innovative concepts and technological advancements, these digital disruptors ultimately faltered in gaining traction and adoption due to various factors, such as market competition, usability issues, pricing strategies, and consumer preferences.

While technological disruption holds immense potential, it's important to recognize that the mere existence of a disruptive product or service doesn't guarantee consumer demand or affection. Ultimately, it's the experiential differentiation that drives demand and enables impactful monetization business cases. Although technology plays a pivotal role, it's the unique user experiences, value propositions, and consumer-centric approaches that truly resonate with consumers and foster loyalty. By focusing on delivering exceptional experiences and addressing genuine consumer needs and pain points, companies can create meaningful value propositions that attract and retain consumers. Therefore, while technological innovation is essential, it's the ability to create memorable and valuable experiences that ultimately determines the success and sustainability of disruptive ventures.

Predicting Where the Experience Meets Monetization

In today's business landscape, the potential integration of AI and predicting where its impact will provide the most value is crucial. We understand that financial success relies on stakeholder satisfaction. As we explore AI deployment, it's clear that experiential metrics measure the qualitative aspects of consumer engagement—capturing user satisfaction and emotional connection—while monetization strategies quantify success through economic impact. These approaches, though seemingly different, are actually complementary, steering businesses toward their goals. User-centric innovation drives brand loyalty and strength, while strategic market insights enhance fiscal growth. Together, they create a holistic blueprint for modern business success, blending emotional resonance with stakeholders and the pragmatic pursuit of profit.

Experiential Satisfaction

The experiential satisfaction pattern prioritizes the creation of value through enhancing user experiences and fulfilling emotional needs. This approach emphasizes understanding and catering to the desires, preferences, and emotions of users or consumers. Companies following this pattern focus on aspects such as usability, aesthetics, and emotional engagement to create products or services that resonate with their target audience. Success in this pattern is measured not only by financial metrics but also by indicators of consumer satisfaction, loyalty, and brand perception. Industries such as hospitality, entertainment, and consumer goods often adopt the experiential satisfaction pattern to differentiate themselves and build strong relationships with their consumers.

Monetization of Success

This pattern revolves around the idea of translating innovation into tangible financial gains or economic value. In this approach, the primary focus is on creating products, services, or solutions that generate revenue or profit. Key elements of this pattern include identifying market opportunities, developing scalable business models, and executing strategies to capture value from innovation. Companies following this pattern often prioritize metrics such as revenue growth, market share, and return on investment. Monetization of success is commonly associated with industries such as technology, finance, and healthcare, where there is a clear link between innovation and financial outcomes.

Pulling It All Together: What and How Do I Measure?

When deploying AI, the core principles of measuring experiential satisfaction and monetization success remain, but the metrics might include additional AI-specific elements to account for the unique aspects of AI technologies. Here's how some metrics can be adapted or expanded for AI deployment.

Experiential Satisfaction with AI

AI deployments often focus on enhancing user experiences through personalization, automation, and improved service efficiency. Therefore, the metrics should reflect these aspects. Here are some examples of metrics for experiential satisfaction with AI:

- Consumer effort score (CES): Assesses how easy it is for consumers to interact with AI functionalities.
- AI interaction success rate: Tracks the percentage of successful interactions or transactions completed using AI, such as chatbot resolutions or automated service tasks.
- Personalization effectiveness: Measures how well the AI personalizes user experiences, which can be tracked through user feedback or engagement metrics.
- Churn rate: Measures the percentage of users who stop using the AI-enhanced product or service over a specific period.

Monetization of AI Success

Monetizing AI involves demonstrating the financial benefits derived from AI investments. This can include direct revenue from AI products or cost savings from AI efficiencies. Examples of some metrics for AI monetization include:

- Gross margin: Measures the difference between revenue and the cost of goods sold, with a focus on improvements from AI-driven efficiencies.
- Time to market: Monitors the reduction in time to develop and launch new products or features due to AI.
- Error reduction rate: Measures the decrease in errors or defects due to AI implementation, leading to cost savings and improved quality.
- Scalability: Assesses the ability to scale AI solutions across the organization or consumer base without proportionally increasing costs.

Validating AI Monetization

To validate AI monetization, businesses should do the following:

- Quantify financial metrics
    - o Monitor traditional financial metrics (revenue growth, ROI, market share) alongside AI-specific ones (cost savings, error reduction).
    - o Compare these metrics against industry standards and past performance.
- Predict future performance
    - o Use AI-driven predictive analytics to forecast future revenue streams, consumer behavior, and market trends.
    - o Model different scenarios to evaluate potential financial outcomes from AI deployment.
- Validate through real-world data
    - o Conduct A/B testing and pilot programs to test AI features and assess their impact on revenue and cost.
    - o Continuously track AI-specific metrics to ensure AI deployment meets expected financial outcomes.

By integrating these AI-specific metrics with traditional business metrics, companies can ensure that their AI deployments not only enhance user experiences but also drive substantial economic value, creating a robust framework for sustained business success.

It's not just the idea...., it's the demand for it that matters

Figure 3.4. Monetization of success. You may have great ideas—
but you need demand and perceived value for those ideas.

So What?

The essence of this chapter is a call to action for businesses to not only embrace AI but to do so with a strategic lens. It's about understanding that AI is not just a tool for efficiency but a transformative force that can redefine consumer experiences and create new value propositions. The "so what" factor lies in the realization that AI investment is not just a financial decision but a strategic one that touches every aspect of the business, from operations to consumer engagement. Understanding the difference between traditional automation and AI is crucial for effective measurement and implementation. Traditional automation focuses on repetitive, rules-based tasks, optimizing for frequency, complexity, volume, and error rates to enhance efficiency and reduce costs. In contrast, AI targets tasks requiring human cognition, like natural language understanding, decision-making, image recognition, and predictive analytics. This shift from automation to AI integration enables businesses to enhance both operational efficiency and strategic decision-making.

Now What?

Armed with this knowledge, businesses must now take a calculated approach to AI integration. This means:

- Identifying key areas where AI can have the most significant impact.
- Measuring the right metrics to ensure that AI initiatives align with broader business goals.
- Learning from past digital transformations to predict future trends and consumer behaviors.
- Focusing on consumer-centric outcomes to ensure that AI solutions meet real consumer needs and desires.
- Evaluating the cost-benefit ratio of AI projects ensures that the value they bring exceeds the investment made.

In essence, the next steps involve a meticulous assessment of AI's potential and a thoughtful integration plan that prioritizes consumer satisfaction and business growth. The goal is to leverage AI not just for the "wow" factor but for its ability to deliver enduring value to both the company and its consumers. To maximize AI's potential, businesses should prioritize tasks that involve human cognitive abilities and measure key metrics like task complexity and cognitive dependency. Integrate AI to improve user experiences and monetize innovations. Focus on:

- Natural language understanding (NLU): Implement virtual assistants and translation apps to enhance consumer engagement.
- Decision-making and problem-solving: Use AI analytics for better strategic decisions.
- Image and object recognition: Deploy AI in security and healthcare to improve accuracy and efficiency.

- Predictive analytics and forecasting: Utilize AI to predict trends and optimize supply chains.

By blending experiential satisfaction with monetization strategies, businesses can create a holistic approach to success, balancing emotional resonance with stakeholders and the pragmatic pursuit of profit.

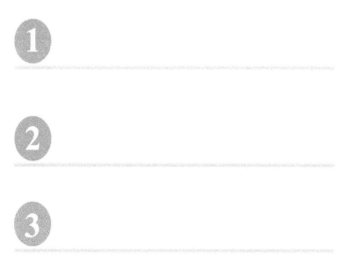

Figure 3.5. What are your metrics for success?

ACCOUNTABILITY

PART 2

WITH THE FOUNDATIONAL groundwork laid out, encompassing the historical context of AI and its practical applications, we pivot toward a deeper exploration of accountability, interwoven with the concepts of touchstone and choice architecture. An AI touchstone emerges as more than a mere buzzword, embodying a pivotal concept guiding individuals within the vast AI landscape. It serves as a fusion of understanding and engagement with AI, intimately tied to individual purpose.

In chapter 4, we examine the profound impact of AI on personal development within contemporary workplaces. Drawing from established theories in psychology, sociology, and organizational behavior, we'll explore how AI shapes job roles, organizational dynamics, and individual aspirations. The concept of the AI touchstone is introduced as a framework for navigating AI integration at the individual level. Through case studies and real-world examples, readers gain insights into assessing their own position relative to AI and identifying avenues for personal growth and professional development. Practical strategies are offered to align personal goals with the evolving AI landscape, empowering readers to thrive amidst technological disruption.

Transitioning into the realm of choice architecture, chapter 5 emphasizes its significance as a powerful framework for effective decision-making in the AI era. Acknowledging readers' progress in defining their AI touchstone, it underscores the importance of proactive choices in navigating the evolving AI landscape. Choice architecture, with its key principles of play, grow, and disrupt, empowers individuals to craft personal growth plans while guiding organizations in aligning AI strategies with their overarching objectives. The PACT method outlined in chapter 5 further reinforces the need for accountability, urging swift pivots toward AI transformation, alignment of internal processes, and fostering a culture conducive to change.

Through personal anecdotes and practical insights, chapter 5 illuminates the transformative potential of knowing your touchstone and choice architecture, illustrating how intentional decision-making shapes individual and organizational journeys amidst the complexities of AI integration. As readers explore, they are invited to delve into touchstone and Choice Architecture, recognizing these concepts as allies in crafting optimal paths in the age of AI and unlocking their personal growth potential.

THE AI TOUCHSTONE

WHERE THE TRANSFORMATION STARTS

Introduction

AS AI CONTINUES to revolutionize workplaces, the necessity for personal transformation and introspection has reached a critical juncture. To be specific, AI is going to reshape organizational systems, workflows, and societal structures. This creates an urgent demand for everyone to take ownership of their personal development and uphold professional accountability.

Let's level set. So far, we have learned about the value of a North Star and how it needs an upgrade for AI. We detailed the evolution of technology, talked about prior transformations, and highlighted what to do when things are going well or how to course-correct when needed. We used the lens of large corporations, leaders, and their consumers. Now we want you to look internally to assess where you are in the realm of AI. This is where the AI touchstone comes into play. This is a new concept that we are going to define and describe, and it will set you up for defining your choices as you move forward in this book.

Here is an example of why there is urgency. Prior to AI, we had digital transformations. To be successful in a digital transformation, you typically need to learn a tool, process, or build a program to help you achieve success. A new technology or feature was introduced, and teams were created to rally around bringing that new feature to market. Looking back at digital transformations, you had time to plan and execute. AI transformations are different. First off, you don't have as much time. Secondly, human intelligence will need to scale with artificial intelligence. Consider the changing landscape as it is shaped by automation and AI. Roles that are task-oriented or data-driven, such as data-driven decision-making, will change or be replaced by AI-powered technology. Naturally, AI will take on tasks that will simplify and speed up work and outcomes. Because of this, it is table stakes to stay relevant and be proactive on an AI-powered planet.

To figure out where you want to go, you need to know where you are today. The purpose of this chapter is to help you identify your AI touchstone and evaluate your willingness, awareness, and readiness to move forward. We also want to introduce an aspirational goal: scale human intelligence with artificial intelligence. To define the AI touchstone and kick off your journey to scale human intelligence at pace with AI, we need to take a moment to look inward and ensure we have context in five areas, which are the objectives of this chapter.

1. Understand your touchstone. This will require personal introspection.
2. Distinguish between automation and artificial intelligence. These are the nuances that are required to understand your current state and where to go.
3. Identify the areas where human thinking is transitioning to AI-driven augmentation.
4. Consider the evolution of roles in an organization.
5. Assess the readiness of self, role, and hiring trends.

This approach ensures the synchronization of human intelligence with the dynamic evolution of AI. By incorporating the objectives in this section, the goal is to blend personal aspirations with organizational needs. This chapter is the baseline that you will need to get you to chapter 5 where you make choices for action.

Defining Your Touchstone

Your touchstone is your current state married to your why. It is a state of purpose you have set for yourself that has driven your choices personally and professionally. It is your motivator and what drives you to change, take chances or not, and influences your decisions. It is a multifaceted concept. Like using a GPS, you need the current location to map your course. When you map your course, you typically get three or four options (routes) you can take to get to your destination. In this book, to get to your North Star, determine whether to go fast or slow or which coordinates to use, you need to know your touchstone—your current state and your why.

Antara and I both have unique nuances to our touchstones. For me, large-scale transformation and change are my professional drivers. I want to lead the biggest baddest work in an organization and will continually look for those transformative efforts to lead or even be a part of. For me, AI is new and fascinating, with a huge runway for growth and learning, and I am super motivated to learn everything I can about it. That is my driver, that is my touchstone.

Antara innovates to disrupt and disrupts to innovate. She likes to stir the pot. As product leader, it was apparent to her at the tail end of digital transformation that a pivot was necessary to embed AI into all things and products from this moment forward. To get a clear picture of what to invest and where to invest, she knew she needed to learn everything about AI. She kicked off her journey by reading and writing and testing the waters with me. And now, together, we have evolved our shared AI touchstone. Our AI touchstone is this book. This book is a part of AI for All, which is our North Star. We want AI to be understandable for everyone and feel empowered to own their future with AI. AI for All is driven by our core belief—humanity drives technology. After all, we are in charge of how we play, grow, and disrupt with AI.

An AI touchstone, however, is the fusion of your present state of understanding and engagement with artificial intelligence intimately bound to the driving purpose behind your involvement. It represents the foundational principle or set of principles that guide your decisions and actions in the realm of AI. Your AI touchstone serves as a compass, influencing your choices and motivating your pursuit of progress within AI personally and professionally. It provides the framework through which you evaluate options and chart your course within your career and role in the context of AI objectives. In the context of this book, understanding your AI touchstone is essential for navigating toward your North Star, determining the pace of your journey, selecting the appropriate strategies, and aligning with your overarching purpose in AI exploration and implementation.

To understand your touchstone, we will help you measure your willingness, awareness, and readiness to move forward.

Willingness

Willingness means being accountable, persistent, and determined to achieve a goal or fulfill a commitment.

- Accountability starts with taking responsibility for your actions, decisions, and promises. It's about being willing to be honest with yourself and ready to follow through.
- Being prepared to take action is essential for willingness. Understanding what needs to be done and being willing to do it, despite challenges.
- Persistence is key to willingness. It means staying determined and not giving up, even when faced with setbacks or slow progress.
- "Keep going until you get there" captures the essence of willingness. It's about committing to your goals and pushing forward until you succeed, staying focused and resilient along the way. Remember in *The Untouchables* when Sean Connery asks Kevin Costner, "What are you prepared to do? . . . And then what are you prepared to do?" (feel free to google this for some funny memes).

If you read these four bullets and believe you are accountable, prepared, persistent, and will keep going no matter what, simply put, you are willing.

Willingness was the first hurdle to cross in writing this book. We had to be willing to invest time, resources, and energy into learning about AI. That said, we have some other great real-life examples of what it means to us. Antara, when trying to get her healthcare startup off the ground, was pitching to investors and potential partners around the clock. One time, she was really close to a collaborative relationship with a healthcare system, and her husband gave her this advice as she was leaving the house. Sam said, "Be like a postage stamp—stick to the letter until it gets to the reader." Not only did it keep her focused that day until she made the deal with a large healthcare conglomerate, but she also internalized that advice and has been using it ever since. Mind you, she was a solo entrepreneur with a vision in a startup business who went into a healthcare system of over one thousand employees, five hospitals, and an insurance arm. Makes you think of David and Goliath. The message here—know what you want, and stick to it until you get there.

Awareness

Willingness is great on its own, but without awareness, it can lead you down the wrong path and keep you from the desired destination. Let's review what we mean by awareness.

Awareness involves several key attributes:

- Self-awareness: Understanding your current state and level of self-awareness is fundamental. It means being conscious of your thoughts, emotions, and behaviors, as well as recognizing your strengths and weaknesses.
- Situational awareness: Being aware of your current "touchstone" or context is important. This includes understanding your surroundings, circumstances, and environment. With AI, updating your touchstone involves leveraging technology to gather information and insights that can enhance your understanding and decision-making.
- Understanding strengths and weaknesses: Awareness also encompasses knowing your strengths, weaknesses, and opportunities. This involves recognizing your skills, talents, and areas for improvement. By identifying these aspects, you can make informed choices and pursue growth opportunities effectively.

In summary, awareness involves self-awareness, situational awareness, and an understanding of personal strengths, weaknesses, and opportunities. Embracing awareness allows for informed decision-making and personal growth.

Readiness

The final aspect of touchstone is readiness. Are you ready to embark on an AI journey? Are you ready to define your AI touchstone? You can be ready for the journey, but without the AI touchstone, how will you get to where you need to go? What steps do you need to take? To start off, you need to understand your touchstone before AI to figure out your touchstone with AI.

A state of readiness has unique properties:

- It is a proactive state of mind characterized by continuous learning to build expertise, prompt action to eliminate procrastination, and a proactive approach to creating opportunities rather than waiting for them to appear.
- It's about being prepared mentally and emotionally to embrace challenges, take initiative, and seize opportunities for growth and advancement.
- Readiness is the true precursor to action.

Willingness, awareness, and readiness—with these three attributes assessed and understood, your touchstone becomes evident, the steps to evolve your touchstone for AI become clear, and the movement into choice architecture becomes the natural next step. Remember, not knowing your touchstone puts you in a place where you drift with no clear direction. And to quote Antara, "It breaks my heart to watch people who don't know their purpose and move though their careers and life in misery and unable to figure out how to change." When we are in this state of misery, we don't know our touchstone or how to define it. We have all been there.

So, let's pull this all together: We are in a whirlwind of change. Roles are changing, organizations are changing, technology is evolving rapidly at scale. But with a defined touchstone, you are driven, filled with purpose, and can create "fit-to-purpose" paths that you can quickly adjust to in the face of these unknown challenges. If someone throws an obstacle in your way, you can easily navigate around it. Understanding willingness, awareness, and readiness will help you navigate the choices that are available to you and even help identify some you may want to make available.

One more example for baseball enthusiasts. After a hit, a player must swiftly get to first base to avoid being tagged out. In AI, individuals must discover and adhere to their personal touchstone to navigate successfully through the evolving challenges of AI in the workplace. Failing to do so will leave them vulnerable to being "tagged out" in the competitive game of professional growth and adaptation.

Our touchstone does not exist in a vacuum. At work, we typically exist within an organization; in our personal lives, we exist within communities. Hence, our touchstones are nested. Introducing the concepts of organizational, functional, individual, and personal transformation will broaden the scope and impact of the transformation touchstone. Beyond guiding organizational change, the touchstone resonates deeply with individuals at all levels, inspiring personal growth and collective advancement. It fosters a culture of innovation and collaboration, driving functional and individual transformations across any organization.

Distinguishing Between Automation and AI

We have highlighted the touchstone, the AI touchstone, and your role in defining it for yourself. To really embrace the AI touchstone, there is a deeper level of understanding required. To some degree, we need to scale human intelligence alongside artificial intelligence to fully gain the benefits of the advances in technology. If you are not mindful of the change, chaos will reign. Humanity, after all, drives technology

AI is often mistaken for mere automation, but they're not the same. Automation involves using technology and a set of rules to mechanize repetitive tasks, streamline processes, and reduce manual work. It mostly impacts roles that are labor-intensive. On the other hand, AI imitates human intelligence, allowing it to analyze large datasets and make decisions across various stakeholders or time frames. While automation improves efficiency in repetitive tasks, AI goes beyond, enhancing decision-making in complex situations and transforming roles with significant stakeholder involvement and temporal complexity. Think back to our car example in chapter 3. Cruise control is automation, but driverless cars are powered by AI.

Cruise control
Automation

Driverless Car
AI

Figure 4.1 Cruise control is automation, but
driverless cars are powered by AI.

Automation and AI stand as two pillars of technological innovation, each making distinctive contributions to the evolving landscape of industry and daily life. At its essence, automation signifies the process of mechanizing tasks to operate seamlessly without direct human intervention. This approach is instrumental in optimizing efficiency and diminishing manual efforts, particularly in activities characterized by repetition and rule-based structures. From the precision of manufacturing processes to the routine tasks in administrative workflows, automation serves as a catalyst for enhancing accuracy, speed, and overall productivity.

In contrast, AI represents a more expansive and intricate realm within technology. It encompasses the development of computer systems endowed with capabilities akin to human intelligence, ranging from learning and reasoning to problem-solving and adaptability. Unlike automation, which predominantly concerns itself with task execution, AI delves into the domain of decision-making. This distinction becomes apparent when considering the adaptability of these technologies. Automation follows predefined rules, making decisions within the established parameters but lacking the sophistication for complex decision-making beyond these boundaries. In contrast, AI systems are designed to autonomously make decisions by analyzing data, recognizing patterns, and adjusting their behavior based on feedback. This cognitive prowess is a defining feature that sets AI apart as a technology capable of nuanced and context-aware decision-making.

Practically, examples of automation include robotic manufacturing processes, scheduled data backups, and automated email responses, all adhering to predefined rules and operational parameters. In contrast, AI finds expression in virtual personal assistants like Siri and Alexa, image and speech recognition systems, and recommendation algorithms in streaming services. For example, the way voice technology has evolved, right now these tools are using natural language processing. These tools aren't making decisions, they are using the vast amount of data at hand to answer your questions. At some point in the future, you may be able to ask these tools for advice or guidance. Instead of asking where the nearest Italian restaurant is, you may ask an opinion-based question on the quality of food in nearby restaurants that would require a deeper layer of response.

These applications highlight AI's capacity to transcend routine tasks, adapting and learning dynamically from interactions and diverse data inputs. Additionally, the adaptability of AI is evident in its capacity to handle complex decision-making processes, making it a technology that evolves based on feedback and changing circumstances. This cognitive prowess is a defining feature that sets AI apart as a technology capable of nuanced and context-aware decision-making.

Now that we understand the difference between automation and AI, what else should you look at to evolve your AI touchstone? Let's circle back to our objectives.

- Understand your touchstone. This will require personal introspection.

- Distinguish between automation and artificial intelligence. These are the nuances that are required to understand your current state and where to go.
- Identify the areas where human thinking is transitioning to AI-driven augmentation in everyday life.
- Consider the evolution of role in an organization.
- Assess the readiness of self, role, and hiring trends.

Let's jump to the next objective.

Identifying the Areas Where Human Thinking is Transitioning to AI-Driven Augmentation

Here comes the next layer. We have defined the touchstone and the difference between automation and AI and why that matters. Now we need to go a layer deeper and figure out what parts of human thinking and decision-making can be augmented by AI. This will help you figure out where you need to scale your own capabilities and where you can leverage AI to take some of the load. In this space, we need you to expand your mindset and open up to using AI for your own evolution. This will help you further define your AI touchstone.

Identifying the optimal transition point from a state reliant on human intellect to one driven by AI involves pinpointing tasks or processes where AI technologies can provide advantages over human capabilities. In this context, you really need to be able to see clearly. You need to look at what you do, ways of working in your environment, and see what is changing or can change with AI. For example, recently I was building some reports at work using a popular reporting tool. I noticed for the first time that Copilot, a Microsoft tool, was an option. Rather than spend the rest of the afternoon building a report manually, I used Copilot and had what I wanted in thirty minutes. I had to see and be aware of what was changing around me. No one sent a memo that we had access; there weren't any training classes; the option just showed up. So I used it.

This transition will occur when you can see how AI can enhance efficiency, accuracy, or speed in performing specific tasks, allowing for a more streamlined and effective workflow. When you can see and experience how AI can help, AI will unlock you—not the other way around. You need to see and be aware and open in your mindset. Like in our core belief: humanity drives technology.

Individual Objectives for AI Integration

As an individual, you need to see and understand your touchstone, acknowledge where you are at, and consider your motivators. To measure that, we need some data points from your journey to date. You need to look to the past to learn for the future. For example, assess your own resume, skill sets, and general readiness for AI adoption. Understanding these data points will help you craft personalized strategies that align with your goals when you get to choice architecture (chapter 5).

In the dynamic job market shaped by AI, adapting for relevance is essential. Steps you will take include setting clear objectives: assess current skills, analyze job roles considering AI, identify transferable skills, and create a learning plan. Reflect on your personal history of change, understanding past experiences as a foundation for moving forward. It's crucial to leverage transferable skills while learning new ones, ensuring a seamless integration into the evolving landscape. Stay informed about industry trends, build a network, and seek mentorship. Prioritize soft skill development, stay agile, and regularly assess progress for continual improvement. Another crucial aspect is goal alignment, which centers around harmonizing individual goals with the broader objectives of AI transformation.

Essentially, these objectives form a roadmap for individuals to navigate the evolving job landscape by drawing insights from both past experiences and forward-looking strategies, ensuring adaptability and success in the AI-driven workplace. For future reference, a roadmap is a strategic plan that outlines a sequence of steps or milestones to achieve a particular goal. It can be personal or something that drives priorities in an organization. A milestone is something big that is accomplished along a roadmap—a necessary step to get you to the destination. We could use milestone birthdays like turning twenty-five or fifty, getting a college degree, or getting your black belt in jujitsu. We get deeper step-by-step in the chapters to come, with Choice Architecture (chapter 5), Play (chapter 6), Grow (chapter 7), and Disrupt (chapter 8).

Organizational Objectives for AI Integration

Being able to see where to go at the individual level is not enough. You are likely an employee. You need to see how your touchstone fits in the context of your organization to help you see AI-related opportunities. Key considerations for leaders and individual contributors include understanding the complexity of tasks or work, the availability of relevant data for AI training, and the potential for AI to augment human decision-making. Organizationally, you need to be willing to conduct a thoughtful assessment of the specific functions and their alignment with AI capabilities to help guide your organization in determining the right place for this transition.

If you want to look for low-hanging fruit, look for activities in your organization that are repetitive, rules-based, or data-intensive, as these are potential candidates for AI automation. Assess the complexity of tasks and the availability of relevant data, favoring those that align well with AI capabilities. Consider opportunities for collaboration, allowing AI to handle routine aspects while humans focus on higher-level decision-making. Prioritize tasks based on their impact and feasibility for AI integration. Train and involve the workforce to ensure a smooth transition. Start with small-scale pilot projects, continuously evaluate AI performance, and gather feedback for ongoing adaptation. This methodical approach ensures a strategic and effective transition, harnessing the strengths of both human and AI intelligence.

Situation @ Work	Action
1 The Organization and Roles are growing	Keep Growing
2 Role and Organization are not aligned in growth	Transform Role
3 The Organization and Roles are shrinking	Transform Personally

Figure 4.2. Define your situation at work, to
help you choose which path to take.

Evaluating the Organization in a Broader Sense

We can not forget the organization in a broader sense. In the quest to establish a transformative touchstone, the organization leverages its rich history of navigating change, embodying adaptability, implementing robust measurement frameworks, and crafting strategic roadmaps. Recognizing its pivotal role in not only transforming functions but also shaping individuals and processes, the organization cultivates a culture of continuous improvement and innovation. Through targeted initiatives and collective efforts, it endeavors to redefine operational paradigms, fostering a dynamic environment conducive to growth and success.

In today's dynamic organizational landscape, the rapid growth of AI introduces a mix of challenges and opportunities. Successfully navigating this evolution requires organizations to adapt their objectives while staying unwaveringly aligned with their overarching mission—the North Star. This adaptive approach positions organizations to fully harness the potential of AI, driving both innovation and sustainable success.

What it comes down to, is that the organization is reevaluating its North Star in the face of AI. You are updating your touchstone to evolve with AI. As the organization refines its North Star and you refine your touchstone, you need to make sure you are in alignment to prevent friction and fatigue and reduce the risk of being out of sync.

AI transformation brings a unique challenge compared to traditional transformations because it is broader and nonlinear. What is truly encouraging is that as this change happens, you begin to scale your human intelligence along with AI. Let's examine four scenarios, each with an explanation and use case, providing valuable insights for organizations navigating the complexities of AI transformation while aligning with their goals.

Evolution of Role: How Emerging Trends Are Reshaping Roles in Organizations

As we researched the impact of AI on roles, it's clear that certain outcomes emerge and are heavily influenced by the state of the organization. Consider figure 4.3.

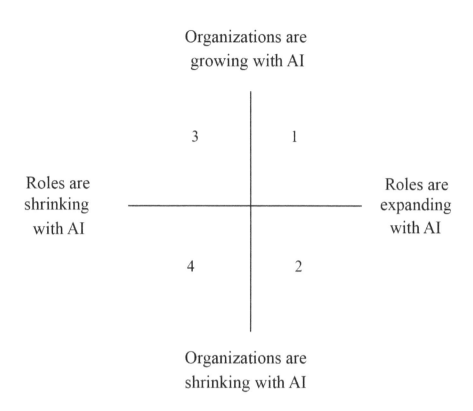

Figure 4.3. Emerging trends for the evolution
of roles with the integration of AI.

Embracing a transformative mindset becomes crucial in this swiftly
changing AI landscape, prompting us to ask: How can I best align in my
current job or get ready for a new role?

We believe there are four trends for roles today.

- **Organization is expanding with AI and your role is expanding with AI.** In this area, you can naturally grow in sync with AI
  advancements and within your organization, leading to career
  development and a happy path progression.

- **Organization is shrinking because of AI, but your role is expanding with AI.** In this example, while the organizational footprint is shrinking, your role has the potential to scale a pivot and grow in relevance with AI.
- **Role is shrinking but the organization is growing.** Your job is becoming obsolete but the organization is opening up opportunities you can grow into. Roles can face material change due to AI's influence, making them more streamlined and efficient.
- **Role is shrinking and organization is shrinking.** In this scenario, you may have to cut and run. Personal transformation is your only option. Roles can be slated for gradual reduction and elimination over time or on a fast track, prompting more immediate organization restructures in the professional landscape.

By acknowledging that we may have some insights into future AI developments as it comes to changing jobs and roles, we must position ourselves for success and build a runway for our careers going forward. You need to own your path, and you need to own your change. In terms of action, there are two pathways that empower you to control your own destiny within the realm of AI:

1. Role transformation
2. Individual Transformation

In both scenarios, personal accountability is key. You own the next steps with your role and your individual development. We emphasize "taking ownership" in both areas for very specific reasons. Those that take ownership will be able to not only demonstrate their ability to adapt, but they will also develop and grow their ability to adapt. Efficient adaptation will be the key to managing the frequent change that is at the heart of AI. By taking ownership, you not only maximize your opportunities, but you also create autonomy and empowerment of choice. Additionally, you fortify a personal resilience layer, which, coupled with efficient adaptation, positions you as a formidable, confident player in the AI arena.

Transforming a role, an individual, and assuming ownership for personal transformations represent distinct but interconnected processes within personal and professional development.

Transforming in a Role

Transforming a role involves redefining and reshaping the responsibilities, objectives, and functions associated with a specific position or job within an organization. This process may entail restructuring workflows, revising job descriptions, and implementing new technologies or methodologies to enhance efficiency and effectiveness in fulfilling the role's requirements. Transforming a role often aligns with broader organizational goals and strategies, aiming to optimize performance and adapt to changing business environments.

Transforming as an Individual

Transforming an individual focuses on enhancing personal skills, capabilities, and behaviors to adapt to new challenges, seize opportunities, and achieve professional growth. This process encompasses self-reflection, learning, and development activities aimed at expanding knowledge, acquiring new competencies, and refining existing strengths. Individual transformation may involve seeking mentorship, pursuing further education or certifications, and actively participating in professional development programs to unlock potential and advance career objectives.

There is also the option of creating a personal North Star. To create a personal North Star you need to assess three things.

1. Figure out what you are good at.
2. Figure out what you love to do.
3. Make sure there is growing demand.

Creating a personal North Star helps you proactively prepare for AI.

Personal Northstar

Figure 4.4. Crafting your personal North Star.

Taking Ownership of Your Personal Transformation

Assuming ownership for personal transformations entails taking proactive accountability and responsibility for one's growth, development, and well-being. It involves recognizing the need for change, setting meaningful goals, and committing to a journey of continuous improvement and self-discovery. Ownership of personal transformations requires resilience, perseverance, and a willingness to embrace discomfort and uncertainty as catalysts for growth. It empowers individuals to take charge of their destinies, navigate transitions, and cultivate a sense of purpose and fulfillment in both personal and professional domains.

So while transforming a role focuses on organizational adaptation, transforming an individual emphasizes personal growth and development. Assuming ownership for personal transformations empowers individuals to drive meaningful change in their lives, careers, and relationships, fostering a sense of agency and self-actualization in the pursuit of success and fulfillment.

Grounded in the transformation touchstone, the shift from human to artificial intelligence represents a profound evolution in our technological landscape. This transition serves as the plane of transformation, where machines increasingly integrate with human capabilities. Guided by the touchstone, we navigate this change, ensuring our values and goals steer the course. As we embrace this paradigm shift, we explore its vast potential while remaining mindful of the ethical and societal considerations it entails.

Assessing the Readiness of Self, Role, and Organization

Are You Ready?

Now we get to the meat of the chapter. You need to take what you have learned and figure out where you are at and begin to define your AI touchstone and figure out how to scale your own human intelligence in parallel with AI, which will influence your path for individual and/or role transformation. Let's regroup.

Navigating the ever-evolving landscape of AI requires a nuanced evaluation of one's own preparedness, the roles and availability within an organization, and the broader industry context. As AI continues to reshape processes, products, and services, individuals find themselves at the intersection of personal development and technological advancement. Understanding the intricacies of AI's impact on the self, the role one plays, and the overall organizational dynamics becomes imperative.

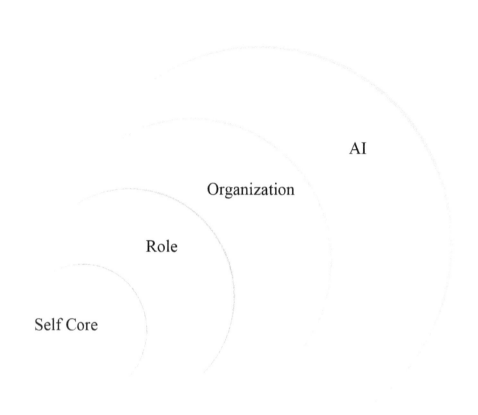

Figure 4.5. Aligning self to surroundings.

Let's consider you are in an organization that is shrinking with AI and your role is growing. For example, you are a product manager who manages voice technology for an organization. Your team leverages virtual assistants to help its consumers. You are likely in a great spot and need to show up and continue to make the same great choices that got you here.

In this scenario, the organization is shrinking because of AI, but your role is expanding with AI. So, if you work in marketing operations, for example, it is likely that this overall function will shrink with AI advancements, reducing the organization's footprint. However, the leaders in this space that leverage generative AI to solve for the work will be in a role that expands. In this scenario, you need to embrace role transformation and take ownership of it.

Let's say you work for a retail company that has decided to implement AI-driven automation to streamline operations and improve efficiency. As a result of this implementation, several departments within the organization, such as manual data entry, inventory management, and consumer support, are experiencing a reduction in workforce needs due to tasks being automated by AI systems.

However, your role as a data analyst or AI specialist is expanding with the integration of AI technologies. Your responsibilities now include designing and implementing AI algorithms to optimize pricing strategies, personalize consumer recommendations, and forecast demand patterns. You're also tasked with analyzing data collected from AI systems to identify market trends, consumer behavior patterns, and opportunities for innovation.

While the overall organizational footprint may be shrinking as certain tasks are automated, your role is scaling and growing in relevance with AI. By leveraging your expertise in AI technologies, you're able to contribute to the company's strategic initiatives, drive revenue growth, and stay ahead of competitors in the rapidly evolving retail landscape. Your ability to adapt and pivot with the changing technological landscape positions you as a valuable asset to the organization despite the overall reduction in workforce size. Again, you need to focus on role transformation and take responsibility to enhance your skills and continue to evolve with the role.

Let's say your role is shrinking, but the organization is growing. Your job is becoming obsolete, but the organization is opening up opportunities you can grow into. Let's imagine you work in a manufacturing company that has recently adopted advanced AI-powered robotics and automation systems to optimize production processes. These AI technologies have significantly streamlined operations, leading to increased productivity, reduced costs, and improved quality control. However, as a result of this automation, your role as a manual assembly line worker or quality control inspector is gradually becoming obsolete.

While your current role is shrinking due to AI's influence, the organization is experiencing growth and expanding its operations. With the implementation of AI technologies, new opportunities are emerging within the company, particularly in roles that involve overseeing, maintaining, and optimizing the AI systems.

Recognizing the need for skilled personnel to manage and operate these AI-driven technologies, the organization is investing in training programs and upskilling initiatives to reskill employees for roles such as AI system technicians, data analysts, or process automation specialists. These roles require a combination of technical expertise in AI systems and a deep understanding of the company's manufacturing processes. By embracing these opportunities and acquiring the necessary skills and knowledge, you can adapt to the changing needs of the organization and position yourself for growth and advancement in your career.

In our final scenario, your role is shrinking and the organization is shrinking. Roles can be slated for gradual reduction and elimination over time or on a fast track, prompting more immediate organization restructures in the professional landscape.

Let's say you work for a local newspaper that's been impacted by the rise of digital media. As more people turn to online news sources and social media for information, the newspaper's circulation and advertising revenue decline. To stay afloat, the company invests in AI technology to automate article writing and optimize content distribution. However, despite these efforts, the newspaper continues to struggle financially, leading to layoffs and budget cuts. As a result, your role as a journalist or editor is shrinking and the organization itself is shrinking as well. With fewer resources and opportunities for career advancement within the newspaper industry, you may need to explore alternative career paths or consider retraining for roles in digital media, content marketing, or related fields.

All's not lost. In fact, you are in a great space even in this type of role. You have today. If you are self-aware, you can solve this before it happens. There will be a multitude of people who will continue to search for what really isn't there anymore. But not you. You bought this book, you know you have to change and grow. Personal transformation is the crystal clear path for you.

My AI Touchstone: Scaling Human Intelligence with AI

In reflecting on the crucial aspects outlined—understanding our touchstone through personal introspection, distinguishing between automation and artificial intelligence to map our current state, identifying areas of AI-driven augmentation in daily life, contemplating the evolution of roles within organizations, and assessing readiness at personal, professional, and market levels—we lay a strong foundation for the next phase: defining our AI touchstone. This transition signifies not only a comprehensive understanding of AI's implications but also a commitment to harness its potential to scale human intelligence.

Think of this as building blocks. You know your touchstone, your motivation; you understand the difference between automation and AI—this will ensure that you know what to look for in your organization. You can see where pieces of work will be replaced by AI in your role and in other roles. You can now look at your organization's footprint with a new lens and anticipate if it will grow or shrink. With this knowledge, you will take accountability to chart your course and define your AI touchstone to prepare you for the choices that lie ahead.

For instance, if you're a data analyst in a tech company embracing AI, you should continue mastering data science tools and methodologies. Instead of relying solely on traditional statistical methods, start learning machine learning algorithms and actively contribute to AI-driven projects. Take ownership of your career by pursuing advanced AI certifications and participating in cross-functional AI teams.

So What?

This chapter emphasizes the transformative impact of AI on the workplace and the imperative for personal growth and adaptability. It underscores the need for individuals to proactively engage with AI, understand its implications, and align their personal development with the changing technological landscape. This chapter gave you the tools to look at yourself and your organization and how it will all change with AI. We reinforced the fact that you must know your "why" so you can forge a path forward. The urgency is clear: AI is not just another digital tool; it's a paradigm shift that requires a new mindset and approach to work.

Now What?

Define your AI Touchstone—Recognize your current position and motivations in relation to AI. This self-awareness will guide your decisions and actions.

Moving forward, it's crucial to take action and:

- Distinguish AI from automation: Grasp the subtle differences to better navigate your journey.
- Identify AI-driven transitions: Understand where and how AI can augment human thinking in your role.
- Evolve with your role: Stay ahead by anticipating changes in your job and the industry.
- Assess readiness: Evaluate your own, and your organization's, preparedness for AI integration.

By doing so, you'll be able to craft a strategic path that harmonizes your personal goals with AI advancements, ensuring you remain relevant and thrive in an AI-centric future. The path forward is clear: to scale human intelligence with artificial intelligence, we must align our personal development with the rapid advancements in technology. This chapter lays the groundwork for the subsequent exploration of choice architecture, where you will make strategic decisions that resonate with your AI Touchstone and propel you toward a future where human potential and artificial intelligence converge.

The AI revolution calls for a proactive stance—a readiness to learn, adapt, and innovate. As we continue to explore the implications of AI, let us do so with a sense of purpose and a commitment to personal and professional growth. The future is ours to shape, and with AI as our ally, the possibilities are limitless.

Before you move forward, take a moment and ask yourself, are you and your organization growing with AI? What is your mindset when it comes to embracing AI? Are you willing, aware, and ready?

My Touchstone situation

My
Employer

Is Growing with AI

✓ ✗ Circle one

My
Role

Is Growing with AI

✓ ✗ Circle one

Figure 4.6. Situational Checkpoint.

My Touchstone mindset

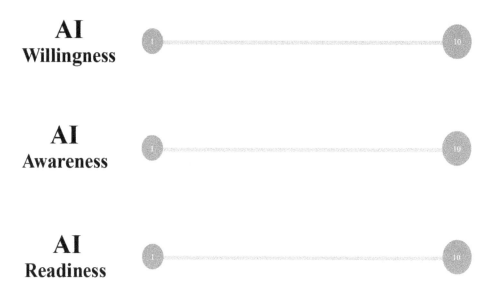

Figure 4.7. Mindset checkpoint.

CHOICE ARCHITECTURE

DESIGN YOUR DECISIONS

Introduction

LET'S KICK OFF your roadmap to empowerment. But first, let's recap: You understand your organization's North Star. You know how to measure progress and success and when to course correct because something is not working or needs refinement. You have gone through the process of defining your touchstone, and you understand the trends for your role and organization and can chart your AI touchstone. Based on your willingness, awareness, and readiness, we want to help you make the best choices for you, your role, and your organization.

You have choices, and acting on them proactively to shape the future is in the best interests of both individuals and organizations in the AI era. We need to talk about choice architecture in the face of change we know is coming. Unlike previous transformations, the AI revolution is already here—just check any of your social media accounts. One of the reasons we wrote this book is because we believe, wholeheartedly, that people and organizations have to design and plan their choices to stay ahead of the AI curve and to truly reap the rewards.

The chapter defines choice architecture within the context of AI and introduces the concepts of play, grow, and disrupt as the primary choice pathways for personal growth and development amid AI advancements. For individuals, it emphasizes understanding options and key decision-making factors. It prompts readers to craft their personal plans, fostering growth alongside AI advancements. It is action-oriented.

Organizations, on the other hand, are encouraged to use choice architecture to align their AI strategies with their objectives, stressing the need for swift decision/making and the ability to course correct dynamically. Organizations are prompted to employ choice architecture through our method, PACT, which stands for pivot, align, culture, and transform. Employing our method helps organizational leaders determine how to pivot to drive AI transformation and align internal roadmaps and budgets while caring for the cultural nuances and change needed within the workforce, ultimately leading to a successful AI transformation.

In the end, readers will be armed with the cognitive knowledge of how to craft personal plans that foster growth alongside AI advancements, recognizing choice as a critical influencer in organizational design, roadmaps, and change adoption.

Choice architecture aims to achieve several objectives for both individuals and organizations:

1. Personal and professional use of choice: understanding the concept of choice architecture and leveraging it strategically in personal and professional contexts. This involves exploring how choices can be utilized for personal growth and innovation, especially in response to the impact of AI.

2. Choice architecture in personal transformation: exploring the embedded choice architecture within the individual's journey of transformation. This includes defining concepts such as play, grow, and disrupt and examining the virtues of different paths through everyday examples. The goal is to encourage experimentation, development, and innovation.

3. Choice architecture in organizational context: describing how choice architecture, coupled with AI, operates within organizational settings. This involves establishing clear objectives and frameworks aligned with the organization's transformational goals, particularly amid AI disruption. It's about sculpting the decision-making landscape to harmonize with organizational objectives and navigate industry evolution.

All About Choice

During my early days at JPMorgan Chase, I worked for a leader who really opened my eyes about choice. My three kids were little, and I constantly struggled to move from work to after-school sports and homework to bedtime and back to work. I was the classic working mom, trying to do it all and feeling like I was failing across the board. At a particularly low point, one of the leaders, a managing director, said to me, "Winnie, I make choices every day. One day I choose my son's soccer game, and the next I choose a steering committee meeting."

There is a layering of choices. Think of it this way: I wanted to make choices to help care for my young children, but at the same time, I wanted to make choices that would help further my career and my personal development and growth. So, I had to evolve my mindset to accept that I had more than one driver and that I had to make fluid choices to not sacrifice my priorities. I had to use choice to navigate among family, career, and personal growth to keep all three objectives moving forward in a positive way. And it wasn't easy.

The key concept is to first understand that we are making daily choices whether we know it or not. For example, hitting the snooze button is your first choice of the day. With AI, you can't take a leap of faith that it will all work out. You need to choose cognitive action and evolve it into instinctive action (like the snooze button). That is what choice architecture should become. It is the beacon that will drive your AI touchstone and scale your human intelligence. It's personal to you.

It is important to us that you feel empowered and that the choice is yours, as is the action that must follow. The best part—the outcome—is yours to celebrate.

Choice Architecture

Choice architecture refers to the intentional design of the way choices are presented to individuals to influence their decision-making behavior. It involves structuring the environment in which choices are made to guide people toward certain decisions while still allowing them to retain their freedom of choice. Key elements of choice architecture include how options are framed, ordered, and presented, as well as the use of defaults and incentives to influence decisions. This concept is often applied in various fields such as economics, marketing, public policy, and behavioral science, to encourage desirable choices and behaviors.

The term *choice architecture* was popularized by Richard H. Thaler and Cass R. Sunstein in their influential book titled *Nudge: Improving Decisions about Health, Wealth, and Happiness.* In this book, Thaler and Sunstein discuss various ways that decision-making can be influenced through subtle changes in the choice architecture, such as the use of defaults, framing, and incentives. They advocate for designing choice environments that make it easier for individuals to make better decisions without restricting their freedom of choice, a concept they refer to as "libertarian paternalism."

Connecting Life Choices and Daily Decisions

The top three choices humans make in their lives vary greatly depending on individual circumstances, beliefs, and values. However, some common choices that many people face include:

- Career and education: Choosing a career path and pursuing education or training to achieve career goals is a significant decision for many individuals.
- Relationships and family: Deciding whom to form relationships with, whether to marry or start a family, and how to navigate relationships with family members are crucial life choices.
- Personal growth and development: Opting for personal growth and development involves decisions related to health, hobbies, interests, spirituality, and overall well-being.

These choices shape the trajectory of one's life and contribute to personal fulfillment and happiness.

The top three choices humans make every day are often routine decisions that impact daily life, such as:

- Food and nutrition: Deciding what to eat and drink is a fundamental choice people make multiple times a day. It involves considerations of taste, health, dietary restrictions, and convenience.

- Time management: Allocating time for various activities such as work, leisure, exercise, and personal responsibilities is a daily choice. Prioritizing tasks and managing time effectively is essential for productivity and balance.
- Communication and interactions: Choosing how to communicate and interact with others is a constant decision. This includes conversations with family, friends, colleagues, and strangers, as well as interactions through digital channels like email, phone calls, and social media. Effective communication shapes relationships and fosters connection.

The top three life choices—career, relationships, and lifestyle—greatly affect daily decisions. Career decisions shape work routines, relationships impact emotions and interactions, and lifestyle choices influence habits and priorities. Conversely, daily choices like diet, time management, and communication can have immediate impact and impact over time, and they influence long-term goals and satisfaction. These choices interact with one another other, shaping overall well-being.

With AI's rise, these dynamics may change. Automation could reshape job markets, prompting career reassessment. AI-driven communication might alter relationship dynamics, while health apps may impact lifestyle choices. As AI advances, ethical issues like privacy and bias will require consideration. Consequently, the relationship between life choices and daily decisions will evolve alongside AI integration.

Choice Architecture When Surrounded by AI

Fundamentally, choice architecture is personal and starts with you. It is equally important for organizations to leverage choice architecture with discipline into AI system development to grow and scale AI responsibly. As the organization frames its choice architecture, they need to be inclusive of you in that process. Within the context of you and the organization, it is a two-way street when it comes to choice and AI. As AI systems increasingly influence decision-making processes and user behaviors, the design of choice architectures becomes paramount in fostering fairness, transparency, and user autonomy. Choice architecture emerges as a critical element in navigating the opportunities and challenges posed by the proliferation of AI technologies within the organization as well as within society and both influence personal transformation.

Navigating the intricate terrain of AI and choice architecture demands a strategic approach to personal evolution. Many have read Spencer Johnson's *Who Moved My Cheese?* The book is a metaphor for how people deal with change and choices in their work and personal lives. It emphasizes the importance of anticipating change, adapting to one's environment, and not being paralyzed by fear. The main characters all make different choices leading to different outcomes. Recognizing the necessity for proactive adaptation, individuals can chart their transformative journey through a combination of foundational learning, community engagement, and strategic partnerships.

Choice Pathways

Planes, trains, and automobiles. From our perspective, there are three pathways you can choose. It simplifies the first steps of the journey with a balanced selection that is not overwhelming. It allows for easier comparison and leads to more thoughtful decision-making.

We don't consider not choosing a choice for our reader because you already bought and are reading the book. We believe your choice can influence the dynamics of the journey, the speed of the journey, and the iterative outcomes. The pathways we have defined are play, grow, and disrupt.

Play

One effective approach to becoming part of AI involves embracing the concept of play, creating a dynamic playground where individuals can experiment and explore AI's potential applications to discover how they can effectively incorporate it into their endeavors. Play, as a concept, encourages individuals to embrace AI with an open mind and actively participate in the AI playground. We'll cover this more in-depth in chapter 6.

Grow

Embracing growth with AI is a smart move for those aiming to stay ahead. By partnering with AI to develop, individuals can excel in the rapidly changing world of artificial intelligence.

To grow alongside AI, individuals can make several choices with specific results. First, continuous learning is essential. Keeping up with the latest AI advancements through education ensures acquiring new skills and staying relevant. Second, specializing in specific AI areas aligning with interests and career goals can lead to career advancement and more job opportunities. We will expand on this in chapter 7.

Disrupt

The type of person who wants to disrupt is often characterized by traits such as innovation, creativity, ambition, and a willingness to challenge the status quo. They are forward-thinking individuals who are not content with the way things are and are driven by a desire to make a meaningful impact and drive positive change. They possess a strong sense of curiosity and are not afraid to take risks or embrace uncertainty in pursuit of their goals. Disruptors are often visionaries who see opportunities where others see obstacles, and they are passionate about pushing boundaries, experimenting with new ideas, and creating innovative solutions to complex problems. They thrive in dynamic environments where they can leverage their skills and expertise to drive transformation and shape the future. You will learn a lot more about this pathway in chapter 8.

What Stops Someone from Choosing to Evolve with Change?

Why don't some people proactively make the choice to evolve with change? What is it about change or their personal perspective that makes them think it will all be ok?

One of the primary psychological barriers to change is known as "loss aversion." Loss aversion refers to the tendency for people to strongly prefer avoiding losses over acquiring equivalent gains. In other words, individuals tend to weigh potential losses more heavily than potential gains of equal value.

This psychological phenomenon can create a strong resistance to change because change often involves letting go of familiar routines, habits, or ways of thinking, which can be perceived as losses. People may fear losing aspects of their identity, status, or sense of security associated with the current state, leading them to resist change even if the potential benefits outweigh the perceived losses.

Additionally, change can evoke feelings of uncertainty, discomfort, and anxiety, which further exacerbate the psychological barrier to change. People may feel overwhelmed by the unknown and prefer to stick with the familiar rather than venture into unfamiliar territory.

Other psychological barriers to change include the following:

- Fear of failure: Change often involves risk, and people may fear that they will not be able to successfully navigate or adapt to the new circumstances, leading to a reluctance to change.
- Cognitive biases: Cognitive biases, such as confirmation bias (favoring information that confirms existing beliefs) or anchoring bias (relying too heavily on initial information), can distort perceptions and decision-making processes, making it difficult for individuals to objectively evaluate the need for change.
- Comfort zone: People tend to seek comfort and stability in their daily lives, and stepping out of their comfort zone to embrace change can be daunting and uncomfortable.
- Status quo bias: This bias refers to the tendency for individuals to prefer the current state of affairs over potential changes, even if the changes offer potential benefits.

Figure 5.1. People will move forward when they are
curious but will be stalled when they are fearful.

Addressing these psychological barriers to change requires a combination of awareness, education, support, and leadership. By understanding the underlying reasons for resistance to change and providing individuals with the resources, incentives, and encouragement they need to overcome these barriers, organizations can foster a culture that is more open to change and better equipped to adapt to new circumstances.

Choice Architecture in the Organization

Any and all transformation starts with choices. To lay the foundation for the choices, it is important to understand where we are headed and what our starting point is. In the context of this book, the North Star represents the ultimate destination or goal that a product, company, or institution is aiming to achieve with regard to AI adoption and development. On the other hand, the touchstone is an assessment of each individual's current position and readiness in relation to that goal. By evaluating the gap between the touchstone (starting point) and the North Star (desired outcome), individuals can understand their personal journey and the steps needed to progress toward the overarching goal of AI proficiency.

In essence, choice architecture acts as a step-by-step move toward embracing AI at large. Everyone at every level of the organization is having some sort of reaction to AI—some are fearful, some are curious, some are just confused. The point here is that everyone at every level is having some type of emotional response.

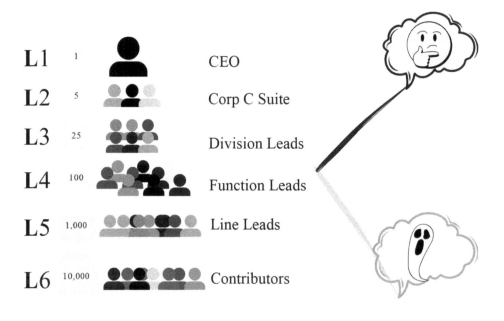

Figure 5.2. Everyone at every level of an organization is having some type of emotional response to AI. For many, it is either curiosity or fear.

In the age of AI disruption, organizations encounter new challenges, opportunities, and considerations (see figure 5.2). As AI transforms industries and business models, organizations need to navigate this changing landscape with clarity and foresight. Choice architecture plays a crucial role by setting clear objectives and frameworks that help organizations adapt and succeed amid change.

By aligning decision-making processes with the transformational touchstone and North Star of the organization, choice architecture ensures that strategic decisions are made with a clear understanding of their impact on the organization's long-term goals and vision.

Changing Organization Design with AI

Organizations can navigate the transformative landscape of AI by making strategic choices aimed at adaptation and growth. First, investing in AI technologies offers opportunities to automate tasks, enhance decision-making processes, and gain a competitive edge. This investment not only streamlines operations and reduces costs but also positions the organization as a leader in leveraging cutting-edge technology for innovation. Second, prioritizing the acquisition and development of AI talent ensures that the organization possesses the expertise and capabilities necessary to effectively harness the power of AI. By recruiting skilled professionals and providing ongoing training, organizations can build internal capacity and drive digital transformation initiatives forward. Integrating AI into existing business processes is another strategic choice, enabling organizations to meet evolving consumer needs and stay ahead of market trends. Whether through AI-powered products and services or solutions for consumer service and operations, integrating AI fosters agility and responsiveness in a rapidly changing business environment. Additionally, organizations must establish clear policies and practices for data governance and ethics to ensure responsible AI usage and compliance with regulations.

Finally, fostering collaboration and partnerships with AI startups, research institutions, and industry peers enables organizations to access cutting-edge technologies and resources, accelerating innovation and driving digital transformation initiatives more effectively. Overall, these strategic choices empower organizations to adapt and thrive in the era of AI by leveraging technology, talent, and partnerships to drive innovation, improve efficiency, and create value.

What Is PACT?

PACT is a method that will aid organizations and individuals define their path with AI. It is an ecosystem and a critical part of *AI for All*. Within PACT, there are four key parts:

- **Pivot:** Change from just scaling up to focusing on what sets you apart in the market, and using AI to make it a reality.
- **Align:** Linking finance, business strategy, operational challenges, and technology to stay laser-focused on what matters.
- **Culture:** Empowering everyone who's curious, bold, and cares about AI to integrate it into products, platforms, processes, and daily lives.
- **Transform:** Reshaping of processes, strategies, and cultures to leverage artificial intelligence for unprecedented innovation, efficiency, and competitive advantage.

Pivot

A pivot typically refers to a point or axis around which an object can rotate or turn. AI can act as a pivotal force to repurpose operational savings, fund innovation, and grow topline metrics. While introducing AI can force a pivot one use case at a time, the strategic recommendation is to orchestrate a pivot that is cohesive and drives deliberate performance change. The pivot can not be decoupled from financial strategy or metrics. It involves significantly more than a simple budget-allocation exercise.

Align

To align means to arrange or adjust something in a way that is in harmony or agreement with a particular purpose, goal, or direction. In a broader context, it refers to ensuring that actions, strategies, or objectives are consistent and coordinated to achieve a common aim. Alignment often involves bringing different elements or stakeholders into agreement or synchronization to work toward a shared vision or objective. It can also entail adjusting one's actions or plans to fit with broader organizational goals or strategies. Overall, alignment is about ensuring cohesion and coherence within a system or organization to maximize effectiveness and achieve desired outcomes.

Culture

Embracing AI universally to change how organizations solve business problems and interact with their consumers, needs to be backed by a meticulous change approach that will foster an AI-friendly culture and ultimately speed up adoption. Ultimately, people drive organizational change. The change approach, when leveraged, will create a space for personal growth with flexibility and choice that will make this universal move to AI consumable for the people, their leadership, and the organization. It will foster a sustainable culture for AI, but it is also the force that can sabotage transformational change if fear trumps curiosity and control.

Transform

The steps in PACT drive the ability to transform, offering a methodical approach that coordinates organizational transformation across various dimensions. By interconnecting these elements, organizations can establish a holistic approach to transformation, effectively leveraging AI to drive innovation, efficiency, and sustainable growth.

Using PACT and Choice Architecture

Let's level set. You understand your organization's North Star. You know how to measure progress and success and when to course correct because something is not working or needs refinement. You have gone through the process of defining your touchstone, understand the trends for your role and organization, and can chart your AI touchstone. Based on your willingness, awareness, and readiness, we want to help you make the best choices for you, your role, and your organization. We have shared a quick view of our method PACT, which will be the in-depth topic in a future book written for executives driving AI transformations in large corporations. As such, we need to set the stage to answer the question "Why do we introduce PACT as part of Choice Architecture?"

Pivot, defined above, is an imperative for corporations to stay relevant in AI and shift with the paradigm. The company has to pivot. This pivot, when executed at the highest of leadership levels and not through incremental changes, guarantees a unified and synchronized effort to steer the entire organization toward its AI-infused North Star.

It involves aligning roadmaps and budgets to the new direction while also addressing cultural shifts necessary to solve the people problem. This alignment ultimately leads to transformation, vital in the face of AI's disruptive impact. Choosing not to pivot will impede the organization's ability to operate with speed and adaptability, potentially hindering its capacity for growth and innovation amid the evolving landscape shaped by AI.

As the organization works to align roadmaps and budget and foster a culture of change adoption, AI transformation becomes straightforward and choices along the journey are evident to the individuals driving the change.

Choice architecture guides stakeholders toward decisions and actions that resonate with the core values and objectives of the transformation journey. It involves crafting the environment in which choices are made to prioritize initiatives that align with the organization's strategic direction and leverage the transformative potential of AI technologies.

Choice architecture can influence how AI initiatives are prioritized and integrated into organizational processes. By presenting options that emphasize alignment with the transformational touchstone and the organizational North Star, choice architecture encourages stakeholders to embrace AI solutions that drive innovation, efficiency, and strategic growth. For example, imagine a healthcare organization that aims to integrate AI to improve patient care. The leadership team, using choice architecture, presents the staff with several AI implementation options. Each option is designed to align with the organization's North Star of delivering exceptional patient care and the transformational touchstone of leveraging technology for better health outcomes.

One option might be the adoption of an AI-powered diagnostic tool that can analyze medical images with greater accuracy and speed than traditional methods. Another could be implementing an AI system that predicts patient admission rates, helping to manage hospital resources more effectively.

By framing these options in a way that highlights their alignment with the organization's core goals and values, choice architecture nudges stakeholders toward embracing AI solutions that not only drive innovation and efficiency but also contribute to the strategic growth of the organization in the long term. This approach ensures that AI initiatives are not just randomly selected but are thoughtfully prioritized to support the overarching mission of the organization.

Moreover, choice architecture fosters a culture of innovation and collaboration essential for success in the AI-driven landscape. By promoting transparency, inclusivity, and accountability in decision-making processes, choice architecture cultivates an environment where stakeholders are empowered to explore AI-driven opportunities, experiment with emerging technologies, and contribute their insights toward achieving transformative goals.

In essence, choice architecture, infused with an AI flavor, serves as a strategic compass guiding organizations through the complexities of transformation. By designing decision environments that reflect the values and aspirations of the organization's AI-enabled future, leaders can navigate uncertainties, capitalize on opportunities, and chart a course toward sustainable success in the age of AI disruption.

What Happens When Choice Is Removed?

When choice is not utilized in the described scenario, organizations face significant consequences. Without the option to pivot, organizations become stagnant and unable to adapt to changing circumstances or capitalize on emerging opportunities. This lack of flexibility inhibits their ability to operate with agility and responsiveness, ultimately hindering their capacity for growth and innovation in an AI-driven landscape. The absence of choice to pivot prevents organizations from realigning their strategies, resources, and culture to align with their defined touchstone and North Star. As a result, they risk falling behind competitors and failing to harness the transformative potential of AI technologies. In essence, without the choice to pivot, organizations face the prospect of being left behind in an increasingly dynamic and disruptive business environment shaped by AI.

For example, imagine a car manufacturer that hesitates to implement AI-driven enhancements in the in-car experience due to uncertainty and initial investment concerns. By not leveraging choice architecture to pivot toward modern AI features like voice-activated controls and advanced navigation systems, they risk losing consumers to competitors offering more innovative and tech-savvy vehicle experiences. This underscores the critical role of choice architecture in guiding organizations to adapt and align with evolving consumer preferences driven by AI innovations, ensuring long-term competitiveness and market relevance.

The Impact of Opt In vs Opt Out

Opting in to evolving with AI involves actively embracing technological advancements, seeking opportunities for learning and skill development, and adapting to changes in personal and professional environments. It signifies a proactive stance toward leveraging AI to one's advantage, potentially leading to competitive advantages, personal growth, and innovation. On the other hand, opting out may reflect resistance to change, limited opportunities for advancement, and risks of obsolescence in an increasingly AI-driven world. Individuals who opt out may miss out on opportunities for career growth, efficiency improvements, and contributions to innovation. Ultimately, the choice to opt in or opt out of evolving with AI can significantly impact individuals' ability to thrive and succeed in an AI-driven landscape.

Addressing Choice Overload

Choice overload, exacerbated by the proliferation of AI-driven technologies, presents a significant challenge for individuals and organizations alike. The abundance of options in the digital age can lead to decision paralysis, decreased satisfaction with chosen outcomes, and increased levels of stress and anxiety. To address choice overload, it's essential to streamline decision-making processes by providing clear guidance, curated options, and personalized recommendations tailored to individual preferences and needs. This can be achieved through the strategic use of AI algorithms to filter and prioritize choices based on relevant criteria, reducing cognitive burden and facilitating more informed decisions. Additionally, fostering a culture of mindfulness and reflection can help individuals cultivate awareness of their values, priorities, and decision-making tendencies, enabling them to make choices that align with their long-term goals and aspirations. Furthermore, organizations can play a crucial role in mitigating choice overload by designing user interfaces and consumer experiences that simplify complex decision-making tasks and empower users to navigate choices more effectively. By addressing choice overload through thoughtful design and targeted interventions, individuals and organizations can enhance decision-making outcomes, reduce stress, and foster a more positive and fulfilling user experience in the AI-driven digital landscape. A smart home AI system streamlines user preferences for daily routines, presenting simplified choices for lighting, temperature, and entertainment. This addresses choice overload, enhancing user experience and decision-making efficiency.

To elaborate, a smart home AI system is designed to learn from a user's habits and preferences over time. For instance, it might observe that a user prefers a certain temperature at bedtime or enjoys dim lighting when watching movies. By gathering this data, the AI can anticipate the user's needs and automate adjustments without requiring the user to make those decisions manually every time. A smart home AI system mitigates choice overload by narrowing down the options based on the user's past behavior and preferences. Instead of the user having to sift through numerous settings for lighting, temperature, or entertainment options, the AI presents a few tailored choices or automates the decision entirely. A smart home AI system not only learns and adapts to user preferences but also presents these preferences in a simplified manner, thereby enhancing the living experience by reducing the number of choices a user has to make and improving the efficiency of those decisions. This leads to a more seamless and enjoyable interaction with technology in the home environment

So What?

The emergence of AI as a transformative force necessitates a proactive approach to choice architecture for both individuals and organizations. Unlike previous transformations, the AI revolution is not just on the horizon; it's here and happening. This reality demands that individuals and organizations design and plan their choices strategically to stay ahead of the AI curve and capitalize on its potential benefits.

Choice architecture offers a roadmap to empowerment in the AI era, urging stakeholders to adeptly utilize it in shaping their futures. For individuals, understanding options and key decision-making factors is crucial, prompting the crafting of personal plans for growth alongside AI advancements. Organizations, on the other hand, are encouraged to align their AI strategies with their objectives and employ choice architecture through methodologies like PACT (pivot, align, culture, transform) to navigate the transformative landscape effectively.

In essence, choice architecture serves as a guiding framework for both individuals and organizations to harness the power of AI strategically, fostering personal and professional growth amid AI advancements and driving organizational innovation and success in the face of AI disruption.

Now What?

Moving forward, stakeholders must recognize the significance of choice architecture in shaping their responses to AI-driven change. For individuals, this means embracing play, growth, and disruption as pathways to personal transformation, leveraging choice architecture to navigate the evolving AI landscape with confidence and adaptability.

For organizations, integrating choice architecture into decision-making processes becomes imperative, particularly in the context of AI-driven transformation. By implementing methodologies like PACT and aligning strategies with organizational touchstones, leaders can steer their organizations toward sustainable success in the age of AI.

Moreover, the consequences of ignoring choice in the face of AI disruption must be acknowledged. Failure to pivot and adapt to changing circumstances risks stagnation and obsolescence, highlighting the critical role of choice architecture in guiding strategic decisions and fostering innovation in the AI era.

Embracing choice architecture as a strategic tool for navigating AI-driven change is essential for individuals and organizations alike. By leveraging choice effectively, stakeholders can unlock the transformative potential of AI and chart a course toward a future of growth, innovation, and success. Remember, in the chapter about touchstone, we discussed how important is it for you to figure out your touchstone and where you are at in your journey. We asked you to assess your own willingness, awareness, and readiness. Now, we want you to make a choice to embrace AI, starting either with play with AI, grow with AI, or maybe you jump straight to disrupt with AI. Where do you choose to go next? Play, grow, or disrupt?

My choice architecture

I am ready to

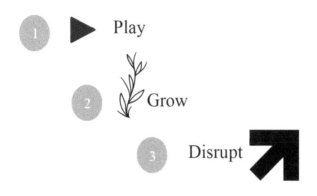

(circle one)   *with AI*

Figure 5.3. I choose to start with . . .

APPROACH

PART 3

WE'VE ESTABLISHED A solid foundation with Axis, laying the groundwork for understanding the historical, technological, and organizational perspectives of AI. You've gained insights into your organization's North Star, mastered the art of measuring progress, and learned when to adjust course for refinement. Delving into Accountability, you've embarked on defining your touchstone, grasping the trends shaping your role and organization, and can now confidently chart your AI journey. Assessing your willingness, awareness, and readiness to make informed choices, you're poised to navigate the landscape effectively for yourself, your role, and your organization. Proactive decision-making is paramount in shaping the future, offering choices such as play, grow, or disrupt, with play being the choice at hand.

Approach offers a strategic roadmap for individuals and organizations venturing into the realm of artificial intelligence. Through three chapters, readers are guided through the stages of play, grow, and disrupt, each offering unique insights and actionable strategies.

In chapter 6, *Play*, the focus is on the exploration and playful engagement with AI concepts and applications. Readers are encouraged to embark on a journey of discovery through diverse avenues such as community exploration, article writing, and participation in hackathons. The emphasis is on actively shaping the future by deepening understanding, contributing to collective knowledge, and driving meaningful change.

Transitioning from playful exploration to intentional growth, chapter 7, *Grow*, underscores the importance of hands-on experience and active participation in AI projects. Readers are urged to reflect on their journeys and leverage their newfound knowledge to drive personal and organizational development. The narrative encourages a shift from complacency to curiosity, from routine to innovation, highlighting the imperative of continuous learning and adaptation in the AI era. With a focus on leveraging choice architecture for strategic decision-making, readers are empowered to chart their course for growth and success in the dynamic landscape of AI.

In the final chapter of the section, *Disrupt*, the spotlight is on disruptive innovation and transformative change. Drawing from economic theories and strategic frameworks, readers are equipped with the tools and methodologies to challenge norms, reshape industries, and drive growth with AI. The narrative navigates the complexities of disruption, guiding readers through the process of defining their role as disruptive leaders and architecting change within their organizations. By leveraging choice architecture and implementing the PACT method for disruption, readers can systematically approach innovation, mitigate risks, and seize opportunities for enduring growth and innovation in the AI-driven landscape.

"Approach" serves as a strategic compass for individuals and organizations navigating the dynamic landscape of AI. By fostering curiosity, nurturing expertise, and empowering disruptive innovation, readers are equipped to harness the transformative potential of AI for the benefit of all.

PLAY WITH AI

SPARKING CREATIVITY AND CURIOSITY

Introduction

SO FAR, YOU understand your organization's North Star. You know how to measure progress and success and when to course correct because something is not working or needs refinement. You have gone through the process of defining your touchstone, understanding the trends for your role and organization, and can chart your AI touchstone. You have figured out if you are willing, aware, and ready to move forward with the art of making choices for you, your role, and your organization. You have choices, and acting on them proactively to shape the future is in the best interests of both individuals and organizations in the AI era—choices like play, grow, or disrupt. The first choice is play.

If you remember in *Touchstone* (chapter 4), we talked about four types of trends related to roles in the organization:

1. Organization is expanding with AI, and your role is expanding with AI.
2. Organization is shrinking because of AI, but your role is expanding with AI.
3. Role is shrinking, but the organization is growing.
4. Role is shrinking, and organization is shrinking.

If you fall in the first two buckets, play is a great option. You can take more time to get acclimated with AI because you are likely already heading in that direction anyway. If you fall in the other two buckets, however, we recommend you do what it takes to grow as fast as possible.

All you need for play is to be willing. If your awareness and readiness are high, you can likely jump to *Grow* (see chapter 7). We assume, in this case, that you want to start with play. Play and AI together seems like an oxymoron. These are two terms that don't intuitively go hand in hand. But this is where we ask our readers to give it a chance. When we discussed choice architecture, we talked about the criticality of making a choice. When it comes to AI and what will happen in the workforce, we believe you have a defined hierarchy of choices. The first choice in the hierarchy is do nothing or do something. The folks who are independently wealthy, at the end of their careers, or are afraid to try or can't see a pathway to learn can potentially opt to do nothing. We don't fall into this group—at least not today. Nor do the folks that have FOMO (fear of missing out), nor do the readers of this book (you).

We have all been members of the "do-nothings" at one time or another. There are always instances in our careers when things aren't going right, you didn't get that promotion, or you are buried in minutiae and can't see a path out. We have had plenty of moments when we dread going into the office, doing the job, and knowing you have to because you have a mortgage, family, bills, and other responsibilities. And sure, you know you should take a class, get certification, or do *something*, but you just can't get your feet under you. We have all been there. However, in this case, doing nothing comes at a much higher cost than in the past . . . and you'll see why.

In the past, some could find comfort in doing the same job in a different place with a new team. But eventually, the doldrums kick in, as does dissatisfaction. You get it, you know the drill. As AI scales and you are in the same old space, you will become further behind. The speed at which AI scales is exponential, so it will be increasingly difficult to catch up.

Part of the reason we embarked on this journey is because we won't be left behind—and we don't want you to be left behind either. This brings us to the second choice at the top of the hierarchy—do something and be a part of the AI revolution. If this is you (and we believe it is), you have three pathways that we mentioned in chapter 5, Choice Architecture—play, grow, or disrupt.

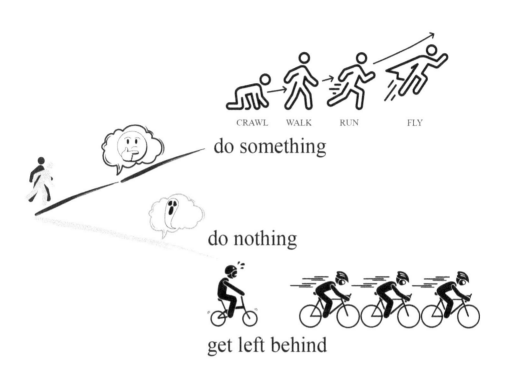

Figure 6.1. Hierarchy of choices. When you are curious, you are more likely to do something. If you are fearful, you will likely do nothing, and in the case of AI, you get left behind.

The objectives of this chapter are the following:

1. Expand on the concept of play, the psychology, and why play as a choice is the path of least resistance to being part of AI.
2. Play for personal development to gain real-time exposure to AI. Start training your AI muscle with ideas that may work for you

personally. The goal is to show you how play can demystify AI when you are learning in a safe space.

3. Play for professional development delves into how play in the workspace can reduce the fear of the unknown and help you figure out where to start your AI chapter and build your awareness.

The outcome will be that you can decide how to use the concept of play in your own AI journey. You need to figure out how you can make this fun. We are giving you the recipe—you need to make the meal.

Let's Talk about Play

We are not the only people who like to play. People smarter than us also think it's important:

Albert Einstein: "Play is the highest form of research."
George Bernard Shaw: "We don't stop playing because we grow old; we grow old because we stop playing."
Carl Jung: "The creation of something new is not accomplished by the intellect but by the play instinct."

The term *play* refers to activities, often recreational or leisurely in nature, that are engaged in for enjoyment, amusement, or creative expression rather than for practical purposes. Play can encompass a range of behaviors, including physical activities, imaginative games, intellectual pursuits, and social interactions. It often involves elements of spontaneity, exploration, experimentation, and freedom from strict rules or goals, allowing individuals to express themselves, learn, and develop skills in a relaxed and enjoyable manner.[19]

---

[19]   Human Kinetics, "Definitions of Leisure, Play, and Recreation," accessed June 23, 2024, https://us.humankinetics.com/blogs/excerpt/definitions-of-leisure-play-and-recreation.

The Psychology of Play

Play is deeply intertwined with human development, particularly in childhood, serving as a vital pathway for learning. It encompasses intrinsic motivation, driving individuals to engage in activities for the sheer enjoyment and exploration they offer rather than external rewards. Through play, individuals actively participate in experiential learning, immersing themselves in hands-on exploration that fosters cognitive development. This engagement encourages problem-solving, critical thinking, and creativity, nurturing a deep understanding of concepts and skills. Moreover, play facilitates social development by providing opportunities for interaction and collaboration, nurturing skills like communication and empathy. Emotionally, play acts as a safe space for expression and regulation, allowing individuals to explore feelings and develop coping strategies. Physically, play promotes activity and motor skill development, enhancing coordination and spatial awareness. Its dynamic nature stimulates brain development, enhancing executive function, memory, and neural connectivity. Embracing play as a fundamental aspect of the human experience supports holistic development, creating environments conducive to optimal learning and growth.

Why Play Works

We did a little soul-searching when we discussed play as a pathway. There are specific characteristics related to how and why play has worked in the past in our personal experiences.

1. We tend to play in a safe space.
2. We play with people we like—it is a comfortable peer group; they typically want to play for the same reasons.
3. We play games we like. For example, we tend to play or do things we like or feel proficient at, and even when we are not, we are with a group we aren't afraid to make mistakes in front of.

The experts, the psychology, and our own experiences are why we believe play with AI makes the AI pill easier to swallow. And it's fun if you give it a try. The first step is sometimes the hardest step to take.

You say to yourself, "I want to become part of the AI revolution, I have chosen play as the pathway." Together, we need to figure out what you actually do for fun, both for personal development and professional development. We are going to take both areas (personal and professional), separately and give a few ideas and share a few of our own past experiences using play. If they are not for you, we want you to be able to take the use cases/examples and reformat them for yourself. This has to be fit for purpose and based on things that are relevant to you. Like painting a room, we can all pick up a paint brush and paint, but in the end, you need to pick the colors to make it your own.

Personal Development

It's time for your own soul-searching. Consider the questions below, and write down your answers. These are the same questions that got us started in the introduction. Your answers will help you forge a path to play and will help to determine what games and activities will meet your needs. We'll offer some common approaches to make AI fun that embody the concept of play with AI.

1. Do I know about AI?
2. Do I know how AI will impact my life?
3. Do I know how to turn AI into an opportunity?

For every question that you answer with a "maybe," "a little bit," or "no idea," you can design your play to change that answer to a yes. Because you are at "play," what you do will be in a safe space, with people you like. By doing things you like, you will be able to retain everything you learn along the way. When you use play to learn AI and internalize AI concepts, they stick.

The lessons learned become the baseline and framework for continued learning and growth. For example, we don't need to relearn how to play Monopoly every time we get it out of the closet. Once you play it, you know the basic rules. However, every time you play the game, the moves and outcomes are different. It depends on the pieces you get, the roll of the dice, what happens with chance, and the people you play with.

In leadership development, there are normally three tiers that illustrate how you move out of your comfort zone. We have constructed a view that shows how you step from one area of your world to the next. This will influence what you do and how you interact with AI changes. We also want you to see that you need to move out of your comfort zone (aka inner circle) to continue to learn and grow. As you expand out, your levels of comfort can shift and expand. To quote Antara's father, you won't find the big opportunities in your backyard. That doesn't mean you don't use your inner circle; you just need to expand out of your circle to make the opportunity happen. Also, it is critical to understand that your personal and professional comfort zones complement each other. You can't expand professionally unless you expand personally and vice versa.

Comfort zone and beyond

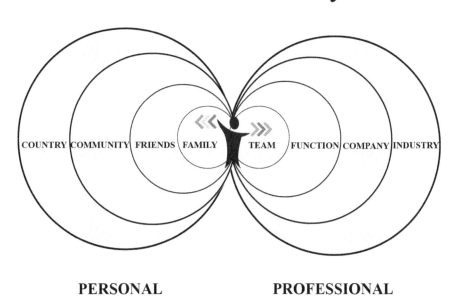

Figure 6.2. Navigating your comfort zone.

Engaging in play with your family, friends, and community within the context of AI can be a powerful tool for overcoming fear, igniting your curiosity, and fostering creativity. By experimenting with AI technologies in a supportive environment, you'll not only gain practical skills but also develop the confidence to navigate the ever-evolving landscape of technology.

If you have friends like I do, whenever they engage in basic play, there is always one person who is uber-competitive. You know that person—the one who sulks when they lose a round or who wants to be the most knowledgeable in a conversation. We both have a few family members like this. They keep us on our toes. For example, Winnie has a brother with seven higher education degrees. Any time Winnie anticipates that he may get technical at a holiday dinner, she prepares for a potential debate. For example, lately, he has been focused on cyber security. So Winnie has been researching cyber security and AI impacts. While that may ruin a dinner party at some houses, at her table it will keep attendees engaged. Human nature suggests she can't let her brother one-up her with information. Many of us have family or friends like that, where we can pose a question that will spark conversation, debate, and a little slice of competition—and in the end, it will help us all learn a little more about a topic like AI.

How Can I Learn More about AI?

When we don't know about a topic, we are vulnerable. To help with that, we have suggested a number of examples to help you find a safe space to play and learn.

Comfort zone and beyond

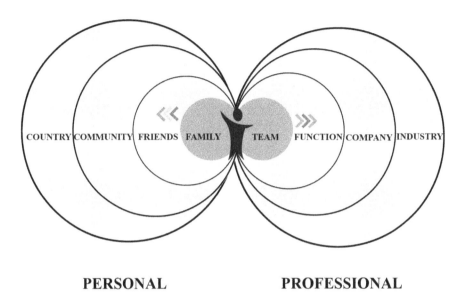

PERSONAL   **PROFESSIONAL**

Figure 6.3. Navigating family and team.

- Happy hours: As memory serves, folks still go to happy hours. We engage in happy hours with coworkers, gym buddies, and friends often (and you can always get a mocktail if you are not a fan of alcohol). This is a great environment to pose an AI question, see what others know, and create an environment of informal learning. In a happy hour scenario, there are no bad questions and no wrong answers. In this environment, someone will always step up with the need to share everything they know about AI. From there, you can reframe the next happy hour as an AI happy hour, and folks can share what they have learned since you last shared cocktails.

- Dinner parties: People like to eat, especially when someone else cooks and serves. My family *loves* to gather around my kitchen table because I cook, serve, and clean up (while I work full-time, prepare to disrupt with AI, and feed my five siblings, multiple nieces and nephews, and my own kids. Item to note: choice architecture is my friend). Now if you are a foodie or like to host dinner parties, how about hosting a "potluck & pitch" AI edition? Invite your friends, family, or fellow AI enthusiasts for an evening of food, fun, and futuristic ideas. Each participant can bring a dish, you can order in (Uber Eats, DoorDash), or gather in the kitchen and cook together. Conversation starters can be ideas for an AI startup, what you have heard in the news this week, any new AI topics related to schools in your neighborhood, or anything you saw in an app or heard on the street.
- Book clubs: There are book clubs in organizations, communities, schools, parent groups, libraries, and beyond. If this is an activity you like, it may be a great way for you to play with AI. For example, if you are part of a book club, add this book to your reading list. Read it, debate it, and share with us on linked in.
- Coffee chats: One of my favorite things to do now that I am back in the office is to go out for coffee with colleagues, friends, gym buddies, and my college-age kids. There is something about going to a local coffee space and focusing on the person in front of you. We encourage you to try it. You can either have a one-on-one coffee date and bring up AI as a topic or can take it a step further and create an "AI Coffee Chat" with your colleagues and friends. Once a week or once a month, talk about the latest breakthroughs and inventions in the world of AI. Maybe someone recently tried a new AI training course that may interest you or read something about a new innovation.

These fun examples to play with AI give you a baseline foundation for the topic. With the baseline, you can use that newfound information along with the initial chapters to then really look inward at your personal life.

How Will AI Impact My Life?

Now that we have played with AI in a safe space, we can look outward. AI's impact will be interspersed between both the personal and professional sides of your life and will become increasingly evident in the ecosystem where you exist. There are examples everywhere you look and in almost every personal use case. Consider the many industries where you, your friends, or your family members are either a consumer or a provider. In each industry, across all walks of life, there are multiple roles—some are consumers, some are providers of the goods or services that a consumer seeks. AI will change each of these roles on both sides of the table. Where you sit will influence the impact of AI in your life. Take a look at the table below. We have illustrated a number of industries with providers and consumers.

Industry	Providers	Consumers
Education	school, colleges, professors, teachers	applicants, students, parents, alumni
Construction	developers, contractors, architects	home buyers, home sellers, homeowners, home renters
Retail	malls, stores, online commerce sites, wholesalers	consumers, shoppers
Hospitality	hotels, airports, chefs, travel agents	tourists, travelers, hotel guests, restaurant patrons
Sport	arenas, TV channels, commentators, players	fans, sports betting consumers
Entertainment	theaters, movie studios, event organizers	moviegoers, concert attendees, gamers
Logistics	shippers, distributors, retailers, e-commerce platforms	gift senders, small business owners
Manufacturing	car manufacturers, distributors, wholesalers	car owners, lawn mower owners

Health	healthcare providers, hospitals, insurance companies	patients, family caregivers
Banking	credit unions, global banks, regional banks	account holders, investors, borrowers

Table 6.1.

Let's take an example that we are all familiar with—education. If you are a teacher, how you use AI is likely to evolve how you do your job. For example, you can use the AI tool SimCheck to check for plagiarism. If you are a student, you can leverage Copilot to get content with sources. Bottom line: how players in the education system use AI is evolving.

When ChatGPT first came out, one of my daughters' teachers suspected his class used it in an assignment based on the similarity of their submission. He had to quickly learn and use a detector that would find sentence patterns and words common to ChatGPT. As a teacher, he had to evolve quickly, and based on his guidance, the students had to change quickly—and they also had a quick lesson in ethics. The key message is that the tools are here for our use, but we need to use them responsibly and ethically.

Another example is healthcare. The consumers are patients and their families. The providers are hospitals, doctors, nurses, insurance companies, and so forth. If you are a patient, AI can enhance your patient experience with personalized treatment and faster diagnostics. For personalized treatment, AI algorithms can analyze medical history, genetic data, and lifestyle choices and provide treatments unique to you. AI tools can also help providers in remote locations where medical help is limited, to accelerate diagnosis with AI tool sets.

So what is the role of Play here? No matter which angle you approach it from, consumer or provider, the response revolves around the novel experiences of AI-driven changes. Play serves as a platform for both learning and pushing boundaries, allowing you to view the world through the lens of AI. By engaging in play, you not only educate yourself but also confront challenges, ultimately guiding you toward setting goals for your personal development in this field. To us, playing with AI encapsulates not only fun experiences but the practical experiences within your everyday life.

We are outcome-focused. With play with AI, there has to be an outcome and a purpose. In the previous section, we gave some examples of how to get the foundations with AI in your personal interactions. Now we are going to highlight some examples for you to consider.

How Can I Turn AI into an Opportunity?

First, let's outline the difference between personal development versus professional development. Personal development involves activities geared toward improving oneself on various levels, encompassing emotional, physical, intellectual, social, and spiritual aspects of life. This includes setting personal goals, cultivating self-awareness, honing communication skills, and fostering healthy habits and relationships. On the other hand, professional development focuses specifically on enhancing skills, knowledge, and effectiveness within one's career or chosen profession. This involves attending workshops, pursuing further education or certifications, networking with peers, and staying updated on industry trends. While personal development targets holistic self-improvement, professional development is geared toward career advancement and excellence in the workplace. Both are crucial for overall growth and success, with personal growth often contributing to professional success and vice versa.

Comfort zone and beyond

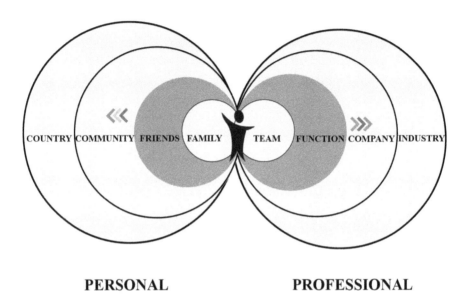

Figure 6.4. Navigating friends and function.

When we think about personal development with AI, we have to understand what we need intellectually to stay current and what the impact is on our personal goals. You need to feel empowered to determine what makes you curious and what is your version of play. It is different for everyone. The other consideration is that AI is still relatively new in the workspace and there may not be well-defined, easily accessible professional development pathways.

Below we have developed a personal development pathway example that you can use to create a bridge to your professional development.

Imagine Delightful Consumer Experiences

One way we want AI to impact our lives is to have it help design delightful consumer experiences. It isn't just about creating seamless interactions—it is about adding a layer of fun. The objective is to create an experience that makes a consumer (or you) happy. For example, when thinking about a delightful experience, Antara was able to rattle off her wish list. For her to be delighted, she would like to have her very own avatar, chatbot, or virtual assistant. Her requirements, to some degree, are simple. She wants it to do everything. It should know her wants, needs, likes. It should manage all her passwords, logins, and profiles including health, financial, social, and work. It should manage her calendar, and if something goes wrong, the AI chatbot fixes it. It makes the calls needed to schedule appointments and follows up until issues are at resolution. Sounds like a dream come true. That being said, this is the kind of stuff AI can do, and with play, your imagination is the limit.

With the chatbot example, we want you to think of consumer experiences as opportunities to experiment with AI technologies in real-world scenarios. Instead of viewing AI as a complex concept, approach it as a toolkit filled with exciting possibilities for enhancing user interactions and adding value to your consumers' lives. Mind you, you have just started to think about designing AI capabilities like Antaras's friendly assistant, capable of understanding and responding to her inquiries as its primary consumer with ease. What you are really doing is delving into the nuances of natural language processing and machine learning algorithms and uncovering the magic behind creating conversational experiences that feel natural and intuitive. Pretty impressive. As a reminder, these concepts are defined in chapter 1.

Throughout this journey, embrace experimentation and playfulness as essential components of the learning process. Treat each consumer interaction as a puzzle to solve and a chance to stretch your creative muscles. Whether it's designing intuitive user interfaces or crafting compelling storytelling experiences, let your imagination soar as you explore the endless possibilities of AI-driven design.

In summary, we have used play to create a nonthreatening place to start learning about AI capabilities. We helped you identify your baseline, figure out what you know about AI, how it will impact your life, and how you can easily expand your AI capabilities in a personal playground where you test and learn. This allows you to assess in real-time how AI can be used to solve common life problems. It opens your eyes to help you see others who struggle with getting up to speed on AI, how they learn, and what they are learning. Finally, it sets you up to define your personal pathway to kick off your professional development so you can eventually evolve into a growth mode. In chapter 7, titled *Grow*, you'll enhance your learning through practical action, guided by a strategic approach designed to keep you relevant and advance your career.

Professional Development

Recalling the definition of personal development and professional development, at this point, you are ready to take targeted steps to set yourself up before you can grow with AI. In this section, you are playing professionally before you get to those targeted career development paths. It is like being in a competitive sport—you have bumped up from learning the sport and playing on an intramural team, to a pro team. For example, in college, Winnie played on an intramural volleyball team. The primary focus was to finish a few games in order to get to the bar afterward and celebrate with team members regardless of a win or loss with a few beers. With professional development, the prize at the end is not a happy hour, it is a better-defined career path in a monsoon of technical change.

Both personal and professional networking groups, retreats, conferences, and meetups are all great candidates for a starting point for work-adjacent options. Things that could happen at work are collaborative projects, hackathons, and design sprints. Workplace training programs, workshops, and team-building activities can foster a culture of curiosity, experimentation, and continuous learning around AI technologies. Here are some ideas of paths you can take for professional development.

Comfort zone and beyond

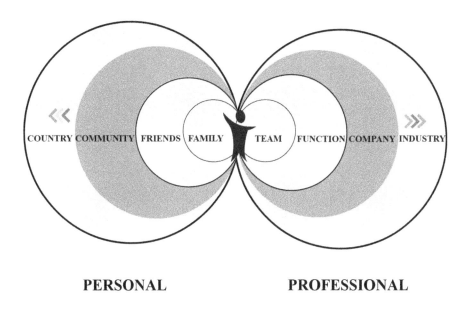

PERSONAL   **PROFESSIONAL**

Figure 6.5. Navigating community and company.

Cross-Industry Exploration

Another development pathway is to explore across industries, with a personal flair. Cross-industry idea exploration offers a unique opportunity to broaden our understanding of AI's applications by crossing traditional industry boundaries. By delving into various sectors, we can uncover innovative uses of AI technologies that span diverse fields, showcasing the versatility and adaptability of these solutions. For example, remember our healthcare example from above? To learn more about changes in the industry, it helps to talk to people in that industry or to research AI advancement in the field. Reach out to the medical providers you know and ask. Everyone we speak to, we ask them about AI. Our editor/colleague recently had to go in for a routine colonoscopy.

When she awoke after the procedure, still blurry and relaxed from the sedatives, she immediately started telling the nurse that she was editing a book on AI and began to pepper her with questions. Did she know that her job was going to be completely transformed? The nurse was a little taken aback. "Oh no! I'm going to be replaced by a robot?" "No, no," our colleague started to explain. Another nurse chimed in, "What we'll have to do is kill the robots before they come for us!" Seeing the conversation quickly deteriorating, our colleague said, "Calm down, people. It's not going to be that bad!" The message is that you should start to have conversations across industries.

Every industry will have its own timeline for AI adoption, some faster than others. At its core, cross-industry exploration encourages us to think beyond the confines of a single domain and embrace the interconnectedness of different industries. By venturing into uncharted territories, we'll gain valuable insights into how AI principles and techniques can be leveraged to address common challenges across industries. For instance, predictive maintenance algorithms used in the aviation sector can be repurposed to improve equipment reliability in energy production facilities, minimizing downtime and maximizing operational efficiency.

We can all agree on the benefit of cross-industry exploration. But where and how? Here are a few more ideas.

Toastmasters

Toastmasters is a great space for cross-industry networking—"The mission of a Toastmasters club is to provide a mutually supportive and positive learning environment in which every individual member has the opportunity to develop oral communication and leadership skills, which, in turn, foster self-confidence and personal growth."

Community Clubs

Clubs in your community like Rotary clubs typically focus on community service to others. Rotary membership spans industries and communities and is focused on action, problem-solving, and community building. A number of people join rotary with the intent to solve for both personal and professional development opportunities. Some use them for networking, others use them to give back. Either way, they are a great place to test AI in the community and foster a space for shared learning.

Coffee Chat with Colleagues: Simulating Cross-Functional Capabilities

Coffee chats are used personally and professionally as well. They can be ad hoc or meticulously planned. For example, Winnie has engineered planned coffee chats with leaders at one of her financial institutions. The intent was to create a group-mentoring environment and give leaders a chance to really get to know some of the people at various levels across organizational layers.

This is another great environment to enhance AI capability development. A coffee chat is the path of least resistance to creating a cross-functional space. While you start with the conversations, you then have the opportunity to simulate cross-functional capabilities across different organizational functions, providing valuable insights into the amplified impact of AI integration.

Simulated scenarios help you to get buy-in and create awareness with others so you can explore how AI technologies intersect with diverse operational areas, such as marketing, sales, operations, and consumer service. For example, we might simulate a scenario where AI-driven consumer insights from marketing campaigns are seamlessly integrated with sales forecasting models, enabling more accurate predictions of consumer behavior and demand.

By engaging in these simulations, we gain a deeper understanding of how AI can facilitate data-driven decision-making processes across multiple departments. For instance, we might simulate a scenario where AI-powered analytics tools analyze data from various sources, including sales transactions, consumer interactions, and market trends, to provide actionable insights that inform strategic decision-making at the executive level.

Moreover, simulation exercises allow us to identify potential bottlenecks and challenges that may arise during the integration of AI across different functions. For instance, we might simulate a scenario where data silos hinder the flow of information between departments, highlighting the importance of establishing robust data governance policies and implementing interoperable systems.

Through these simulations, we can also explore the transformative potential of AI in optimizing cross-functional workflows and enhancing organizational efficiency. For example, we might simulate a scenario where AI-driven automation streamlines repetitive tasks across departments, freeing up valuable time and resources for more strategic initiatives.

Ultimately, simulations of cross-functional capabilities serve as a valuable tool for fostering collaboration, promoting cross-disciplinary thinking, and accelerating the adoption of AI across organizations. By engaging in these simulations, we can unlock new insights into the synergies between different functional areas and unleash the full potential of AI to drive innovation and growth.

Crowd Pitch Picnic: Investing in Startup Dreams

The crowd pitch picnic is a personal initiative pathway that can lead to a professional development opportunity. A crowd pitch picnic is a picnic set up by you to host a contest-like event where people, or peers, pitch AI ideas. You can do this at work, or with your personal network. In most organizations, there are often events designed to promote engagement—to get people to expand out of their comfort zone or to do something other than their day job. Creating, watching, judging pitch contests, or investing in crowdfunded startups presents a unique opportunity to gain practical insights into the dynamic landscape of AI and emerging technologies. By participating in crowdfunding campaigns, we not only support innovative ventures but also immerse ourselves in the exciting world of startup ecosystems where groundbreaking ideas and disruptive innovations come to life.

Crowdfunding platforms serve as catalysts for innovation, enabling entrepreneurs to showcase their ideas, attract early-stage funding, and validate market demand for their products or services. As investors, you have the opportunity to explore a diverse range of AI startups across various industries, from healthcare and finance to education and e-commerce.

Monitoring the progress of crowdfunded startups allows us to understand the challenges, opportunities, and trends shaping the AI landscape. By staying informed about market dynamics, technological advancements, and regulatory developments, we can make informed investment decisions and identify promising startups with high growth potential and innovative business models.

Witnessing firsthand how AI technologies are shaping emerging businesses provides valuable insight into the transformative power of AI across different sectors. From AI-powered healthcare solutions and predictive analytics platforms to autonomous vehicles and smart city initiatives, startups are leveraging AI to revolutionize industries, disrupt traditional business models, and address complex challenges facing society.

Creating pitch contests can serve as a catalyst for getting innovative ideas out of basements and paper napkins and into early funding within local communities and friends and professional networks. By organizing pitch events, we provide aspiring entrepreneurs with a platform to showcase their ideas, receive feedback from industry experts and investors, and access early-stage funding to kick-start their ventures.

Pitch contests not only foster innovation and entrepreneurship but also build vibrant startup ecosystems where ideas flourish, collaborations thrive, and connections are forged. By connecting entrepreneurs with potential investors, mentors, and collaborators, pitch contests empower startups to accelerate their growth, scale their operations, and bring their innovative solutions to market.

In summary, investment in crowdfunded startups offers a compelling opportunity to gain firsthand experience and insights into the AI landscape. By monitoring startups' progress, understanding their challenges, and participating in pitch contests, we can actively contribute to the growth and success of the AI ecosystem while potentially reaping financial rewards and supporting groundbreaking innovations that have the potential to shape the future.

Capital Conclave: Investment Club Meetup

Another great place to enhance your AI understanding is using the investment club concept. After all, who doesn't research their investments? Create an investment club meetup, where you can delve into the exciting realm of investing in emerging financial vehicles. By exploring various investment options, such as stocks, funds, and other products, you can gain invaluable insights into the financial implications of AI advancements.

Participating in investment clubs fosters a collaborative environment for sharing insights and discussing investment strategies. Through research sessions, portfolio reviews, and market analysis discussions, deepen your understanding of investment principles and financial markets.

Diversifying our investment portfolio across different asset classes allows us to spread risk and capture potential returns from various sectors. Allocating a portion of our capital to AI-related stocks or funds enables us to directly engage in the growth potential of companies driving AI innovation.

Tracking the performance of AI-related investments helps us stay informed about market trends and technological developments. Analyzing financial statements and monitoring key performance indicators empowers us to make informed investment decisions. Exploring emerging financial products linked to AI, such as robo-advisers and algorithmic trading platforms, allows us to witness firsthand how AI is reshaping traditional financial services. By experimenting with these tools, we gain insights into their impact on investment decision-making processes.

Continuous learning and staying updated on AI trends are essential for navigating the evolving landscape of AI-driven finance. Attending seminars and networking events focused on AI and finance helps us expand our knowledge and exchange ideas with industry professionals.

Professional Associations

Professional networking groups are a great source for cross-industry networking and discussion. For example, PMI (Project Management Institute) has monthly networking meetings and plenty of opportunities to become involved with the project management community, as they are always looking for presenters and people to participate. Recently, PMI started publishing content on the project management role and how AI can be leveraged in that function. Project management is a cross-industry function—meaning, you will find the role of project manager in pharmaceutical, finance, petrochemicals, manufacturing, retail, and beyond.

Joining a Community of Practice Focused on AI

Communities of Practice (CoPs) equate to networking opportunities and fall under our umbrella of play. CoPs should be fun. They provide an immersive cohort experience for AI enthusiasts to share insights, explore novel ideas, and collaborate on transformative projects. Within CoPs, members engage in lively discussions, delve into advanced AI concepts, and dissect real-world applications, enriching their understanding of AI and fostering a collaborative learning environment.

Leveraging Article Writing and Publication

This is not for everyone. We debated if this is play or not. For us, your authors, it is, in fact, play. Antara has consistently put pen to paper and published articles in the *Delaware Business Times*, Delaware Online, and LinkedIn, covering topics on small business ownership, socio-economic parity issues, transformations, healthcare, and beyond. While Winnie had created trainings and facilitated continuing education sessions, she was reluctant to write and post articles. Antara pushed Winnie out of her comfort zone to get her to try publishing on LinkedIn as well, knowing that the ideas were there—but so was the fear of putting something out there, where they could be judged by the masses. But Antara made it fun; she made it play. Once the idea of writing became play, the floodgates of ideas opened. We started writing articles on AI for fun as a creative outlet that the day job wasn't consistently providing. For us, AI was and is a high-interest, high-potential topic. Writing articles about AI has allowed us as individuals to delve deeper into various concepts, clarify our understanding, and synthesize information from different sources. The other "Aha" is that there is no topic we can't research and learn. In the face of AI, that is truly a comfort. By sharing expertise and perspectives, individuals contribute to the collective learning of the community, showcase their knowledge, and foster collaboration and exchange within the AI community.

Choice Architecture from Play to Grow to Disrupt

The journey from play to growth and disruption with AI is characterized by continuous learning, experimentation, and adaptation. As individuals playfully engage with AI, they grow their skills, insights, and capabilities, positioning themselves to drive meaningful change and disruption in their respective domains.

Play as a Driver to Grow with AI

In the above personal and professional development examples, we have illustrated how to use play to learn AI. Grow with AI is the doing, so while you were doing coffee chats and investment clubs, you were playing with the intent to grow with AI. You now need to determine what to do with what you have learned. But more on that in chapter 7.

Play as a Driver of Disruption

Playfulness ignites the spirit of innovation and disruption, empowering individuals and organizations to challenge the status quo and reimagine traditional approaches to problem-solving. By encouraging experimentation and risk-taking, playfulness fosters a culture of innovation where bold ideas can flourish and transformative solutions can emerge. This disruptive potential of play in the context of AI enables individuals and organizations to push boundaries, disrupt industries, and create positive change on a global scale.

Back in 2009, Antara's banking career was soaring high until the market abruptly crashed. It felt like a sudden storm had swept through, leaving her career in disarray.

As the economy took a downturn, Antara's once-stable job became uncertain and she was uncertain if she even wanted to stay in that field. She was at a crossroads, trying to determine which path would give her professional and personal fulfillment. The path she had thought was the right one was now on shaky ground. Antara felt a need to reinvent herself in a space with purpose and a potential to be part of the greater good. With a new sense of direction coupled with a natural inclination for pushing boundaries and exploring new ideas, she evaluated her choices. The choice was whether to do something or do nothing. She could stay in a space where she was no longer satisfied or try something that met her altruistic North Star. Antara decided to take a leap of faith. She started with play. She knew she had a passion for healthcare. At a very young age, she faced some health challenges as a first-generation immigrant, and with limited financial resources and the savvy of navigating the ecosystem, she truly felt the gaps in healthcare. Her success in banking and her profession gave her the tools and confidence to solve large complex problems. She took that, looked at the gaps, and applied it to learn how to be an entrepreneur in a safe space to start a business that would incite her passion. Armed with the understanding of the value of test-and-learn instead of diving headfirst into the world of entrepreneurship, she chose to bring clarity to a path of uncertainty by starting small.

Antara tested the waters, playing around with different ideas. Volunteering with SCORE, a federally funded organization that helps small businesses, provided her with invaluable learning experiences and opportunities for growth. Since 1964, SCORE has helped more than seventeen million entrepreneurs start, grow, or successfully exit a business (see https://www.score.org).

As Antara became more involved with SCORE, her confidence grew, and she realized she was ready to make a real impact. No longer content with just playing around, she was determined to disrupt the status quo. She took the plunge, embracing change as an opportunity rather than a setback. It turned out to be the best decision she ever made. From experimenting with new ideas to empowering others, she found a whole new purpose in life. And amid the uncertainty, there was a thrill unlike anything she had ever experienced before. She launched her healthcare disruptor—Ayuvya, but that's a story for another day. The takeaway is she played to disrupt when faced with a choice architecture of shrinking.

So What?

Play is a strategic approach to AI integration for individuals in their personal and professional lives. We chose play because of the psychology—play makes learning something complex fun. Play as a viable pathway for those whose roles or organizations are impacted by AI, emphasizing the need for willingness to engage with AI. We acknowledge the challenges faced by those in shrinking roles or organizations, and we urge them to adopt a growth mindset quickly. From our perspective, this chapter is a call to action—a gentle way to encourage our reader to step out of their comfort zone. But it's also a firm way to find a path to growth. It's about recognizing that the landscape of work and business is changing because of AI and you need to adapt to stay relevant.

So, say to yourself as you wrap this chapter up, "I am choosing to do something and be part of the AI revolution. There are three pathways laid out before me: play, grow, or disrupt. And I'm starting with 'play.'"

Now What?

We reinforced the concept of do nothing vs do something. We want you to take action. Take the tools we discussed in this chapter, and use them to expand your AI knowledge in a safe and fun space. Do some personal soul-searching, figure out what you know about AI, how it will impact your life, and then strategize on how to turn it into an opportunity. Assess your role and where you sit in the organization. As AI expands, try to predict if your role is growing, adapting to the new technology, or shrinking in certain areas. Bottom line is to lean into growth wherever you find the best path for it.

You have to contextualize to memorialize. Try the games, happy hours, social endeavors we suggested to make AI fun, entertaining, and not threatening. It might seem surprising, but in addition to your reading and research on the technical progress of AI, you also need to converse and interact with others. This is essential not only to make AI enjoyable but also to broaden your understanding and gauge the AI knowledge of those around you. With this foundation, you are ready to grow.

My Plan to Play

Network
    Friends
    Family
    Team.....

AI Topics
    Chat GPT
    Computer Vision
    Prompt Engineering...

Fun Events
    Coffee
    Happy Hour
    Pitch Picnic

Figure 6.6. Before you move forward, what is your plan to play?

GROW WITH AI

CULTIVATE YOUR POTENTIAL

Introduction

BY NOW, YOU are truly internalizing the concepts we have introduced. When we talk about grow, understanding AI concepts—the North Star, measurement, and your AI touchstone—is super important. If you need to, now is a great time to skim or reread those concepts as they will help you navigate growth. If you started from play, then you should be very insightful about how you move into the growth phase of your AI journey.

Organizations use AI and technology to grow and continue to the North Star, while leaders guide and inspire everyone to contribute to this growth. For the individual, you need to either drive the growth or join the growth path in your organization. At the end of grow, you have two options: (1) You are ready to explore a new role—either a new job or an elevated role because you have learned and practiced and are confident in your ability to grow with AI. (2) You have taken the concepts from play, have the abilities to leverage AI, and are now ready to disrupt.

When you grow with AI, you are going to grow within the context of your business, role, and career. It is institutionally focused on helping you stay relevant or become relevant in the organization. It is also about doing. When you choose grow, you are prepared to execute.

The key to mastering AI lies in gaining knowledge through hands-on experience and learning from the outcomes. There are a number of ways to do this. For example, you can seek out and participate in pilot projects and proof of concepts, regardless of whether you are a team member or a leader. By taking the initiative to kick-start projects, you not only contribute to the advancement of AI initiatives but also accelerate your own growth trajectory. Remember, if you followed the path of play, you will have built the AI muscle you need to flex in this space. The next step is to train that muscle by doing and generating outcomes. The measurement is in speed to market and metrics that evolved with AI. This is when you have grown with AI, and you are able to demonstrate the value to your stakeholders and leaders.

Another thing to consider is that you need the right environment for growth to happen. Growth is not just about size—it's about purposeful expansion that strengthens an organization's position and resilience in the marketplace. AI-inspired and enabled growth needs a transformative culture and mindset: growth in terms of intellectual capacity, talent, and maturity for transformation represents a holistic evolution encompassing various dimensions of an individual's or organization's development.

In this chapter, we delve into insights and practices that empower both personal and institutional development, positioning you at the forefront of AI advancements. The following are our objectives for this chapter:

1. Define what we mean by growth. *Grow* is a fairly common term, and we are adopting and adapting it for AI.
2. The pursuit of growth. There is a history of growth strategies and methods that have been leveraged over time. We have taken these methods and added an AI flavor to help you assess what could work for you.
3. Apply choice architecture to determine how you choose a method of growth to solve for your personal growth outcomes.

At the end of "Grow," you will be geared up to transition from personal transformation into delivering organizational or institutional value. You will be able to reap the benefits of your AI learning pathway in your professional endeavors.

My Plan to Grow

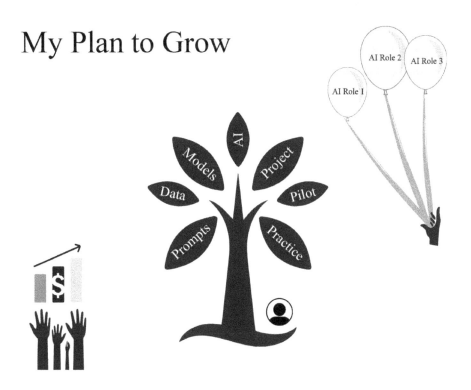

Figure 7.1. First, you raise your hand and become part of
the AI evolution. You then watch your skills expand and
evolve. From there, you reach for the next opportunity.

Figure 7.1 demonstrates the growth process: first, you raise your hand and become part of the AI evolution. You then watch your skills expand and evolve. From there, you reach for the next opportunity.

The ultimate outcome is the ability to scale human intelligence as AI scales to factorially or exponentially scale the benefits and outcomes of investments in technology. In layman's terms, you create a win-win scenario, personally and professionally.

What Is Growth?

Growing is about action and results. We often think of it like how we grew as kids, with parents using a pencil and tape measure to track our height on a door frame or wall every few months.

Growth in an organization signifies its expansion in size, capabilities, and resources. It involves increasing revenue, market share, consumer base, and product offerings. Pursued strategically, growth enhances competitiveness, creates value, and ensures long-term viability. It can be achieved organically through internal initiatives or inorganically through mergers and partnerships. Ultimately, growth strengthens an organization's position, resilience, and success in the marketplace.

We categorize growth two ways—incremental and exponential. Incremental growth involves gradual improvements and advancements in processes, products, or services, often driven by optimizing efficiency and effectiveness. This type of growth relies on leveraging existing strengths and gradually increasing market share or revenue streams. For example, when we plant our garden each year, we plant tomatoes. Each year, we start to germinate seeds in late winter, and the seedlings begin to evolve as plants from early to mid summer. It is slow and measurable but takes time, and we consider this incremental growth.

Exponential growth involves harnessing breakthrough innovations, disruptive technologies, or transformative strategies to rapidly scale operations and impact. It often requires bold initiatives, strategic partnerships, or disruptive business models to unlock new opportunities and propel the organization into new markets or industries. So in our tomato example, what starts as an incremental growth explodes into exponential growth in late June and through July when we are producing so much fruit (tomatoes) that it becomes a challenge to harvest and consume all of the outputs.

There are a number of organizations that grew incrementally, then exponentially, that became disruptors. Consider Airbnb or Uber. Their growth started incremental, building a base of consumers, and then, as their popularity increased, the consumer focus became enhanced and the growth skyrocketed and became exponential as disruptors in the marketplace. With AI, we need to leverage strategic pivots to trigger exponential growth and keep pace with AI change. As with our examples, they represent a paradigm shift from doing more of the same.

Let's look at incremental and exponential growth as it is displayed in the diagram in Figure 7.2. Here, we illustrate incremental growth over time, using a traditional bar chart. Incremental growth characteristics show steady growth over time at a predictable rate. In the other illustration, we display exponential growth. Exponential growth can be viral or explosive, where the increase becomes dramatically larger in a shorter period of time.

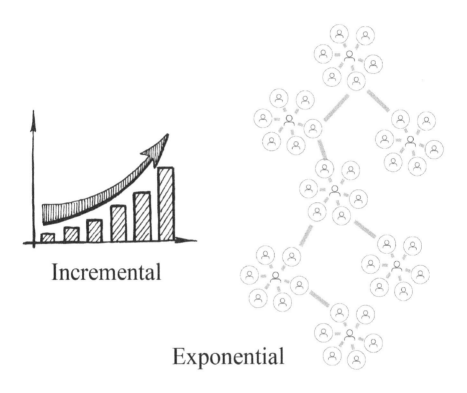

Figure 7.2. Incremental vs. exponential growth.

Now in the case of AI, we can look at the marketplace on a broad scale or look at work in our own organizations and see where there is a potential to be upgraded, enhanced, or replaced by AI. Again, do this while keeping disruptive growth in mind. As individuals, we are empowered to engage and be a part of the growth. Hopefully, the message is clear—don't do more of the same, and course correct quickly as needed

In the introduction, we mentioned that environmental conditions facilitate growth. The organization needs the leadership and the openness to invite growth opportunities. It needs a tolerance to be able to fail and iterate with learnings. In organizations experiencing exponential growth through AI opportunities, effective leadership is paramount to paving the path forward. Visionary leaders with a deep understanding of AI technologies and their potential applications can chart the course for innovation and success. These leaders inspire confidence, foster a culture of experimentation, and drive strategic initiatives that capitalize on AI-driven opportunities. Equally important are the first followers, individuals within the organization who embrace the vision set forth by leaders and actively contribute to its realization. These early adopters play a crucial role in championing change, galvanizing support, and catalyzing momentum across the organization.

For individuals seeking opportunities to grow within this dynamic landscape, there are two primary paths to consider: (1) Aspiring individuals can strive to step into leadership roles themselves, leveraging their skills, expertise, and vision to drive meaningful change and innovation. By assuming leadership responsibilities, individuals have the opportunity to shape organizational strategies, inspire teams, and drive impactful outcomes in the AI-driven ecosystem. (2) Alternatively, individuals can seek out visionary leaders within their organizations or broader professional networks and align themselves as first followers. By supporting and collaborating with visionary leaders, individuals can contribute their talents, insights, and energy toward collective goals, accelerating the pace of innovation and growth within the organization.

Whether assuming leadership roles or aligning with visionary leaders as first followers, individuals have the opportunity to shape the trajectory of their organizations and contribute to the realization of AI-driven opportunities. By fostering a culture of leadership, collaboration, and innovation, organizations and individuals alike can harness the full potential of AI to drive exponential growth and create lasting impact in an ever-evolving digital landscape.

Pursue Growth—Learn by Doing Something New

Growth methods refers to a variety of psychological and educational approaches aimed at fostering personal development, critical thinking, creativity, and overall well-being. These methods often focus on empowering individuals to realize their potential, understand themselves and others better, and navigate challenges effectively. They may involve encouraging self-reflection, promoting curiosity and inquiry, providing opportunities for holistic problem-solving, addressing basic human needs for optimal learning, resolving conflicting beliefs or attitudes, utilizing insights from psychology to shaping behavior, fostering a supportive and empowering learning environment, and recognizing the importance of social interactions in the learning process. Overall, growth methods seek to enhance individuals' cognitive, emotional, and social capacities to facilitate continuous learning and growth. Below are a handful of growth methods that can help individuals and leaders shape growth journeys:

- Existentialist empowerment
- Positive reinforcement
- Socratic questioning
- Gestalt principles of creativity
- Maslow's hierarchy of needs in learning
- Cognitive dissonance resolution
- Behavioral economics in incentives
- Social learning theory

The question we answer in this section is: How do we use these tried and true methods with an overlay of AI? The methods are actions we take to help us master AI in our role to grow and lead us to disrupt. Let's dive deeper into each method and assess each AI use case. That can help you find out what works best for you.

Existentialist Empowerment

Existentialist empowerment is a philosophical and psychological concept rooted in existentialism that emphasizes individual freedom, responsibility, and the search for meaning in life. In organizational contexts, existentialist empowerment encourages employees to find personal significance and purpose in their work, aligning their values with the mission and goals of the organization. It involves recognizing the inherent autonomy and agency of individuals to make choices and take ownership of their actions within the workplace. Existentialist empowerment encourages employees to explore their passions, interests, and talents, fostering engagement, creativity, and intrinsic motivation. By empowering individuals to find meaning and purpose in their work, existentialist empowerment enhances job satisfaction, productivity, and overall well-being within the organization. It acknowledges the importance of personal fulfillment and self-expression in driving organizational success and creating a fulfilling work environment for employees.

In a dynamic tech firm embracing existentialist empowerment, let's spotlight Mia, a software engineer keen on leveraging AI to tackle societal challenges. Inspired by her passion for education equality, Mia proposes an AI-driven personalized learning platform aimed at underserved schools. Supported by the company's ethos, Mia's project gains traction.

Mia collaborates with a diverse team to develop the AI-powered platform, harnessing machine learning algorithms to adapt teaching methods to individual student needs. Through existentialist empowerment, Mia guides the team with purpose, aligning their efforts with the vision of democratizing education.

As the project unfolds, Mia's commitment to meaningful innovation drives her to explore advanced AI techniques, such as natural language processing and recommendation systems. With autonomy and support, Mia's creativity flourishes, leading to groundbreaking solutions that redefine personalized learning.

The AI-powered platform, championed by Mia, revolutionizes education delivery in underserved communities. By providing tailored learning experiences, the platform empowers students and educators alike, bridging educational disparities and fostering lifelong learning.

Through Mia's journey, the enterprise witnesses the transformative impact of existentialist empowerment in driving AI innovation with purpose. By empowering individuals like Mia to pursue purpose-driven AI initiatives, the company advances its mission of harnessing technology for societal good while fostering a culture of creativity, collaboration, and collective impact.

Positive Reinforcement

Another approach to pursue growth is to utilize positive reinforcement to reward and recognize curiosity and creative problem-solving. This approach reinforces desired behaviors and reduces reluctance to change. Positive reinforcement psychology is a psychological principle that focuses on encouraging and reinforcing desired behaviors through positive stimuli or rewards. It involves providing favorable consequences immediately following a desired behavior, which increases the likelihood of that behavior being repeated in the future. Positive reinforcement can take various forms, including verbal praise, tangible rewards, social recognition, or privileges. The key aspect of positive reinforcement is that it strengthens the association between the behavior and its consequences, motivating individuals to continue engaging in the desired behavior. Positive reinforcement psychology is widely applied in various contexts, including education, parenting, organizational management, and behavior therapy, to promote learning, motivation, and behavior change.

In a forward-thinking organization embracing positive reinforcement psychology, let's spotlight Mark, a data scientist passionate about leveraging AI to enhance consumer experiences. Motivated by the principles of positive reinforcement, Mark proposes an AI-driven consumer engagement platform designed to delight users and foster brand loyalty. Supported by the company's culture of recognition, Mark's idea gains enthusiastic support.

Mark collaborates with cross-functional teams to develop the AI-powered platform, employing reinforcement-learning algorithms to personalize consumer interactions and anticipate their needs. Guided by positive reinforcement psychology, Mark fosters a supportive environment where team members feel valued and empowered to innovate.

As the project progresses, Mark's dedication to uplifting consumer experiences drives him to explore cutting-edge AI techniques, including sentiment analysis and predictive modeling. With encouragement and acknowledgment, Mark's creativity thrives, resulting in transformative solutions that redefine consumer engagement.

The AI-powered platform, championed by Mark, revolutionizes the company's approach to consumer service, delivering personalized and proactive support at every touchpoint. Through tailored recommendations and empathetic interactions, the platform strengthens consumer relationships and drives long-term loyalty.

In this case, the positive reinforcement is the fact that the organization champions and supports Mark's idea. Through Mark's journey, the organization witnesses the profound impact of positive reinforcement psychology in driving AI innovation with empathy and purpose. By empowering individuals like Mark to pursue consumer-centric AI initiatives, the company advances its commitment to delivering meaningful experiences while nurturing a culture of positivity, collaboration, and continuous improvement. Thus, Mark grows with positive reinforcement.

By the way, positive reinforcement is bidirectional. While the organization cheered for and supported Mark, Mark can do the same for the organization by continuing his innovative growth behaviors. When you make positive reinforcement bidirectional, you become someone others want to work with or emulate.

Socratic Questioning

The Socratic method of questioning is another approach to grow that can stimulate critical thinking and foster a culture of curiosity and continuous inquiry. The Socratic questioning approach is a method of inquiry and dialogue developed by the ancient Greek philosopher Socrates. It involves asking probing questions to encourage critical thinking, reflection, and deeper exploration of ideas. Rather than providing answers, the Socratic method prompts individuals to examine their assumptions, challenge their beliefs, and arrive at their own conclusions through reasoned discourse. This approach aims to stimulate intellectual curiosity, foster open-mindedness, and promote a deeper understanding of complex issues by engaging individuals in a structured and dialectical exchange of ideas.

In an organization embracing the Socratic questioning approach, let's introduce Camilla, a project manager leading AI integration initiatives. Camilla employs the Socratic method to stimulate critical thinking and foster innovation within her team. During brainstorming sessions, Camilla poses thought-provoking questions that encourage team members to explore diverse perspectives and challenge assumptions.

Camilla initiates a new AI use case focused on optimizing supply chain logistics through predictive analytics. Leveraging the Socratic questioning approach, Camilla engages her team in rigorous analysis and inquiry to identify key variables and potential challenges. Through a series of probing questions, Camilla prompts her team to consider alternative approaches and anticipate potential roadblocks in the AI implementation process.

As the project unfolds, Camilla's Socratic approach encourages her team to delve deeper into the nuances of supply chain dynamics and AI technology. Through collaborative dialogue and critical inquiry, team members uncover insights and uncover innovative solutions to complex logistical challenges.

With Camilla's guidance, the team develops an AI-driven predictive analytics platform that optimizes inventory management, reduces transportation costs, and enhances operational efficiency across the supply chain. By leveraging the Socratic questioning approach, Camilla empowers her team to think critically, adapt to change, and drive meaningful outcomes through AI innovation.

Through Camilla's leadership, the organization embraces a culture of inquiry and continuous learning, leveraging the Socratic questioning approach to navigate the complexities of AI integration with confidence and clarity. By encouraging curiosity and intellectual rigor, Camilla inspires her team to explore new possibilities and unlock the full potential of AI technology in transforming supply chain operations. The other value is the collaborative outcomes for Socratic questions, as it gives the team a voice, improving end-state solutions.

Camilla's growth with AI is evident in her leadership of a project aimed at optimizing supply chain logistics using predictive analytics. Employing the Socratic questioning approach, she guides her team through rigorous analysis and inquiry to identify key variables and potential challenges. Through collaborative dialogue, her team uncovers insights and develops innovative solutions to complex logistical challenges. The outcome with Camilla's guidance is an AI-driven platform that unlocks the full potential of AI technology within their supply chain operations.

Gestalt Principles of Creativity

Gestalt principles of creativity encourage people to consider the whole picture and think about things in a connected way. These principles, based on Gestalt psychology, highlight how we perceive visual information as a whole. They include ideas like objects appearing related when they're close together and grouping similar objects. Other principles involve mentally filling in missing parts of a picture and seeing interrupted lines as coherent. Applying these principles helps creators make designs and artworks that are clear and impactful.

Gestalt refers to a school of psychology that emerged in the early twentieth century, primarily associated with German psychologists, such as Max Wertheimer, Wolfgang Köhler, and Kurt Koffka. The term *Gestalt* roughly translates to "form" or "shape" in German. Gestalt psychology emphasizes the idea that humans perceive objects and patterns as whole entities rather than as a collection of individual parts. This holistic approach to perception influenced various fields, including psychology, philosophy, and design, and laid the foundation for the Gestalt principles of creativity mentioned earlier.

The Gestalt principles of creativity are a great way to grow because they help you see the big picture and think in a connected way. They teach you to understand patterns and relationships better, which makes you more creative and better at solving problems. Plus, using these principles can help you learn more about yourself and express yourself better. They also teach you how to communicate more clearly and build stronger relationships with others. Overall, they're a helpful tool for personal growth.[20]

Incorporating the Gestalt principles of creativity, let's delve into an AI use case centered around enhancing user experience in e-commerce platforms. Meet Alex, a UX designer tasked with optimizing the visual layout and design of an online marketplace. He opts to leverage generative AI and computer vision (defined in chapter three) and, drawing upon the Gestalt principles, to create cohesive and intuitive user interfaces that maximize engagement and conversion rates.

Alex begins by applying the principle of proximity, grouping related elements such as product images, descriptions, and prices to create visual clusters that guide users' attention and streamline navigation. By organizing content based on proximity, Alex enhances the user's ability to quickly identify relevant information and make informed purchasing decisions.

Next, Alex integrates the principle of similarity, employing consistent colors, shapes, and styles to establish visual patterns that convey hierarchy

---

20   Interaction Design Foundation, "What Are the Gestalt Principles?" accessed June 26, 2024, https://www.interaction-design.org/literature/topics/gestalt-principles.

and reinforce brand identity. By aligning visual elements according to similarity, Alex creates a cohesive and harmonious user experience that fosters trust and familiarity among users.

To leverage the principle of closure, Alex strategically employs white space and negative space to create fluid and dynamic layouts that invite users to explore and interact with the platform. By allowing elements to visually connect and complete patterns, Alex encourages users to fill in the gaps and construct meaningful narratives as they navigate the e-commerce interface.

Finally, Alex incorporates the principle of continuity, employing smooth transitions and visual flow to guide users through the browsing and checkout process seamlessly. By aligning content along continuous lines and pathways, Alex creates a sense of progression and coherence that enhances the user's journey from discovery to purchase.

Through the application of Gestalt principles, Alex transforms the e-commerce platform into an immersive and engaging digital experience that resonates with users on a subconscious level. By harnessing the power of AI-driven design, Alex empowers businesses to deliver personalized and intuitive user experiences that drive consumer satisfaction and loyalty in the competitive online marketplace.

Alex is growing with AI by using Gestalt principles to improve user experience in e-commerce. As a UX designer, Alex applies these principles to create visually cohesive interfaces that enhance engagement and boost conversion rates. By grouping related elements together and using consistent colors and styles, Alex makes navigation easier and reinforces brand identity. Smooth transitions guide users seamlessly through the platform, resulting in an immersive experience that fosters consumer satisfaction and loyalty. Through AI-driven design, Alex helps businesses deliver personalized and intuitive experiences in the competitive online marketplace.

Maslow's Hierarchy of Needs in Learning

Maslow's hierarchy of needs in learning applies Abraham Maslow's psychological theory of human motivation in an educational context. Maslow proposed that individuals have five hierarchical levels of needs: physiological, safety, love/belonging, esteem, and self-actualization. In learning, this theory suggests that learners must have their basic needs met before they can focus on higher-order learning objectives. For example, learners need to feel safe and secure in their learning environment (safety needs) and have a sense of belonging and connection with others (love/belonging needs) before they can fully engage in learning activities. As learners progress up the hierarchy, they strive for esteem and recognition for their achievements, ultimately aiming for self-actualization—the realization of one's fullest potential. Educators can use Maslow's hierarchy of needs to design learning environments that address students' diverse needs and create conditions conducive to optimal learning and growth

Let's explore Maslow's hierarchy of needs in learning within the context of AI-driven personalized education platforms. Consider Seema, an educational technologist tasked with developing a learning platform designed to meet students' diverse needs and facilitate their educational journeys.

At the foundational level of Maslow's hierarchy, Seema ensures that the platform addresses students' physiological needs by providing access to essential resources, such as reliable internet connection, digital devices, and nutritious meals. She explores AI tools to enhance the platform. Through partnerships with community organizations and government agencies, the platform offers support services to students facing food insecurity, housing instability, or other basic needs challenges, ensuring that every learner has the foundational support required to engage in meaningful learning experiences.

Moving up the hierarchy, Seema focuses on meeting students' safety needs within the digital learning environment. The platform employs advanced AI-enabled cybersecurity measures to protect students' personal information and ensure the integrity of their online interactions. Additionally, Seema integrates features such as real-time monitoring and reporting tools to identify and address instances of cyberbullying, harassment, or other safety concerns, fostering a secure and supportive online learning community for all students.

As students progress to higher levels of Maslow's hierarchy, Seema leverages AI-driven analytics and adaptive learning technologies to personalize the learning experience and meet students' belongingness and esteem needs. The platform analyzes students' learning preferences, cognitive styles, and academic performance data to tailor instructional content, pacing, and feedback to each individual learner. By providing opportunities for collaborative learning, peer feedback, and recognition of achievements, the platform cultivates a sense of belonging and competence among students, enhancing their motivation and engagement in the learning process.

Finally, Seema integrates opportunities for self-actualization into the learning experience, empowering students to pursue their passions, interests, and aspirations. The platform offers personalized learning pathways, project-based learning opportunities, and access to mentorship programs and industry partnerships, enabling students to explore their interests, develop new skills, and pursue meaningful learning experiences aligned with their personal and professional goals.

Through the integration of Maslow's hierarchy of needs in learning principles into the AI-driven education platform, Seema creates a supportive and empowering learning environment that nurtures students' holistic development and fosters their lifelong love of learning. By addressing students' physiological, safety, belongingness, esteem, and self-actualization needs, the platform empowers every learner to reach their full potential and thrive in an increasingly complex and interconnected world.

Seema is growing with AI by focusing on students' safety and personalization in the digital learning environment. She ensures students' safety through advanced cybersecurity measures and real-time monitoring for cyberbullying and harassment. Moving up Maslow's hierarchy, Seema uses AI analytics to personalize learning, tailoring content and feedback to each student's preferences and performance. By fostering collaboration and recognition, she creates a sense of belonging and competence. Finally, Seema empowers students to pursue their passions through personalized pathways and mentorship programs, fostering holistic development and a love for lifelong learning. Through AI-driven education, Seema creates a supportive environment that empowers every student to thrive and reach their full potential.

Cognitive Dissonance Resolution

Cognitive dissonance resolution refers to the psychological process of reducing or eliminating the discomfort that arises when an individual holds conflicting beliefs, attitudes, or behaviors. Cognitive dissonance occurs when there is a discrepancy between one's beliefs or behaviors and new information or experiences that challenge those beliefs or behaviors. To resolve cognitive dissonance, individuals may engage in various strategies, such as changing their beliefs or behaviors to align with the new information, seeking out additional information that supports their existing beliefs, or rationalizing and justifying their beliefs or behaviors in light of the new information. Cognitive dissonance resolution is an important aspect of cognitive and emotional adaptation, as individuals strive to maintain internal consistency and reduce psychological discomfort in the face of conflicting information or experiences.

In the bustling headquarters of a top telecommunications company, Emily, a seasoned project manager, took on a challenging task—upgrading the outdated IVR (interactive voice response) system to a cutting-edge consumer service solution.

As Emily delved into the project, she saw the vast potential of integrating AI capabilities into the IVR system. With determination, she embarked on her AI-powered journey. Emily's first move was exploring AI-powered virtual assistants. She envisioned a future where these assistants, driven by natural language processing, could interact seamlessly with consumers, providing personalized solutions and even predicting their needs.

Next, Emily aimed to implement sentiment analysis. Using AI, the system could detect consumer emotions in real-time, prioritizing those needing urgent assistance. Driven by predictive analytics, Emily foresaw a system anticipating consumer needs before they spoke. By analyzing data, the IVR system could tailor options to each consumer, creating a personalized experience. Emily also considered AI-driven voice biometrics to enhance security and streamline authentication, and AI-driven call routing to reduce wait times.

Throughout her journey, Emily embraced a culture of continuous improvement. AI-driven analytics and feedback mechanisms allowed her to monitor interactions, identify trends, and enhance the system with each iteration. In the end, Emily's AI-powered journey transformed the company's IVR system. Consumers experienced unmatched convenience and efficiency, setting new industry standards.

This experience helped Emily realize the transformative power of AI. With pride and gratitude, she looked forward to unlocking more possibilities in project management. Emily encountered uncertainty as new AI ideas challenged her understanding. However, by remaining openminded and learning, she found innovative ways to leverage AI, leading to the successful transformation of the IVR system.

Behavioral Economics in Incentives

Behavioral economics in incentives uses insights from psychology and economics to design rewards that encourage desired behaviors. It recognizes that people don't always make decisions rationally and considers factors like loss aversion, social norms, and framing effects. For instance, emphasizing potential losses can be more motivating than focusing only on gains. Incentives can also leverage social proof and frame rewards positively to drive behavior effectively. By understanding these behavioral principles, organizations can design incentives that better influence people's actions and help achieve their goals.

Consider this use case. Diego is a software engineer at Tech Innovations Ltd. Recently, his company added a performance management program powered by AI. The system analyzes Diego's work patterns, identifies areas for improvement, and suggests personalized incentives to enhance his productivity and job satisfaction. Through the AI-driven platform, Diego receives real-time feedback on his performance metrics, such as code quality, project completion rates, and collaborative contributions to team projects. Based on his performance data, the system generates tailored incentives designed to motivate Diego and reinforce positive behaviors.

For example, when Diego consistently exceeds his coding targets or demonstrates exceptional teamwork skills, the AI platform rewards him with recognition badges, virtual tokens, or access to professional development resources. These incentives are strategically designed to tap into Diego's intrinsic motivations, such as mastery, autonomy, and purpose, to drive sustained performance improvements.

Moreover, the AI system leverages behavioral economics principles, such as loss aversion and social proof, to enhance the effectiveness of incentives. Diego receives notifications highlighting his progress relative to his peers, fostering a sense of competition and social recognition. Additionally, the platform introduces time-limited challenges and rewards, creating a sense of urgency and excitement around achieving performance milestones.

As Diego engages with the AI-driven performance management system, he experiences a positive reinforcement loop, where his efforts are consistently recognized and rewarded, leading to increased motivation and job satisfaction. The behavioral economics-informed incentives not only drive individual performance but also foster a culture of continuous improvement and collaboration within the organization.

Overall, Tech Innovations Ltd.'s AI-driven performance management system demonstrates the power of behavioral economics in designing incentives that effectively motivate employees, boost productivity, and drive organizational success. By harnessing the insights of behavioral economics and leveraging AI technology, the company creates a dynamic and engaging work environment where employees like Diego are empowered to thrive and achieve their full potential.

Social Learning Theory

Social learning theory is a psychological concept that suggests people learn by observing others and modeling their behavior. Developed by Albert Bandura, this theory emphasizes the importance of social interactions and role models in the learning process. According to social learning theory, individuals not only learn from direct experiences but also from observing the actions and consequences of others. This theory highlights the role of reinforcement, imitation, and vicarious learning in shaping behavior. By observing others and the outcomes of their actions, individuals can acquire new skills, attitudes, and behaviors. Social learning theory has significant implications for education, as it underscores the importance of positive role models, social reinforcement, and collaborative learning environments in facilitating skill acquisition and behavior change.

Sarah, a product manager in a bustling tech company named InnovateTech, found herself at a crossroads in her role. With the rapid advancements in AI, she knew that integrating AI into their products could revolutionize their offerings and enhance user experiences. However, she felt overwhelmed by the complexity of AI and unsure of where to start.

Determined to navigate this challenge, Sarah turned to the principles of social learning theory for guidance. She began her journey by identifying role models within her industry who had successfully integrated AI into their products. Through industry conferences, online forums, and networking events, she discovered inspiring stories of companies that had leveraged AI to streamline processes, personalize user experiences, and drive innovation.

As Sarah delved deeper into these success stories, she realized the importance of observation and modeling in her own learning journey. She studied the strategies and techniques employed by these companies, taking note of their approaches to data analysis, machine learning algorithms, and user interface design. By immersing herself in the experiences of others, Sarah gained valuable insights into the practical applications of AI in product management.

However, Sarah knew that learning from success alone was not enough. She also needed to understand the potential challenges and pitfalls associated with AI integration. Through case studies and post-mortems of failed AI projects, she learned valuable lessons about the importance of data quality, algorithmic bias, and ethical considerations in AI development. These insights equipped her with a more nuanced understanding of the risks involved and empowered her to make informed decisions moving forward.

As Sarah continued her journey, she found motivation and reinforcement in the positive outcomes achieved by companies that had successfully embraced AI. She celebrated their successes and used them as inspiration to fuel her own efforts. Additionally, she sought out mentors and colleagues who could provide guidance and support along the way, fostering a collaborative learning environment within her team.

Armed with knowledge, inspiration, and a supportive network, Sarah embarked on her mission to integrate AI into InnovateTech's products. She led her team in brainstorming sessions, experimentation, and iterative development cycles, leveraging the collective expertise and insights of her colleagues. Together, they pushed the boundaries of innovation, delivering AI-powered solutions that exceeded consumer expectations and propelled InnovateTech to new heights of success.

In the end, Sarah's journey exemplified the power of social learning theory in guiding her through the complexities of AI integration. By observing, learning, and collaborating with others, she transformed her vision into reality, demonstrating that with the right mindset and approach, anything is possible.

Choice Architecture with Growth

These industry-leading practices for growth integrate principles from philosophy and psychology to enhance curiosity, foster creativity, reduce reluctance, and remove resistance to growth through change and learning methods in the context of workforce transformation and AI adoption.

The interconnectedness of growth among organizations, their leaders, individuals, AI enablement, and methods of growing beyond today's constraints reflects a dynamic ecosystem of mutual influence and empowerment. Organizations drive growth by embracing AI enablement, leveraging technology to optimize processes, innovate, and expand into new markets. Effective leaders play a pivotal role in orchestrating this growth, providing vision, direction, and support to unleash the full potential of both the organization and its individuals.

Individuals, in turn, contribute to organizational growth through their skills, creativity, and commitment to excellence. By fostering a culture of learning, collaboration, and empowerment, organizations empower individuals to thrive and contribute meaningfully to collective success. AI enablement serves as a catalyst for growth, augmenting human capabilities, automating repetitive tasks, and unlocking new opportunities for innovation and efficiency.

All that being said, as an individual, you have to act if you want to grow. The methods of growth are simply theory or words on a page if you don't act on them. In discussing our collective AI journey, a lot of this book is about growth. To grow, we are researching and writing about AI with a business lens because we believe that AI is for all. Thinking about the growth methods we used, we have adopted social learning theory. By co-authoring a book, we have had the opportunity to debate, discuss, write, and rewrite. We are challenging ourselves to continuously think bigger and out of the box, like employing the Gestalt principles of creativity which, coincidentally, encourage employees to see the bigger picture and promote holistic thinking and innovative solution

In essence, the interconnectedness of growth underscores the symbiotic relationship among organizations, leaders, individuals, AI enablement, and innovative methods of growth. By embracing collaboration, continuous learning, and adaptive strategies, stakeholders can navigate complexity, capitalize on emerging trends, and realize their full potential in the dynamic landscape of the future.

So What?

Methods of growing beyond today's constraints involve embracing transformative approaches, such as existentialist empowerment, positive reinforcement psychology, Socratic questioning, Gestalt principles of creativity, Maslow's hierarchy of needs in learning, cognitive dissonance resolution, behavioral economics in incentives, and social learning theory. These methodologies provide frameworks for fostering personal and professional development, enhancing organizational effectiveness, and driving sustainable growth in the face of evolving challenges and opportunities.

The chapter emphasizes the importance of growth in the context of AI, suggesting that understanding and applying AI concepts is crucial for both personal and organizational development. It encourages readers to reflect on their journey from "play" to "grow" with AI, highlighting the need for hands-on experience and active participation in AI projects to truly master the technology and contribute to organizational success. To create space for this growth, it's an imperative to shift away from doing more of the same. The key is to do something new, be comfortable with failing fast, and iterating. Know that when you have achieved a state of growth, you can get the next role—a promotion, a new job, or even a new career path.

Now What?

If you capture all the concepts, you know that "to grow" is "to do." To grow, you need to actively pursue opportunity and learning. You need to look at the work in your space and evaluate it with an AI lens. When you aren't sure, you need to pursue alternatives to determine the right one, taking everything you learned in play and grow. Finally, the choice is yours. You now employ choice architecture. Do you want to continue your growth in your space, or is it time to emerge as a leader of disruption? First, put pen to paper and document some ideas for your growth plan.

My learnings by using methods

1. Existentialist empowerment

2. Positive reinforcement

3. Socratic questioning

4. Gestalt principles of creativity

5. Maslow's hierarchy of needs in learning

6. Cognitive dissonance resolution

7. Behavioral economics in incentives

8. Social learning theory

Figure 7.3. Tried and true methods to grow.

DISRUPT WITH AI

SHIFT PARADIGMS WITH THE POWER OF AI

Introduction

NOW THAT WE'VE laid the groundwork for personal and institutional growth with AI, it's time to level up and explore the exhilarating world of disruption with AI. In this chapter, we shift gears from simply growing within the AI landscape to actively reshaping it and defining its future. This isn't just about adapting to change; it's about leading the charge in revolutionizing industries, markets, and organizational paradigms through the power of AI. Get ready to challenge conventions, ignite innovation, and make waves in your professional sphere. Disrupt with AI is your guide to becoming a trailblazer in the AI-driven era, so buckle up and get ready to disrupt the status quo like never before.

This chapter is for those with an entrepreneurial spirit, innovators, and disruptors. Don't worry if you're not feeling entrepreneurial yet—this will give you a taste of the mindset needed for a startup or a changemaker, whether it is inside or outside of your organization. We'll explore how AI can disrupt industries and drive innovation, bringing about positive changes for society. Let's dive into the exciting potential of disruption together!

The objectives of this chapter are the following:

1. Understand the concept of disruption, its significance in various industries, and its impact on market competition dynamics.
2. Explore the role of choice architecture and economic theories, such as creative destruction and supply-demand dynamics, in facilitating disruption.
3. Examine the intersection of artificial intelligence (AI) with disruption and its implications for businesses, including the adoption curve dynamics.
4. Learn systematic approaches to disruption, including the PACT framework and strategies for ensuring successful monetization, with practical "how-to" examples.

What Is Disruption?

There is a camp of people who hear the word *disruption* and automatically go to the negative. We and many others who have been part of disruptive change know that, when orchestrated correctly, disruption can lead to positive outcomes for people throughout society. The mindset here is that disruption is actually positive. *Disruption* refers to a significant change or disturbance that alters existing processes, practices, or industries, often by introducing new technologies, business models, or ideas that fundamentally transform the way things are done. Disruption typically challenges established norms and incumbents, leading to shifts in market dynamics, consumer behaviors, and competitive landscapes. Looking at this definition, you can see why we believe that disruption clears the path for something new and better to emerge. Disruption creates space for something new and better. It allows you to take charge in your role to create change with AI that drives either a financial benefit or experiential benefit that is sustainable.

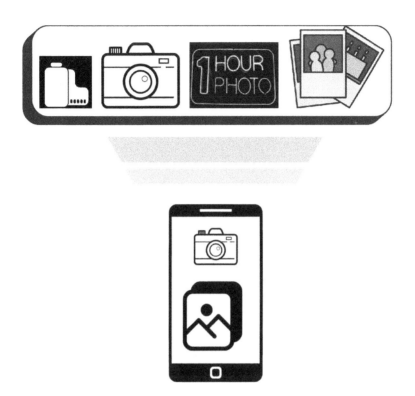

Figure 8.1. The mobile phone disrupted multiple industries.

Think about when you first became aware of disruption around you or in the marketplace. Were you aware that it was actually a disruption? The smartphone certainly disrupted and replaced a number of devices.

Antara and Winnie learned about disruption inadvertently at different times in their careers. Winnie, who leads large programs that take a strategic vision and bring it to the marketplace, learned about disruption early in her career when the question of cryptocurrency came up. The digitization of payments was brought up as a potential thread of work in 2015. Her first reaction was that it wasn't feasible but, over time, the potential became more and more revolutionary. Candidly, Winnie admits that she recognized the work as disruptive after the fact.

We want you to view disruption as stepping into a whirlwind of change. It is the opportunity to transform at lightning speed, with you in the thick of it or even as the orchestrator. Disruption flips the script, tossing old ways aside.

We know AI is a disruptor. We don't know exactly how it will impact us—at home, at work, and possibly on our commutes. But we know it absolutely will and has started. We also know that there are two types of people—the ones who see the storm coming and hide for safety and the ones who get their cameras or tools and seek to harness the storm's path.

If you are the type of person who seeks to harness, read on because there are some great tips ahead. If you are not—how do you find a disruptor whose North Star pulls yours?

Remember, disruption is a complex event that affects people differently based on their roles and viewpoints and place in the organization. There are many examples that we can use to demonstrate the disruption of the past and impact and value. Understanding who you are in the face of disruption will help you pick your path forward. Below are some examples where disruption has left its mark.

Disruption in Healthcare

Even before the pandemic, the healthcare industry was riddled with problems—long waits, expensive appointments, and limited access. The pandemic initially made these problems worse, taking away healthcare almost completely, at least initially, from those who needed it. In the chaos, solutions emerged because healthcare providers were forced to move quickly to provide their services with limited physical interaction. In a profession that needed to be in-person, healthcare providers had to think outside of the box and expand methods to provide the services remotely. Say hello to telemedicine. While originally planned as a stopgap, telemedicine has become a material disruptor.

Telemedicine wasn't just a solution; it was a lightning bolt of innovation, fueled by advancements in technology and the evolving needs of patients. It didn't just tweak the system—it completely rewrote the playbook, offering a lifeline to those who needed it most. And while it was introduced at scale during the pandemic, it has continued to grow with continued advancement in the technology. Computer vision, for example, as a technology has grown in its capabilities. Computer vision plays a significant role in diagnostic imaging by leveraging algorithms and artificial intelligence to analyze medical images with precision and efficiency. Computer vision has many uses, including diagnostic imaging, vitals monitoring, and injury assessments. Computer vision has allowed providers to include throughput and provide outcomes at a speed greater than previously imagined. As a patient, you no longer need to take the day off to go to an appointment and then wait days or weeks to get a diagnosis. Outcomes of the providers and patients are speedier and more efficient.

Disruption in Banking

Think about the money—how we get and how we use it. Back in the day, banking was a hassle. Consumers had to wait in long lines, often struggled to access cash, and they were tethered to banking hours.

Here is some history to ground us in the disruption. The first dollar bill was issued in 1862 as a legal tender note with a portrait of Salmon P. Chase, the treasury secretary under President Abraham Lincoln. The name "Chase," by the way, is still around today—as part of the name of the financial company JP Morgan Chase. The first ATM in the U.S. made its public debut on September 2, 1969, dispensing cash to consumers at Chemical Bank in Rockville Centre, New York. The world's first ATM was installed a bit earlier, on June 27, 1967, at a branch of Barclays Bank in Enfield, North London. The first electronic (wire) transfer was done using the telegraph in 1872 (or shortly before) by Western Union on its existing telegraph network.

Since then, digital transactions have evolved significantly, with the introduction of platforms like PayPal in 1998, which allowed users to send and receive money online using an email address and a linked bank account or credit card. The evolution of digital payments has fundamentally changed the way we conduct transactions, making them faster, more secure, and more efficient.

Let's highlight the disruption of the ATM. Remember, the first dollar was printed in 1862. For consumers, unless you kept your dollars in your home, you needed to use a bank. For more than a hundred years, people were unable to access their money during off hours. ATMs were a game-changer. They broke the chains of traditional banking, offering people a way to access their money whenever they needed it, day or night.

Today—and we're on the brink of another seismic shift—the move toward a cashless society. With the rise of digital payments, mobile banking, and contactless transactions, cash is becoming a thing of the past. Many of us don't use cash at all. Now, in all fairness, both Antara and Winnie have made a living digitizing payments, so this is second nature. But from a usage perspective, digital payments are growing exponentially. Payments are made with a tap of a card or a swipe of a phone, seamlessly integrating into our daily lives. And just like that, the disruption sparked by ATMs has paved the way for a future where cash is no longer king.

Choice Architecture with Disruption

In chapter 5, we defined choice architecture and how it is about deliberately designing how choices are presented to influence decision-making. It's setting up the environment in a way that nudges people toward certain decisions while keeping their freedom intact. It involves things like how options are shown, the order they're in, and even using defaults or incentives to sway decisions. This idea is used in different areas like economics, marketing, and public policy to encourage positive behaviors and choices.

When you disrupt, you need to create the choice architecture structure for impacted stakeholders and the organization. Until now, we have used choice architecture at a personal level when it comes to AI. Disruption with AI requires that we use choice architecture at scale. Think about it this way: At Thanksgiving, you may have to cook for ten people. Imagine if you had to cook Thanksgiving dinner for your entire town. Now we are talking about scale.

Choice architecture to disrupt is deeply ingrained in an organization's pursuit of exponential growth and need to capitalize on emerging opportunities. It revolves around designing the framework and decision-making processes that govern how disruptions are identified, evaluated, and pursued within the organization. This architecture encompasses various elements:

- Strategic vision and goals: At its core, when employing choice architecture, you need to consider the organization's strategic vision and long-term objectives. Choices need to reflect ambitious targets for growth, market expansion, and competitive differentiation.

- Risk appetite and tolerance: Choices should be influenced by the organization's risk appetite and tolerance for uncertainty. Each choice should include a careful assessment of the risks and rewards associated with disruptive initiatives.
- Resource allocation: This is critical. Choices need to be evaluated against resource capacity and allocation. There has to be a clear understanding of how resources are used today. Choices will require allocation of sufficient financial, human, and technological resources to support disruptive endeavors, including strategic investments in research and development, talent acquisition, and technology platforms.
- Organizational culture: Lastly, organizational culture plays a vital role, shaping how individuals and teams approach innovation, risk-taking, and change. A culture that values experimentation, agility, and continuous learning fosters an environment where disruptive ideas can thrive.

By carefully orchestrating these elements, organizations can create a choice architecture that guides and empowers people to challenge the status quo, embrace uncertainty, and pursue bold ideas that drive exponential growth and transformation.

So far, we have discussed what is internal to the organization's landscape within the context of the choice architecture framework needed to disrupt. The external landscape and consumer needs also must be considered to drive choices that will disrupt with AI. To truly disrupt with AI at the forefront, whether you're leading a startup or an established entity there are three pivotal elements:

- Identifying significant market gaps
- Tailoring innovative AI-driven solutions to meet evolving demands
- Establishing a dominant presence that draws consumers in

The choice architecture for disruption involves deliberately designing decision-making processes to influence stakeholders and organizational direction. It encompasses strategic vision, risk assessment, resource allocation, and organizational culture. By orchestrating these elements, organizations empower themselves to challenge norms and pursue bold ideas for exponential growth and transformation, especially when leveraging AI. This approach requires a well-thought-out framework of both internal organizational landscapes and external market dynamics to effectively determine how to innovate and disrupt.

Disrupting with AI

So far, we have defined disruption and its impact and outcomes on society using some examples. We highlighted the choice architecture to help you create the framework to disrupt. We have basically given you the first pieces of the puzzle. Now we are going to explore at a deeper level to help you take your ideas and evaluate them as choices in context. In this section, we are going to cover the following areas to flex your muscle to disrupt:

- Economic theories of disruption: These provide a roadmap for navigating market changes effectively and seizing emerging opportunities. These are well-studied, tried-and-tested methods.
- Risk and reward for a pivot to disrupt: With any change, there will be a risk and reward proposition. This is true of AI change, and certain changes will bring greater reward. Understanding economic theories of disruption is crucial for organizations seeking to disrupt, as it helps them balance risks and rewards. Just as venturing into space involves risks but also offers significant rewards, disruptive innovations entail uncertainties and potential gains. For example, companies investing in space exploration face high costs and uncertainties, yet the rewards, like pioneering new technologies and accessing vast resources, can be immense. Elon Musk's SpaceX demonstrated the benefits of disruptive innovation by reducing the cost of space exploration by a factor of twenty-seven through initiatives like reusable

rocket technology.[21] Similarly, disruptive innovations in other industries require careful consideration of economic theories to navigate uncertainties and seize opportunities, ultimately driving progress and shaping the future.

- Disruption with AI from the perspective of a consumer: When we disrupt AI, we need to keep the consumer at the forefront. The consumer is why we are making changes to drive innovation to the marketplace faster and cheaper. Any planned or orchestrated disruption needs to hold the consumer at the highest level. They are the highest priority.
- Dilemma of disruption without monetization: While the consumer is the highest priority, we can't serve them unless we are getting paid. Plus, if you give something away for free, it is perceived as having no value. Plus, your disruption needs to provide value to the consumer. If you were thinking of a great way to make changing your flat tire easier, for example, it is no longer needed with the emergence of run-flat tires. You can continue driving after a puncture so you can take time to get to an auto shop or find a safe place where your tire can be fixed or replaced.

---

[21]   Wendy Whitman Cobb, "How Elon Musk's SpaceX Lowered Costs and Reduced Barriers to Space," The Wire Science, February 3, 2019, https://science.thewire.in/aerospace/how-elon-musks-spacex-lowered-costs-and-reduced-barriers-to-space/.

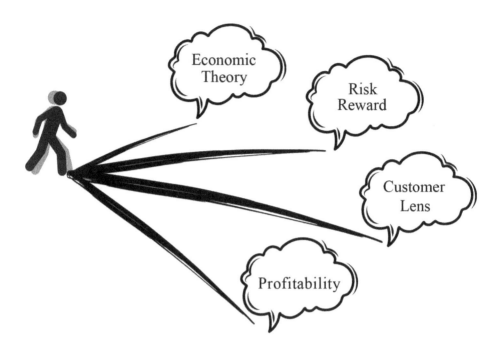

Figure 8.2. Pathways to disrupt with AI.

If you are a disruptive leader, you will define your role and your actions needed to disrupt economies, consumption patterns, demand curves, pricing, experience, and so much more. Using AI as a leader, you will revolutionize traditional processes, systems, and paradigms by introducing novel approaches, efficiencies, and capabilities. All will be within the context of defined choices that consider the organization's structure and the needs of the consumer with a level of clarity on the broader marketplace.

Economic Theories of Disruption

To disrupt with AI, it helps to understand the economic theories of disruption. These theories provide insights into how new technologies can fundamentally reshape industries, drive innovation, and create competitive advantages, enabling organizations to strategically leverage AI for transformative change. The theories also provide valuable insights into market disruptions, helping organizations understand and adapt to these changes. By grasping economic theories, businesses can navigate disruptions effectively and capitalize on emerging opportunities in the shifting landscape. A fundamental piece of economics is supply and demand—with technology-driven transformations, the supply side is the technology and the demand side is the humans and their problems that are hard and expensive to solve. Economic theories will help us target and right the size of the supply to the demand and let humanity drive technology. From our perspective, leaders assess risks all day and every day. They rarely look at economic theory, which sets the stage for profitability. We will be discussing creative destruction, market competition and monopoly power, adoption curve dynamics, network effects and social influence, and supply-and-demand dynamics.

Creative Destruction

Creative destruction, a concept introduced by economist Joseph Schumpeter, describes the process where innovations and technologies replace outdated ones, leading to significant changes in industries and markets.[22] In the context of meal delivery services, companies like HelloFresh and Blue Apron have embraced this concept by leveraging AI to revolutionize the way people shop for groceries and plan meals. These companies utilize predictive algorithms powered by AI to anticipate consumer preferences and optimize inventory management, ensuring that consumers receive personalized meal kits tailored to their tastes and dietary requirements. This application of AI not only enhances the consumer experience but also streamlines the entire supply chain process, from meal planning

---

[22]   Joseph Schumpeter, *Capitalism, Socialism, and Democracy* (New York: Harper and Brothers, 1942).

to delivery. As a result, businesses in the food industry must adapt to these transformative changes and harness the power of AI to stay competitive in a rapidly evolving market landscape. While this adaptation may present challenges, it also presents opportunities for growth and innovation, ultimately driving progress and shaping the future of the food industry.

Market Competition and Monopoly Power

Market competition fuels innovation, driving companies to continually improve their products and services to attract consumers. However, when one company gains excessive market power, it can stifle innovation and limit consumer choice. This is where AI comes in, offering a potential solution to rebalance the scales. Take the travel industry, for example. Traditional booking platforms may dominate the market, controlling prices and options. But with the emergence of generative AI (GenAI), a new era of innovation is unleashed. GenAI, with its ability to analyze vast amounts of data and automate processes, enables smaller players to compete on a level playing field. These newcomers can provide personalized travel experiences, dynamic pricing models, and sustainable travel options, challenging the dominance of established players. As a result, market competition intensifies, driving further innovation and benefiting consumers with more choices and better services. In the face of market dominance by established players, AI presents a transformative opportunity to level the playing field, fostering competition, stimulating innovation, and ultimately providing consumers with more choices and improved services in industries like travel.

Adoption Curve Dynamics

Adoption curve dynamics illustrate the trajectory of how new technologies like AI are embraced across various industries. It's a journey from initial skepticism to widespread acceptance, and understanding this process is crucial for gauging the potential impact of AI adoption. By examining technology adoption patterns and stakeholder engagement strategies, we can anticipate how quickly AI may permeate different sectors and the challenges it may encounter along the way.

In the healthcare industry, for instance, GenAI also holds immense promise. Imagine a scenario where AI algorithms analyze medical records, genetic data, and patient histories to provide personalized treatment recommendations. This application of GenAI not only enhances diagnostic accuracy but also improves patient outcomes. As healthcare providers witness these benefits firsthand, the adoption curve for AI in healthcare may steepen, leading to rapid integration of AI-driven solutions across the sector. Understanding these dynamics helps stakeholders anticipate shifts in the industry landscape and prepare accordingly, ensuring a smoother transition to AI-enabled healthcare. Understanding adoption curves helps stakeholders anticipate how quickly AI will be embraced in different sectors, like healthcare. This foresight allows them to prepare for challenges and ensure a smooth transition to AI-driven solutions, ultimately improving patient care.

Network Effects and Social Influence

Network effects and social influence play a significant role in driving the adoption of products and services, and, with the amplifying power of AI, their impact is even more pronounced. Understanding the potential and scale of disruption in network effects and social influence entails harnessing AI tools to maximize their reach and effectiveness. For example, consider the application of natural language programming (NLP) in news and journalism. By analyzing vast amounts of textual data from various sources, NLP algorithms can generate personalized news feeds tailored to individual preferences and interests. These personalized recommendations leverage network effects by encouraging users to engage more with the content, thus amplifying its influence. Moreover, social media algorithms powered by AI can target specific demographics with relevant news stories and articles, further magnifying the dissemination of information. As a result, AI-driven innovations in NLP revolutionize the way news is consumed and shared, illustrating the profound impact of network effects and social influence in shaping product adoption and market dynamics. Understanding the role of network effects and social influence, especially in the context of AI, is crucial as it highlights the potential for amplified impact in driving product adoption and shaping market dynamics.

Supply and Demand Dynamics

Supply and demand dynamics are pivotal, as AI innovations can alter supply chains and influence consumer preferences, reshaping market dynamics. For example, companies like Greenfield Technology are using AI to improve seed development and crop resilience. Through predictive models, AI helps breeders select seeds that perform well in different climates. This technology also accelerates the development of climate-adaptive seeds urgently needed to combat disease outbreaks and extreme weather events. By analyzing real-time weather information and field sensor data, AI systems assist farmers in making informed decisions and optimizing resource allocation. Additionally, AI aids in understanding genetic diversity among plant populations, helping researchers prioritize conservation efforts and protect vulnerable species. These advancements in AI-driven seed genetic engineering transform the agricultural landscape, ensuring a stable food supply and empowering farmers to thrive in a changing climate. Supply-and-demand dynamics are disrupted as AI innovations reshape market preferences and introduce novel products tailored to evolving consumer needs. So, AI innovations in agriculture, exemplified by companies like GreenFields, are reshaping supply-and-demand dynamics by revolutionizing seed development, optimizing resource allocation, and safeguarding crop resilience, ensuring a stable food supply and empowering farmers to thrive amidst changing environmental conditions.

In summary, these theories provide a roadmap for navigating market changes effectively and seizing emerging opportunities. By grasping concepts like creative destruction and supply-and-demand dynamics influenced by AI, businesses can reshape market preferences and introduce novel products tailored to evolving consumer needs. Moreover, AI helps rebalance market power, fosters innovation, and anticipates adoption trajectories, ensuring a smoother transition to AI-enabled solutions across sectors. Leveraging network effects and social influence, amplified by AI, further magnifies the impact of disruptive innovations, driving product adoption and market dynamics.

Risk and Reward for a Pivot to Disrupt

Risk perception and behavioral economics illuminate how AI insights can mitigate risks and improve decision-making. In traversing the path from the decision to disrupt to achieving scale, organizations encounter various risks that demand meticulous identification, quantification, detection, prevention, and remediation.

One primary risk lies in the failure to accurately identify the potential impact of AI-driven disruptions on existing business models, operations, and market dynamics. Organizations must undertake thorough assessments to quantify the magnitude of disruption and its implications for revenue streams, consumer relationships, and competitive positioning. This involves analyzing market trends, competitor strategies, and consumer preferences to gauge the extent of change required and the associated risks involved. This primary risk is the reason we go so in-depth on choice architecture for disruption. To us, it is critical to document and evaluate your choice through the lens of the organization and the consumer so you truly understand the potential risks and the ultimate rewards.

Detecting risks along the disruption journey necessitates vigilant monitoring of internal and external factors that could impede progress or derail strategic objectives. Organizations should establish robust monitoring mechanisms, key performance indicators, and early warning systems to track progress, identify deviations from planned outcomes, and detect emerging threats or vulnerabilities. By leveraging data analytics, predictive modeling, and risk assessment tools, organizations can proactively identify potential risks and take timely corrective actions to mitigate their impact.

Preventing risks requires proactive measures to establish safeguards, controls, and contingency plans aimed at minimizing exposure to potential threats and vulnerabilities. This entails implementing robust governance frameworks, risk management protocols, and compliance mechanisms to ensure adherence to ethical, legal, and regulatory standards. Organizations should also invest in employee training, awareness programs, and capacity-building initiatives to enhance risk awareness, decision-making capabilities, and crisis preparedness across the organization.

Navigating the path from decision to disrupt and at scale requires organizations to be vigilant, proactive, and agile in identifying, quantifying, detecting, preventing, and remedying risks along the way. By adopting a comprehensive risk management approach and integrating risk considerations into strategic decision-making processes, organizations can effectively navigate the complexities of AI-driven disruptions and capitalize on opportunities for growth, innovation, and sustainable value creation.

Disruption with AI from the Perspective of a Consumer

Disrupting with AI from a consumer perspective involves leveraging artificial intelligence technologies to enhance everyday experiences, access personalized products and services, and make more informed decisions. For instance, AI-powered recommendation systems can offer tailored suggestions based on individual preferences and behaviors, improving the shopping or entertainment experience. Additionally, virtual assistants and chatbots equipped with AI capabilities can provide personalized consumer support, streamline interactions, and resolve queries efficiently. Moreover, AI-driven predictive analytics can empower consumers with insights into trends, pricing fluctuations, and product availability, enabling them to make more informed purchasing decisions. Overall, embracing AI as a consumer means embracing personalized, efficient, and data-driven experiences that enrich daily life and empower individuals in their decision-making processes.

Consider the disruption we talked about earlier with telemedicine from the lens of the consumer. AI is now aiding mental health telemedicine for suicide triage with innovative tools. Stanford Medicine researchers are developing AI tools that analyze speech to predict anxiety and depression severity, offering objective measures. They've also created a crisis-message detector to swiftly identify suicidal thoughts in patient messages. Talkspace, a teletherapy platform, uses AI to detect high-risk behaviors in real-time messages, alerting therapists. Additionally, a pilot study using automated assessment and telehealth technology reported a 73 percent reduction in suicide severity among patients. These advancements offer promising avenues for suicide prevention in mental health care.[23]

Perceptions of telemedicine from the consumer's point of view were initially a mixed bag. Some felt disconcerted by not being able to have a physical office visit while others embraced the change. Today, AI-driven

---

[23]   Nina Bai, "Going Beyond 'How Often Do You Feel Blue?'" *Stanford Medicine Magazine* 1 (April 29, 2024), https://stanmed.stanford.edu/ai-mental-crisis-prediction-intervention/.

telemedicine has fundamentally changed how consumers access and experience healthcare. With the rise of telemedicine platforms powered by AI, individuals now have greater access to healthcare services regardless of their location. Through virtual consultations, patients can connect with healthcare providers conveniently, eliminating the need for travel and reducing geographical barriers.

AI also plays a crucial role in streamlining the healthcare process for consumers. Through efficient triage and diagnosis, AI algorithms help prioritize patient care, leading to quicker and more accurate assessments. Furthermore, remote monitoring enabled by AI-powered telemedicine allows for continuous tracking of patients with chronic conditions or postoperative care needs. This real-time monitoring, coupled with AI analytics, facilitates early detection of health issues and timely interventions, improving health outcomes.

Consumers also benefit from the optimization of healthcare resources driven by AI. Predictive analytics identify trends in patient data, allowing for better allocation of healthcare resources and staffing. This optimization ensures that consumers receive timely care and that healthcare providers can effectively manage patient loads.

Dilemma of Disruption without Monetization

The dilemma of disruption without monetization arises when emerging technological disruptors catalyze significant shifts in consumer behavior, yet sustainable monetization patterns fail to materialize. In such scenarios, disruptive innovations may capture widespread attention and even change the way people interact, consume content, or conduct business. However, if these innovations cannot translate their popularity and user engagement into viable revenue streams, they face a critical challenge. This comes down to a great idea with no monetization strategy. This could have happened with Facebook or Google, but they had the perspective to know the value in using ads and collecting your personal data to make money.

This dilemma often stems from the rapid pace of technological advancement and the dynamic nature of consumer preferences. While disruptors may succeed in attracting a large user base or generating buzz around their offerings, they struggle to find effective strategies for monetizing their products or services. This could be due to various factors, including inadequate market research, a lack of clear value proposition, or difficulties in implementing monetization models that align with user expectations.

In the absence of sustainable monetization patterns, disruptors may encounter several obstacles. They may struggle to secure investment funding or sustain operations without a clear path to profitability. Additionally, the inability to monetize their offerings may hinder their ability to scale, compete effectively with established players, or justify ongoing development efforts.

To address the dilemma of disruption without monetization, disruptors must focus on developing robust business models that balance innovation with revenue generation. This involves conducting thorough market analysis, understanding user needs and preferences, and experimenting with different monetization strategies. Whether through subscription models, advertising, freemium offerings, or other approaches, disruptors must find ways to capture and deliver value to users while also generating sustainable revenue streams.

Moreover, fostering partnerships, exploring new market opportunities, and adapting to evolving industry trends can help disruptors overcome monetization challenges and position themselves for long-term success. By prioritizing innovation, agility, and strategic foresight, disruptors can navigate the complexities of the digital landscape and unlock the full potential of their disruptive technologies.

Bottom line: Ideation that yields disruption with AI must be monetized to be sustainable.

Using Our Method PACT to Disrupt

Disrupting methodically is key to ensuring success in navigating the complexities of innovation and transformation. PACT was born as a scoring model in a spreadsheet. To give you background, anything Antara does starts with a spreadsheet. Whether she is planning her vacation or developing an ROI model to raise private equity, it starts with a spreadsheet. Winnie, however, runs her life with a project plan, from planning her wedding, to graduations, to large organization transformations. Before we started this book, Antara was exploring a startup idea with an early-stage funding on a model that would predict, prioritize, and validate AI use case automation and scaling. As we began to chat, the power of a method emerged. The trajectory of PACT (pivot, align, culture, and transform) serves as a structured approach to guide organizations through the disruptive process and brings all aspects into a single sequenced and aligned playbook.

Pivot

The first step involves recognizing the need for change and pivoting toward new directions or strategies. This may entail reevaluating existing business models, identifying emerging market trends, and exploring innovative opportunities. By pivoting strategically, organizations can position themselves to capitalize on disruptive forces and stay ahead of the curve.

Disruption, in the realm of AI, isn't just about shaking things up; it's about fundamentally reshaping how businesses operate, how they innovate, and how they thrive. It's about leveraging AI as the pivot point—the axis around which everything turns—to repurpose operational savings, fund innovation, and drive growth like never before.

Pivot

Figure 8.3. AI is the pivot point.

Before diving into the pivot, let's talk odds. Disruptive ventures are high-risk endeavors, fraught with uncertainty, resource constraints, and fierce competition. Success hinges on a multitude of factors, from market acceptance to flawless execution and everything in between. But amid this uncertainty lies a beacon of hope: return on capital (ROC). This financial metric serves as a guiding light, illuminating the path toward profitability and efficiency in capital utilization.

Funding a Pivot

How do you fund a pivot? It starts with a strategic reallocation of resources—shifting from business as usual to high-impact AI initiatives. The 70-20-10 investment rule sets the stage: 70 percent keeps the lights on, 20 percent yields nominal returns, and the remaining 10 percent is where the magic happens—the realm of exponential growth through AI-enabled innovation.

Now, who's steering the ship? Leadership levels L2 and L3 take the helm, conducting a thorough analysis of performance gaps and setting the pivot direction. CEO engagement is key, providing the impetus for prioritization and alignment with the North Star. But it doesn't stop there. With priorities defined, teams cascade the vision downward, translating strategic objectives into actionable plans. It's about more than just realigning roadmaps and budgets; it's about driving strategic alignment, empowering teams to innovate, and delighting consumers with groundbreaking products and services.

In the end, a successful pivot isn't just a strategic maneuver—it's a game-changer. It's about driving growth, meeting shareholder commitments, and delighting consumers with speed, depth, and predictability like never before.

Align

Once the pivot has been identified, it's essential to align all facets of the organization, including goals, processes, and resources, toward the common objective. Alignment ensures that everyone within the organization is working toward the same goals and that efforts are coordinated and focused. This may involve realigning structures, redefining roles and responsibilities, and fostering collaboration across departments and teams.

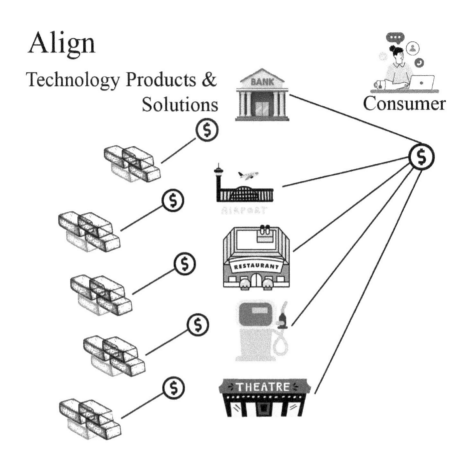

Figure 8.4. Alignment is the secret sauce of organizational success.

Alignment is the secret sauce of organizational success, ensuring that operations, technology, and governance teams march in unison toward shared objectives. At every level of leadership, from business units to functions, this symphony of alignment centers on delivering value to both shareholders and consumers.

Budget alignment sets the stage for success, but traditional methods often fall short in the face of macro disruptions like the emergence of the internet, for example. Organizations stuck in legacy planning models risk being left behind by disruptors. It's time to embrace a modern approach like zero-based budgeting (ZBB), which starts with a clean slate each budgeting cycle and prioritizes initiatives based on market trends and sustaining market leadership.

With funding secured, roadmap alignment becomes paramount. Roadmaps, once linear timelines, have evolved into dynamic tools for navigating complex business landscapes. But they often fall short in capturing synergies and opportunities across silos. By incorporating ZBB principles into agile budgeting practices, organizations can prioritize initiatives that drive maximum value across the organization and foster a culture of financial accountability.

However, alignment doesn't end with budgets and roadmaps—it extends to strategy, vision, and even technology initiatives. Generative AI, for example, promises to streamline workflows and eliminate inefficiencies by introducing algorithmic decision-making in real-time. By aligning tech backlogs with strategic imperatives and embedding GenAI capabilities, organizations can ensure that all work is human-centered and delivers value to both shareholders and consumers.

In essence, *alignment* isn't just a buzzword—it's the linchpin of AI transformation, driving tangible outcomes at every milestone of the journey. So let's pivot toward alignment, steering our organizations toward a future where success is not just a possibility but a certainty.

Culture

Cultivating a culture that fosters innovation, agility, and adaptability is crucial for driving successful disruption. Organizations need to nurture an environment where employees feel empowered to experiment, take calculated risks, and challenge conventional thinking. A culture of innovation encourages continuous learning, creativity, and resilience in the face of change, laying the foundation for sustained success in disruptive endeavors.

Culture

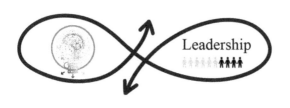

CURIOSITY
OVER FEAR

HUMANITY
OVER TECHNOLOGY

PERSONAL
OVER PROGRAM

CLARITY
OVER CHAOS

Figure 8.5. How to cultivate culture

Embracing AI requires more than just technological advancements—it necessitates a cultural shift that fosters curiosity, control, and transparency. To achieve success with disruption, organizations must embark on a meticulous change approach that addresses the human element at every step.

1. **Replace fear with curiosity.** Humanity must remain in charge of technology, ensuring that every individual impacted by AI feels empowered and informed. Lessons from past transformation journeys provide invaluable insights for planning and succeeding in AI adoption.

2. **Customize the course of change.** Engage leaders at all levels to tailor messaging for their teams, illustrating the bigger picture while incorporating unique details relevant to each

audience. Bidirectional messaging allows for continuous improvement and empowers employees to have a voice in the change process.

3. **Humanize options to transform individuals.** AI transformation must leave no one behind, offering choices for everyone to opt in, learn, and be part of the process. Defining roles, mapping talents to emerging opportunities, and providing personal change arcs are essential for individual ownership and empowerment.

4. **Make the pivot clear and simple.** Collaboratively define the pivot, distinguishing between program-impact communications and human-impact communications. While program-impact communications keep stakeholders informed about progress and risks, human-impact communications focus on empowering individuals with options for personal growth and development.

By leveraging this change approach, organizations can foster a culture that embraces AI, driving sustainable success in the era of disruption.

Transform

The final step involves executing transformative initiatives that translate vision into action. This may include implementing new technologies, redesigning processes, and reimagining consumer experiences to drive meaningful change. Transformation requires a commitment to ongoing evolution and improvement as well as a willingness to embrace ambiguity and navigate unforeseen challenges along the way.

Transforming operations with AI involves balancing short-term projects with transformative initiatives, integrating ongoing digital transformation efforts. Streamlining fundamental functions like finance, marketing, and risk management liberates capital for strategic industry-specific innovations, fostering a competitive edge. Operational expenses across key functions present prime opportunities for AI-driven automation, aiming for cost reduction and standardized efficiency.

Transform to
Transitionary

Figure 8.6. Transform from speed in motion to speed at rest

Consider our bicycle example. Believe it or not, the bicycle and its use have continued to transform since its inception in the 1800s. For over one hundred years, there have been incremental improvements in bicycle technology—the move from aluminum to carbon fiber, tubeless tires, and so on. While the bike was designed for outdoor use, there was also a desire to enjoy a bike indoors. Hence, the stationary bike. This example shows how in the evolution of the bicycle you had to pivot, align, use culture to transform to get the outcome—the stationary bike.

Operational changes must harness AI to substantially reduce costs, enabling innovation that enhances consumer experiences and fosters shareholder trust. Fortune 100 companies, representing various industries, shape innovation agendas by aligning with market-leading trends and leveraging emergent AI capabilities. Use cases across retail, healthcare, energy, financial services, automotive, and food industries demonstrate how AI technologies improve processes, enhance experiences, and drive innovation.

A successful pivot for AI transformation at scale relies on restructuring operational costs, simplifying functional capabilities, and introducing disruptive innovations tailored to industry-specific challenges and opportunities. This transformation drives enduring competitiveness, consumer loyalty, and shareholder value in today's dynamic business landscape.

PACT Scoring

To use the method, you first need to assess everyday metrics and measures that matter. If you put monitors in place, either systematic or human, scoring will continue to occur with every iteration of execution. By following the trajectory of PACT, organizations can methodically approach disruption, mitigate risks, and increase the likelihood of success in a rapidly evolving business landscape. This structured approach provides a roadmap for navigating the complexities of innovation and transformation, ensuring that organizations remain agile, competitive, and resilient in the face of disruptive change guided by comprehensive scoring metrics across diverse operational dimensions. Inputs to score include the following:

- Macro trend analysis, encompassing indices like Nasdaq and S&P Composite, to glean nuanced insights into prevailing market dynamics and our relative standing within the broader technological landscape.
- Forecasted company performance metrics, including stock prices, revenue streams, pretax profits, and PE ratio to furnish invaluable indicators of financial health and market valuation.
- Market share metrics, which will offer critical intelligence to inform strategic decisions aimed at enhancing our competitive edge and market penetration.

- Product and service evolution metrics facilitating the timely retirement of obsolete offerings and the introduction of new, market-aligned solutions.
- Human capital metrics, such as total employees, global footprint, and lines of business, to ensure optimal resource allocation and organizational agility as we adapt to evolving market demands.
- Organizational change metrics, providing insights into the efficacy of strategic realignments, ensuring seamless transitions and operational effectiveness.
- Collaboration and culture metrics as barometers of organizational cohesion and employee engagement, guiding initiatives aimed at fostering a dynamic and inclusive work environment.
- Employing system metrics to offer invaluable insights into operational efficiency and resilience, empowering proactive intervention to mitigate potential disruptions.
- Embrace program metrics, enabling us to gauge the success of strategic initiatives and facilitating data-driven decision-making and ROI optimization.

By envisioning this holistic approach to scoring and metrics integration, we can position ourselves to navigate the complexities of AI-driven disruption with agility and confidence, driving sustained growth and innovation in a rapidly evolving landscape. In essence, we are powered by the data to help drive sustainable choices in AI.

Figure 8.7.

So What?

The choice architecture for disruption involves designing decision-making processes to influence stakeholders and organizational direction. It includes strategic vision, risk assessment, resource allocation, and organizational culture. By orchestrating these elements, organizations challenge norms and pursue growth, especially with AI. This approach requires a framework considering internal landscapes and external market dynamics.

Disrupting with AI involves defining disruption's impact on society, identifying key stakeholders, and creating a choice architecture framework. We delve deeper to help evaluate ideas in context, covering economic theories of disruption, risk and reward for a pivot to disrupt, disruption from the perspective of a consumer, and the dilemma of disruption without monetization.

If you're a disruptive leader, you'll define your role and actions needed to revolutionize economies, consumption patterns, pricing, and more, using AI to introduce novel approaches. All within defined choices considering the organization's structure and consumer needs in the broader marketplace.

Understanding economic theories of disruption is crucial for organizations aiming to disrupt with AI, as these theories offer insights into how new technologies can reshape industries, foster innovation, and create competitive advantages. By strategically leveraging AI in line with economic theories, organizations can drive transformative change and capitalize on emerging opportunities in a shifting landscape. Economic theories provide valuable guidance for navigating disruptions effectively, ensuring businesses can adapt and thrive amid technological transformations. By aligning technology supply with human demand and leveraging economic principles, organizations can empower humanity to drive technological innovation, setting the stage for profitability and success. Implementing the PACT method for disruption ensures organizations can systematically approach innovation and transformation, mitigating risks and increasing success probabilities in a rapidly changing business environment. By following this structured approach, organizations remain agile, competitive, and resilient in the face of disruptive change, guided by comprehensive scoring metrics across various operational dimensions. Through PACT, organizations can leverage data-driven insights to drive sustainable choices in AI adoption, positioning themselves for enduring growth and innovation.

Now What?

Now that we understand the importance of economic theories in disruption and how AI can reshape industries, it's time to take action. Organizations must strategically leverage AI in alignment with these theories to drive transformative change and capitalize on emerging opportunities. Implementing the PACT method for disruption offers a systematic approach, helping organizations navigate innovation and transformation while mitigating risks. By following this structured approach, organizations can remain agile, competitive, and resilient in the face of disruptive change, ultimately positioning themselves for enduring growth and innovation.

For leaders poised to disrupt, armed with awareness, knowledge, methods, models, and maturity, the journey is one of strategic empowerment. With a profound understanding of AI's potential, these leaders leverage awareness to navigate complexities and seize opportunities. Their knowledge base extends beyond theory, incorporating practical methods and models that align with organizational goals. Maturity in handling AI disruptions involves a holistic approach, considering ethical considerations, long-term sustainability, and societal impacts. By embodying these attributes, leaders not only navigate disruptions but actively shape them, becoming architects of transformative change in their industries and beyond.

What is your plan to disrupt?

My Plan to Disrupt

Problem

Access

Experience

Speed

Solution

How Big?

How Unique?

How Expensive?

Figure 8.8.

AMPLIFY

PART 4

IN PART 4, we transition from academic insights to practical application, aiming to catalyze significant impacts. We explore how disruptive innovations shift paradigms and guide organizations in assessing and aligning their actions accordingly.

Established businesses with substantial market presence face a critical decision point. They must choose between embracing disruptive changes on a large scale or risk falling behind more agile competitors.

Failure to seize the transformative potential of AI-driven disruptions risks relegating businesses to a reactive stance, struggling to keep pace with competitors who embrace change. Therefore, the choice to disrupt decisively or risk obsolescence marks a pivotal moment for mature businesses aiming to thrive in a dynamic, AI-driven marketplace.

"Amplify" signifies strategic enhancements in organizational structures and practices to harness the full potential of artificial intelligence. Through coordinated actions and disciplined adaptation, individuals and organizations can enhance their effectiveness, resilience, and success in navigating the evolving landscape shaped by AI.

In this section, we discuss coordinates and speed, cadence, and momentum. Both chapters are designed to help you amplify your integration of AI in our organization.

In chapter 9, we explore how organizational structures, traditionally designed to deliver goods and services, are akin to maps with latitudes, longitudes, and altitudes. These coordinates represent the complex matrix that must adapt as AI integrates into systems, people, and processes. As AI adoption increases, individuals' roles within organizations may shift dramatically, prompting a reevaluation of organizational design principles and scaling factors. We examine how these coordinates influence growth, disruption, and alignment with strategic goals, emphasizing the dynamic nature of organizational evolution in response to AI. The key takeaway is that understanding and adapting to these shifts are crucial for navigating the complexities of AI integration effectively. Looking ahead, individuals and organizations are encouraged to continuously monitor their coordinates, embrace change, and remain flexible to optimize their positions and seize opportunities in an AI-driven landscape.

Chapter 10 focuses on the critical balance of speed, cadence, and momentum in AI transformation within organizations. Here's a summary:

AI is evolving rapidly, altering consumer behaviors and necessitating swift organizational adaptation. This chapter discusses finding the right rhythm for AI transformation by aligning strategic actions with overarching goals, akin to driving a car where speed adjustments are crucial for safe navigation.

Leadership plays a pivotal role in this transformation, with leaders needing to tailor strategies to their organization's unique context. The chapter highlights the importance of moving quickly yet steadily in adopting AI to avoid chaos and ensure success.

Speed is about the quick implementation of changes and achieving objectives promptly, while cadence is the structured, regular pattern of activities that ensures organized progress. Both are essential for effective transformation, with speed focusing on urgency and cadence on consistency.

Momentum is the sustained progress that comes from developing, adopting, and integrating AI initiatives, impacting both the organization and the consumer market.

The chapter aims to help readers:

- understand the necessity of speed to avoid being outpaced by competitors,
- recognize the importance of cadence in maintaining strategic alignment,
- learn to harness momentum to achieve market dominance.

In essence, the chapter guides on calibrating the transformation process to ensure successful navigation through the AI landscape, leveraging speed, cadence, and momentum to respond to market conditions and opportunities effectively.

FIND YOUR COORDINATES

CHART YOUR COURSE

Introduction

ORGANIZATIONS ARE BUILT with a structure that is designed, in theory, to deliver goods and services to a consumer. There are levels of seniority, departments, and functions. There may be different lines of business in different geographies that may even include redundant departments, roles, functions, or hierarchies. We look at organizational structures in terms of latitudes, longitudes, and altitudes. This represents the matrix of coordinates that will have to flex as AI becomes integrated into systems, people, and processes. Individuals are positioned within organizations like cities on a map, with coordinates indicating their roles. This chapter explores how the individuals' positions may shift as the coordinates change while AI adoption increases.

Understanding your coordinates enables you to either reconfigure the organization to align with the integration of AI iteratively or be aware that it is happening. In chapter 8, we talked about disruption. When we disrupt with AI and bring new and enhanced technology to the organization, we need to be able to flex. That means we may need to expand, collapse, converge, or simply adjust the organization in any and all dimensions.

In this chapter, we reinforce how levels, and scale, global footprints will ebb and flow, shift, and change in terms of people and products with the successful adoption of AI. The objectives of this chapter include the following:

1. Apply the concept of coordinates to help readers grasp organization design principles and scale drivers. We will define coordinates within various organizational structures, highlighting patterns in companies of various sizes and maturity.
2. Understand the relationship between coordinates and scale and how that relationship can enhance or impede your AI agenda.
3. Explore the relationship among organizational coordinates, the North Star, and touchstone.
4. Explore the relationships between coordinates and how you use them in plotting your growth and disruption paths.
5. The last objective is all about you. We focus on being able to recognize where you are and predict your future trajectory in the organization.

Organization Design Principles

Applying the concept of coordinates will help you grasp organizational design principles and scale drivers. We will define coordinates within various organizational structures, highlighting patterns in companies of various sizes and maturity. It is imperative to understand where you sit in the organization and the broader structures of the organization because this is what will likely change and optimize with the integration of AI. Ask yourself the following questions:

- Is your organization global?
- Are there repetitive functions—like more than one IT department in different geographies?
- Are there repetitive roles? For example, are there ten CIOS?
- How many people in your location have the same job title as you do?
- How many levels are between you and the CEO of the company?

There are likely a dozen more questions you can ask yourself, but the key here is to look out in the space you are in and determine where you are at. This will help you frame where you are in the organization.

Organization design is the deliberate structuring of an organization's hierarchy, functions, and business units to optimize its performance and achieve strategic objectives. It involves defining clear roles, responsibilities, reporting relationships, and decision-making processes to facilitate effective coordination and collaboration within the organization. Below, we define the concepts in greater depth.

- **Hierarchy:** Hierarchy refers to the formal structure of authority and reporting relationships within an organization. It establishes levels of management and supervision, delineating who reports to whom and how communication flows throughout the organization. Hierarchical structures typically consist of multiple levels, from top executives to frontline employees, each with specific responsibilities and levels of authority.

- **Functions:** Functions represent the different areas of expertise and activities within an organization, such as finance, marketing, operations, human resources, and technology. Each function is responsible for specific tasks and activities related to its area of expertise, and collaboration among functions is essential for achieving organizational goals. Depending on the organization's needs and objectives, functions may be organized hierarchically, cross-functionally, or in matrix structures.

- **Business units:** Business units are semiautonomous divisions or departments within an organization that focus on specific related products, services, markets, or geographic regions. They operate with a degree of independence and accountability, allowing them to adapt their strategies and operations to local or market-specific conditions. Business units may be organized based on product lines, consumer segments, or strategic priorities, and they often have their own functional teams and resources to support their objectives. For example, in a consumer goods company manufacturing toothpaste, perfumes, and home cleaning products, business units would be distinct divisions or departments focusing on each product line. There might be a toothpaste business unit, a perfume business unit, and a home cleaning products business unit. Each of these units operates semi-autonomously with its own set of resources and functional teams. They have the flexibility to adapt strategies and operations to specific market conditions or consumer preferences within their respective product categories. This structure allows for greater focus and specialization, ensuring that each business unit can effectively cater to the needs of its target market while still operating under the overarching umbrella of the consumer goods company.

Effective organization design involves aligning hierarchy, functions, and business units to support the organization's overall strategy, goals, and values. It requires careful consideration of factors, such as organizational culture, market dynamics, industry trends, and technological advancements. By designing structures that promote clarity, accountability, agility, and collaboration, organizations can enhance their ability to innovate, adapt, and thrive in a competitive and dynamic setting.

Organizations have historically scaled both vertically and horizontally to accommodate growth, meet market demands, and enhance operational efficiency. Vertical scaling involves expanding within existing functions or business units by adding more layers of management or increasing the depth of expertise within specific areas. For instance, in the pharmaceutical industry, a company may vertically scale its research and development division to explore new drug formulations or therapeutic treatments, thereby deepening its expertise in specific medical domains. In banking, vertical scaling might involve expanding the depth of financial services within existing branches or divisions, such as offering specialized wealth management services or tailored investment solutions.

Horizontal scaling involves expanding across different functions, business units, or geographic regions to diversify offerings, capture new markets, and leverage economies of scale. By horizontally scaling, organizations can broaden their reach, spread risk, and capitalize on synergies among different parts of the business.

An example of horizontal scaling in business could be observed in German car brands expanding operations into the electric vehicle (EV) market. Brands like Audi and Volkswagen are aiming to capture market share in regions with growing demand for sustainable mobility solutions. Through these initiatives, German car manufacturers are diversifying their product portfolios, tapping into the burgeoning EV market, and positioning themselves for long-term success in the automotive industry.

Historically, as organizations have scaled vertically and horizontally, it's essential to acknowledge the inherent limitations of human intellect in acquiring and mastering a diverse range of skills. While individuals possess remarkable capabilities, there are practical constraints on the extent to which they can learn and practice various disciplines simultaneously. Therefore, the scaling of organizations is not only a function of expanding operational capacities but also of augmenting human intellect and capabilities. To put it simply, previously, when we needed more brain power, we hired more brains. Now, with AI, we have opened up a new way to scale the intellectual capacity.

Coordinates and Scale

In any organization, coordinates pinpoint individual hierarchical and functional locations. Scaling involves expanding revenue, operations, and technology. To effectively harness AI's power, organizations need to be mindful to methodically expand and contract these dimensions.

Coordinates

Let's define *coordinates* first as it refers to sets of numbers used to pinpoint a specific location on Earth's surface. They consist of latitude, longitude, and altitude. Latitude measures the distance north or south of the equator, while longitude measures the distance east or west of the prime meridian. Altitude refers to the height above sea level. These coordinates provide a precise description of a location, allowing for accurate navigation and mapping of Earth's terrain.

In an organization, altitude refers to hierarchy, latitude refers to functions, and longitude refers to business units. In this context, the coordinates identify an individual in a role at the intersection of a unit, function, and level.

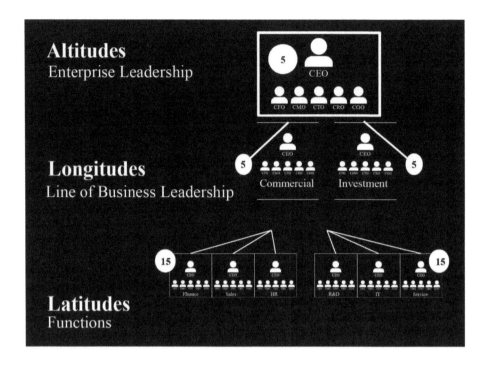

Figure 9.1. Coordinates in the organization.

Scale

You may have noticed that we use the term *scale* often in this book. We want to touch briefly on why scale matters. We can apply scale to a number of organizational factors—we have revenue scale, operational scale, human resource scale, technological scale, and consumer scale. Successful scaling in an organization requires the ability to determine where you want to scale (climb up) and careful planning and decision-making with the ability to adapt. While scaling with AI, you can drop a pin on the coordinate you deem scalable. These points will meet you at your touchstone and take you to your North Star.

Organization scale is based on some overarching principles:

- **Span of control:** This refers to the number of direct reports a manager oversees. While there's no universal figure, factors like business model, supervisory load, and the balance between agility and stability should be weighed.
- **Layers:** The number of hierarchical levels in an organization also impacts its efficiency. Generally, fewer layers (ideally five or fewer) and a higher span of control (seven to twelve employees) tend to be more effective. However, this depends on the nature of work and organizational size.
- **Efficiency:** Spans and layers influence how tasks are delegated across functions, processes, teams, and individuals. Conducting a formal analysis of spans and layers can enhance organizational efficiency and effectiveness.

Several factors should inform decisions about span of control and layers, including the stage of senior executive development, collaboration requirements, time allocation beyond direct control, role scope, and team composition.

The paradigm shift with AI augmentation is in key areas of cognitive capabilities. The four areas below reflect the AI capabilities that will enhance our ability to scale with more targeted teams. These capabilities will, in essence, augment human intelligence. As a refresher, they are as follows:

- Natural language understanding (NLU): Processing and understanding human language, including nuances, context, and semantics.
- Decision-making and problem-solving: Analyzing complex datasets, identifying patterns, and making strategic decisions based on incomplete or ambiguous information are tasks essential for executives, analysts, and decision-makers across various industries.
- Image and object recognition: Identifying objects, faces, patterns, and anomalies in images or videos.
- Predictive analytics and forecasting: Predicting future trends, outcomes, and behaviors based on historical data and current variables requires advanced statistical analysis, machine learning models, and predictive algorithms.

In chapter 3, we illustrated how hours of effort can be eliminated by stitching together these four capabilities and leveraging them in the MBR example. Now we are leveraging the same capabilities in coordinates.

A formal analysis of spans and layers in the context of AI integration can significantly optimize the structural components within an organization. These components can vary significantly among large corporations, medium-sized enterprises, and startups. In a large corporation, coordinates may include multiple layers of management, extensive departments, and specialized roles like chief information officers (CIOs) and risk managers. Medium-sized enterprises may have fewer layers and a more streamlined organizational structure, while startups often operate with minimal hierarchy and cross-functional teams.

The change with AI augmentation will also vary at scale based on the current size and organizational complexity. Some coordinates will converge where others will diverge to gain market share or improve consumer-centricity.

Consider this example: In a retail company, the adoption of AI augmentation may manifest differently based on its size and organizational complexity. For instance, in a large-scale retail corporation with multiple departments and hierarchies, the coordination of AI initiatives may converge around enhancing consumer experience through personalized recommendations, inventory management, and supply chain optimization. AI technologies can be utilized to analyze vast amounts of consumer data to predict trends, optimize pricing strategies, and improve product recommendations both online and in-store. The convergence of coordinates in this scenario would involve aligning various departments, such as marketing, sales, and operations, to leverage AI capabilities for improving overall business performance and consumer satisfaction.

In a smaller retail startup, the focus of AI augmentation may diverge to gain market share and establish a competitive edge in the industry. A startup retailer may prioritize AI-powered consumer engagement platforms, such as chatbots or virtual shopping assistants, to enhance the online shopping experience and differentiate themselves from larger competitors. The divergence of coordinates in this context would involve deploying AI solutions tailored to the startup's specific needs and growth objectives, focusing on targeted consumer acquisition, retention, and brand building.

We talked about healthcare use cases in chapter 8. Now, with the lens of coordinates, we can evaluate the impact on scale. In a healthcare company, the impact of AI augmentation will also vary depending on its scale and organizational complexity. In a large healthcare organization with multiple departments and specialized functions, the convergence of coordinates may revolve around improving patient care, operational efficiency, and clinical outcomes through AI-driven predictive analytics, disease diagnosis, and treatment planning. AI algorithms could analyze medical images, patient records, and genetic data to assist healthcare professionals in diagnosing diseases earlier, personalizing treatment plans, and improving patient outcomes.

In contrast, in a smaller healthcare clinic or telemedicine startup, the divergence of coordinates may involve leveraging AI technologies to enhance accessibility, affordability, and quality of care for patients. For instance, AI-powered virtual health assistants and remote monitoring systems might enable patients to access healthcare services from the comfort of their homes, reducing the burden on traditional healthcare infrastructure and expanding access to healthcare in underserved communities. The divergence of coordinates in this scenario would focus on leveraging AI innovations to address specific healthcare challenges and deliver value to patients in innovative ways.

Scaling the Business, Not the Coordinates, with AI

The traditional hierarchical organizational structures delineated by altitude, latitude, and longitude illustrate the layers of authority, functional specialization, and business focus within an organization. Altitude represents the top-down decision-making hierarchy, latitude defines functional departments, and longitude signifies semiautonomous business units.

Here are a couple of use cases to help you understand how we scale the business and not coordinates with AI.

Use Case: Car Manufacturer

Consider a car manufacturer aiming to scale its business operations while optimizing its organizational coordinates using AI technology. Here's how it could be implemented:

- **Reducing spans and layers:** The manufacturer can leverage AI-powered automation and analytics to streamline its production processes and reduce the number of hierarchical layers. By implementing smart manufacturing systems, AI can optimize inventory management, production scheduling, and quality control, thereby reducing the need for extensive middle management oversight. This consolidation of layers enhances operational efficiency and agility.

- **Opening new markets:** AI-driven market analysis and predictive analytics can help the manufacturer identify emerging market trends and consumer preferences. By analyzing vast amounts of data, including social media trends, consumer behavior patterns, and economic indicators, AI can provide valuable insights into potential new markets and segments. With this information, the manufacturer can tailor its product offerings and marketing strategies to target specific demographics or geographical regions effectively.

- **Optimizing supply chain management**: AI-powered algorithms can optimize the manufacturer's supply chain by predicting demand fluctuations, identifying potential bottlenecks, and optimizing inventory levels. By integrating AI-driven forecasting models with real-time data from suppliers, distributors, and logistics partners, the manufacturer can ensure timely delivery of raw materials and components while minimizing inventory costs and supply chain risks.

- **Enhancing consumer experience:** AI technologies, such as natural language processing and machine learning algorithms, can be deployed to enhance the consumer experience across various touchpoints. For instance, AI-powered chatbots can provide personalized assistance to consumers, address inquiries, and resolve issues in real-time. Additionally, AI-driven recommendation engines can analyze consumer preferences and purchase history to offer tailored product recommendations, driving consumer engagement and loyalty.

By leveraging AI to optimize its organizational coordinates, the car manufacturer can achieve greater operational efficiency, expand into new markets, and enhance its competitive position in the automotive industry. The strategic integration of AI technologies enables the manufacturer to adapt to changing market dynamics, meet evolving consumer demands, and drive sustainable growth in the long term.

Use Case: Cloud Migration

The migration of companies from on-premise data centers to the cloud presents a compelling example of how AI can scale business operations while optimizing organizational coordinates. Traditionally, organizations have maintained extensive on-premise infrastructure, delineated by altitude, latitude, and longitude to support their IT operations. However, the shift to cloud computing revolutionizes this paradigm by leveraging AI-driven technologies to streamline processes, enhance scalability, and optimize resource utilization.

- **Reducing spans and layers:** The transition to the cloud allows companies to streamline their IT infrastructure by consolidating hardware resources and reducing the number of hierarchical layers. Through AI-driven automation and orchestration tools, organizations can optimize workflows, automate routine tasks, and eliminate redundant processes, thus reducing the need for extensive middle management oversight. This consolidation of layers enhances operational efficiency and agility, enabling organizations to respond more rapidly to market dynamics and consumer demands.

- **Opening new markets**: Cloud-based analytics and machine learning capabilities empower organizations to unlock valuable insights from vast datasets, enabling them to identify emerging market trends and consumer preferences. By leveraging AI-driven predictive analytics, organizations can anticipate market shifts, identify new growth opportunities, and tailor their product offerings to meet evolving consumer needs. The scalability and flexibility of cloud infrastructure enable companies to expand into new markets and geographic regions seamlessly without the constraints of traditional on-premise environments.

- **Optimizing supply chain management**: Cloud-based supply chain management solutions leverage AI-driven algorithms to optimize inventory management, logistics planning, and supplier relationships. By integrating real-time data from suppliers, distributors, and logistics partners, organizations can gain visibility into their supply chain operations, identify potential bottlenecks, and mitigate supply chain risks. AI-powered forecasting models enable companies to predict demand fluctuations more accurately, optimize inventory levels, and ensure timely delivery of goods and services to consumers.

- **Enhancing consumer experience**: Cloud-based consumer experience platforms leverage AI technologies, such as natural language processing and sentiment analysis to enhance consumer interactions across various touchpoints. Intelligent chatbots provide personalized assistance to consumers, address inquiries, and resolve issues in real-time, enhancing consumer satisfaction and loyalty. AI-driven recommendation engines analyze consumer preferences and behavior patterns to offer tailored product recommendations, driving engagement and fostering long-term consumer relationships.

The strategic migration to the cloud enables organizations to optimize their organizational coordinates while scaling computing range and space. By harnessing the power of AI-driven technologies, companies can achieve greater operational efficiency, expand into new markets, and enhance their competitive position in the digital economy. In the future, the integration of AI and cloud computing will continue to reshape organizational structures and business models, enabling companies to thrive in an increasingly dynamic and interconnected world.

Touchstone and Coordinates

We talked about touchstone in chapter 4 and defined it from the lens of the individual and where you are within the organization. Your touchstone is your current state married to your why. It is a state of purpose you have set for yourself that has driven your choices personally and professionally. It is your motivator and what drives you to change, take chances or not, and it influences your decisions. So, like using a GPS, you need the current location to map your course. When you map your course, you typically get three or four options (routes) you can take to get to your destination. In this book, to get to your North Star, determine whether to go fast or slow, which coordinates to use, you need to know your touchstone—your current state and your why.

We also shared role/organizational AI impact scenarios and suggested that you or your role will likely fit into one of these areas.

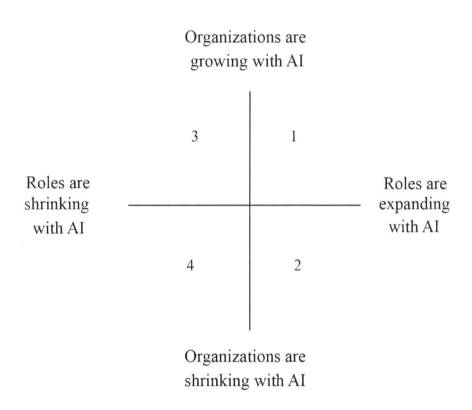

Figure 9.2. Emerging trends for the evolution of roles with the integration of AI.

Finally, we have taken you through grow and disrupt, which enable you to change coordinates and identify disruptive change. We are now spelling out how scale impacts, and we are giving you a bigger picture to assess how the AI change is happening around us, again using coordinates.

People need to understand their touchstone, but they also need to understand the organization's touchstone. The relationship between the touchstone of the organization and its people is integral to understanding the dynamics of AI adoption and augmentation. People form the heartbeat of the organization, and it is their collective intellect, skills, and adaptability that ultimately drive technological innovation and organizational success. While there may be an initial inclination to streamline operations by relying on a select few individuals knowledgeable in AI, the reality is more nuanced for several reasons.

Adjusting the organization to accommodate AI strategies takes time and requires frequent adaptations as technology evolves. It is often more cost-effective to retrain existing employees rather than resort to layoffs, fostering a culture of continuous learning and development within the organization. By investing in the continuous education and upskilling of employees, organizations can maintain scalability and throughput while harnessing the full potential of AI technologies. People make decisions based on their own touchstone to engage in these education and upskilling opportunities. There should be the willingness to take on new ventures.

As AI becomes more pervasive within organizations, its impact extends beyond the cultivation of AI talent to influence the structure of spans and layers. With the integration of AI technologies, traditional hierarchical layers may flatten, allowing for more direct communication and decision-making processes. This shift can lead to a broader span of control for managers as they oversee larger teams and initiatives empowered by AI-driven automation and decision support systems. As mentioned in chapter 4, the role is changing based on AI.

Moreover, the introduction of AI capabilities may streamline processes and workflows, reducing the need for multiple hierarchical layers and enabling organizations to operate more efficiently with fewer management tiers. As a result, spans and layers evolve to accommodate the changing dynamics of AI-driven work environments, emphasizing agility, flexibility, and responsiveness to market demands. This reflects the scenario where organizations are shrinking with AI.

Additionally, the deployment of AI solutions often necessitates cross-functional collaboration and integration, blurring traditional organizational boundaries and restructuring spans and layers to foster interdisciplinary teams and initiatives. This collaborative approach enhances communication and coordination across different functions and departments, optimizing resource allocation and decision-making processes within the organization. Roles will change in scope. Essentially, roles will reshape and the organization will restructure.

As organizations embrace AI technologies, a wave of new roles will emerge, focusing on training, governance, and optimizing AI models. Professionals like AI trainers, data scientists, and AI ethics specialists are crucial in developing and deploying AI solutions effectively. They enable organizations to scale AI capabilities while ensuring regulatory compliance, ethical standards, and data privacy. This evolution in AI-related roles will reshape the organization's hierarchical structures, influencing the ratios of spans and controls. Understanding your touchstone will help you make powerful choices in a timely manner so opportunities in new roles are not lost.

Grow and Coordinates

In the exploration of growth, you have two choices. The first is stretching, expanding, or finding the next level role fed by your newly found confidence in your AI capabilities. The other path is ideal for the disruptors, those who have played with concepts and now wield the prowess to leverage AI for groundbreaking innovations.

Growth is not merely a matter of scale. It's about purposeful expansion that strengthens an organization's market position and resilience. AI-inspired growth demands a transformative culture and mindset. It's about augmenting intellectual capacity, talent, and maturity for transformation—a holistic evolution that spans the many facets of an individual's or organization's development.

The ultimate goal is to scale human intelligence as AI scales, amplifying the benefits and outcomes of technological investments. In simpler terms, it's about crafting a win-win scenario where personal and professional growth are in harmony and the organizational coordinates—altitude, longitude, and latitude—are recalibrated for a future shaped by AI integration.

To simplify, we just learned that when we scale or transform coordinates, we are making changes in altitude, latitude, and longitude. In grow, we shared learning methods designed to help you grow with AI by doing and electing the method that works for you. Coordinates allows you to understand your location in the organization, your industry, and within your role. Based on the changes happening on this coordinate, you need to take the learning method from grow and the coordinate patterns around you to further define your growth strategy and get to where you want to go

This narrative underscores the transformative impact of AI on organizational strategy and the importance of awareness and adaptability as the operational coordinates shift with AI integration. It's a call to action for individuals and organizations to grow and coordinate in harmony with technological advancements. As AI reshapes the organizational coordinates, it offers a dual path: one that leads to personal transformation and readiness for new roles and another that empowers individuals to disrupt and innovate. The ultimate outcome is scaling human intelligence alongside AI, creating a win-win scenario that amplifies the benefits and outcomes of technological investments both personally and professionally.

Disrupt and Coordinates

The largest impact on coordinates will come from disruption. It will likely be the driver to the majority of the job changes in the next five to ten years. If you remember, disruption is a significant change or shift that alters existing processes, practices, or industries, often by introducing new technologies, business models, or ideas that fundamentally transform the way things are done. Disruption typically challenges established norms and incumbents, leading to shifts in market dynamics, consumer behaviors, and competitive landscapes.

Applying this definition, AI is poised to disrupt organizational structures traditionally defined by altitude (hierarchy), longitude (business units), and latitude (functions) in several ways:

- **Flattening hierarchies (altitude):** AI can flatten traditional hierarchies by enabling more decentralized decision-making. With advanced analytics and real-time data, lower-level employees can make informed decisions without waiting for executive approval, thus speeding up processes and reducing bottlenecks.

- **Integrating business units (longitude):** AI can foster greater integration across different business units. By analyzing vast amounts of data from various departments, AI can identify patterns and insights that lead to more cohesive and unified strategies, breaking down silos and promoting cross-functional collaboration.
- **Expanding roles and functions (latitude):** AI can automate routine tasks, allowing employees to focus on higher-value work. This can lead to a redefinition of job roles and an expansion of employee functions, as workers are freed from mundane tasks to engage in more strategic and creative activities.

Coordinates and You

What does all of this boil down for you? When you drop a pin to your current coordinate, are you in a position of power to drive the decisions around the future transformation of your coordinate and the surrounding coordinates? If not, are you at least in control of your own?

In a world transformed by artificial intelligence, recognizing your coordinates—altitude, longitude, and latitude—becomes pivotal for navigating the evolving organizational landscape. As you chart your course within an AI-driven enterprise, understanding your position is key to success.

- **Understanding your current coordinates:** If you're not in a position of power, it's crucial to understand your current organizational coordinates—where you stand in terms of altitude (hierarchy), latitude (function), and longitude (business unit). This self-awareness allows you to prepare for future shifts and align yourself with upcoming changes.
- **Driving disruption:** Being at a place that is driving disruption means you are part of a dynamic environment where innovation and change are constants. It's about being proactive and taking part in initiatives that challenge the status quo and introduce new ways of thinking and working.

- **Aligning with the pivot:** Aligning with the pivot refers to adjusting your strategies and actions to match the organization's changing direction. As AI transforms business models and processes, staying agile and adaptable ensures you remain relevant and contribute effectively to the organization's goals.

- **Undergoing transformation:** You may be undergoing transformation, which involves adapting to new technologies, processes, and mindsets. This personal evolution is essential for thriving in an AI-driven workplace and leveraging the opportunities it presents.

- **Responsible for Culture:** Being responsible for the culture means you play a role in shaping the values, behaviors, and attitudes within your organization. In an AI-influenced environment, fostering a culture of innovation, continuous learning, and collaboration is key to harnessing the full potential of AI for growth and success.

These concepts highlight the importance of understanding one's role and potential within an organization's structure and the need to adapt to the transformative impact of AI on traditional organizational coordinates.

North Star and Coordinates

As you navigate the landscape of AI transformation, each coordinate plays a crucial role in shaping your journey toward the North Star, guiding you to traverse your personal path of growth and disruption. Each change in latitude, longitude, and altitude will provide perspective and direction in your ascent because the shifts you make in coordinates should all aid in the pursuit of the North Star strategy and metric. In chapter 10, *Cadence*, we will show you how to take all you learned at the right speed so you win in the race to the North Star.

So What?

Organizational structures are not static; they are dynamic and must evolve to meet the demands of a rapidly changing business landscape. The integration of AI into systems, people, and processes necessitates a reevaluation of traditional structures. As AI becomes more prevalent, it will inevitably alter the coordinates of organizational design—latitude, longitude, and altitude—requiring a flexible approach to management and operations. This shift presents both challenges and opportunities for individuals and organizations alike. The key takeaway is that the relationship between coordinates and touchstone, growth, disruption, and scale is not linear. AI enablement can create patterns and antipatterns. It's important to understand the complexities and then adjust as needed.

Now What?

A large objective of this chapter is about dropping a pin to your current location and predicting your future trajectory in the organization. AI enablement and the changing of coordinates are two threads of evolution.

To stay ahead in this AI-driven era, it's imperative for both organizations and individuals to take action and take the following steps to continuously monitor and adjust based on changing coordinates. We encourage you to embrace change and recognize that AI integration will alter the way organizations operate and your place in the organization. Be open to learning and adapting to new roles and responsibilities. Regularly assess your position within the organization's coordinates and anticipate where shifts might occur. This can open you up to opportunities. Be flexible and ready to flex. Try experimentation not just in technology but with the coordinate design around it to find the best ways to integrate AI into existing structures.

Take a moment and write down your coordinates today. That will help you figure out where you want to be tomorrow.

My Coordinates in current role

Altitude

*How many levels
between me and our
CEO?*

Latitude

*How many others
reports to my
manager?*

Longitude

*How many other locations
and departments like mine
exist?*

Figure 9.3. Determine your Coordinates.

MASTERING MOTION

SETTING YOUR SPEED, CADENCE, AND MOMENTUM

Introduction

WE CAN ALL see that AI is evolving faster than any previous technology, requiring rapid adaptation by organizations and the people in them. AI is already shifting consumer patterns toward AI-fueled solutions, which means that learning, alignment, and action must match the pace. Going too fast may cause a crash and burn. Not going fast enough may enable competitors to disrupt marketplaces and grab a bigger share of revenue and customers.

In this chapter, we focus on how to find the right rhythm for AI transformation. We discuss synchronizing the pace between strategic coordinates and the North Star to achieve success. Navigating the AI transformation process is like driving a car—knowing when to speed up, slow down, or maintain a steady pace enables you to maneuver through twists and turns efficiently, ultimately reaching your destination safely. When you successfully navigate AI transformation, you create momentum, which helps deliver disruption at scale.

In the fast-changing world of AI transformation, leadership is the key to success. Leaders drive change by adjusting their strategies to fit the unique needs of the organization. This chapter explores the importance of moving quickly while also maintaining a steady pace in adopting AI technology. This matters because speed and cadence, while intuitive, can help you go fast and can also slow you down. Momentum left unchecked or unpredictable momentum fosters chaos.

Speed and cadence are two essential aspects of organizational transformation, albeit with distinct meanings. *Speed* refers to the rate or velocity at which changes are implemented and objectives are achieved within a specific timeframe. It emphasizes the urgency and efficiency required to swiftly adapt to evolving market dynamics and technological advancements.

In contrast, *cadence* refers to the rhythm or pattern of activity over time, characterized by regular intervals or cycles. It emphasizes the importance of maintaining a structured and consistent flow of activities, ensuring that work progresses in an organized manner. While speed underscores the need for quick decision-making and action, cadence focuses on establishing regular checkpoints and reviews to monitor progress and make necessary adjustments. Together, speed and cadence play complementary roles in driving successful organizational transformation, with speed ensuring timely adaptation and cadence providing the framework for consistent and systematic execution.

Momentum, however, refers to the sustained progress and increasing velocity that comes when AI initiatives are developed, adopted, and integrated within an organization. The second aspect of momentum reflects what you are launching in the marketplace and its impact on the consumer.

Speed, cadence, and momentum will help you in the context of your organization swiftly respond and adapt to changing conditions, demands, and opportunities.

The objectives of this chapter are as follows:

1. Understand why speed is key—too slow = too late.
2. Discover why cadence matters in keeping coordinates in synch.
3. Learn how to harness momentum to dominate the market.

Speed, Cadence, and Momentum

Speed refers to how fast products are developed and brought to market or how rapidly organizations adapt to changing conditions or opportunities. Let's measure the success of an AI pivot in terms of speed. The AI landscape is constantly evolving, with new advancements and innovations emerging rapidly. Organizations need to move quickly to capitalize on these developments, stay competitive, and seize opportunities presented by AI. A faster pivot allows organizations to implement AI solutions more swiftly, enabling them to address market demands, respond to changing customer needs, and outpace competitors. Additionally, speed ensures that organizations can navigate disruptions and challenges effectively, minimizing the risk of falling behind in the rapidly evolving AI ecosystem.

The cadence of enterprise alignment and culture is crucial to ensure that a pivot in an organization is both timely and successful. Cadence, in this context, involves maintaining a consistent and structured approach to aligning strategies, processes, and behaviors with the new direction set by the pivot.

In case of alignment, cadence ensures that all stakeholders are synchronized and moving in the same direction at a steady pace. This means regularly communicating the goals and objectives of the pivot, providing updates on progress, and coordinating efforts across different departments or teams. Consistent cadence in alignment activities helps prevent miscommunication, confusion, or divergence from the intended path, ensuring that everyone is working toward the same objectives.

Similarly, cadence plays a vital role in culture by fostering the attitudes, values, and behaviors needed to support the pivot. It involves establishing a rhythm of cultural initiatives, such as training programs, workshops, or team-building activities, to reinforce the desired cultural traits and norms. Consistent cadence in cultural activities helps embed the desired behaviors and mindset changes required for the pivot to be successful.

When it comes to transforming a business, speed is essential, but it's not everything. To ensure your changes are both sustainable and impactful, consider the three key elements of transformation: speed, cadence, and momentum. Speed refers to the pace at which you implement changes. It's important to be able to innovate and adapt quickly to new market demands. Cadence, on the other hand, is the consistent rhythm of innovation and iteration. Maintaining a steady flow of transformative actions is key to driving continuous improvement.

Momentum is the powerful drive that builds as disruptive changes take hold. It's the escalating force that propels your organization forward, fueled by ongoing innovation and adaptation. By keeping these three elements in mind, you can ensure that your transformation is not only swift but also sustainable and impactful.

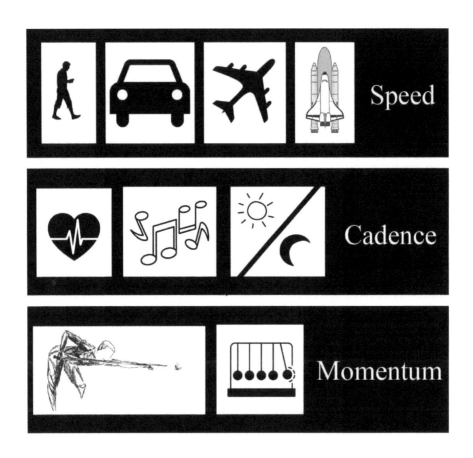

Figure 10.1. Speed vs. Cadence vs. Momentum.

Why Does Speed Matter in an AI Transformation?

Speed matters significantly in an AI transformation due to the dynamic nature of technological advancements and market competition. In the realm of AI, rapid progress is essential to keep pace with evolving technologies and stay ahead of competitors. The speed of implementing

AI solutions determines the organization's ability to leverage emerging opportunities, address challenges, and adapt to changing market demands effectively.

Let's use a common example in the industry where speed is paramount. In the world of information security, speed is key in both eliminating vulnerabilities and preventing fraud. AI-driven hacking techniques evolve rapidly, exploiting weaknesses in systems with alarming efficiency. Conversely, institutions must detect and halt fraudulent activities swiftly, leveraging AI tools to stay ahead. Speed is pivotal across risk management, innovation, solution implementation, scaling, and transformation. Rapid detection curtails financial losses and safeguards reputation. Innovating swiftly with new detection algorithms ensures that institutions stay ahead of evolving threats. Implementing these innovations at scale ensures widespread coverage and effectiveness, transforming traditional money management practices for enhanced security and resilience.

In addition, in AI transformations, it's crucial for organizations to outpace both the customer demand curve and the competitors' supply curve to stay ahead in the market. The customer demand curve represents the evolving needs and expectations of consumers, which are continually changing due to factors like technological advancements, market trends, and shifting preferences. To outpace this curve, organizations must anticipate future customer demands by leveraging AI to analyze data, identify patterns, and forecast trends. By proactively innovating and developing AI-driven solutions that meet emerging customer needs, organizations can stay ahead of the curve and maintain a competitive edge.

Similarly, the competitors' supply curve reflects the offerings and capabilities of other players in the market. To outpace this curve, organizations need to continuously improve and expand their AI capabilities to deliver superior products, services, and experiences compared to competitors. This involves investing in research and development, talent acquisition, and strategic partnerships to enhance AI infrastructure, algorithms, and applications. By innovating faster and more effectively than its competitors, organizations can capture market share, attract customers, and drive growth in the rapidly evolving landscape of AI technology.

Why Cadence Matters in AI Transformation

In an AI transformation, cadence plays a vital role in unlocking the optimal speed of a pivot by aligning coordinates with culture. Cadence refers to the rhythm or pace at which activities are carried out, and it ensures that the transformation progresses steadily and effectively over time. To achieve this, organizations must synchronize their activities with the broader organizational culture and strategic objectives.

Aligning coordinates with culture involves ensuring that all aspects of the transformation, including strategies, processes, and behaviors, are in harmony with the organization's values, norms, and goals. This alignment fosters a supportive environment where employees feel empowered to embrace change, collaborate effectively, and drive innovation.

Cadence helps maintain momentum—and momentum is crucial for driving meaningful progress in an AI transformation. In physics, momentum is a fundamental concept that describes the quantity of motion an object possesses. It basically describes how much power an object has when moving. By establishing a consistent rhythm of activities, organizations can sustain momentum (propulsion forward) and avoid disruptions or delays that can hinder progress.

Cadence strikes a balance between speed and momentum. On one hand, there is the need for speed to create AI capabilities across coordinates and in different parts of the other organization. The value of cadence is that it creates a consistent pace and a steady flow of work. When you create cadence across multiple levels of the organization, you achieve balance and cross-functional progress remains in sync. On the other hand, external forces like demand and the competitive landscape require not only speed and synchronized cadence but momentum to meet the markets in a way that makes monetization predictable and sustainable.

Why Cadence Is More Critical in AI Transformations

Cadence is even more critical in AI transformations compared to previous transformations due to the iterative nature of AI development, particularly in building large language models (LLMs) and training models for efficiency and improved decision-making. Unlike traditional transformations, AI projects require continuous iteration and refinement to achieve optimal results. For example, in building LLMs, researchers often need to train models repeatedly with vast amounts of data, adjusting parameters and algorithms along the way to enhance performance. The cadence at which these iterations occur directly impacts the speed and quality of model development. Similarly, in training AI models for efficiency and improved decision-making, regular updates and adjustments are necessary to adapt to changing data patterns and user requirements. Cadence ensures that these updates are implemented promptly and consistently, allowing organizations to stay agile and responsive in their AI transformations.

A structured and consistent cadence enables organizations to navigate the complexities of AI transformation effectively, stay ahead of the curve, and realize the full potential of AI technologies.

Using Momentum to Maximize Impact

In an AI transformation, leveraging the momentum that is triggered by speed and cadence can effectively maximize impacts on market delivery and return on investment (ROI) by ensuring a balance between speed and momentum.

In the context of AI implementation, leveraging momentum is critical to maximizing its impact. Momentum in this setting refers to the sustained progress and increasing velocity at which AI initiatives are developed, adopted, and integrated. By continuously building on each success, the organization can drive significant and compounding improvements across its operations. This proactive approach ensures that the benefits of AI, such as enhanced decision-making, increased efficiency, and innovation, are realized more quickly and effectively. Ultimately, leveraging momentum in AI implementation enables organizations to not only achieve immediate gains but also build a sustainable competitive advantage in the rapidly evolving digital landscape.

For example, the U.S. Department of Energy has committed substantial funding to AI/machine learning research in fusion energy and plasma sciences. Recent milestones, such as achieving fusion ignition, underscore the pivotal role of AI in advancing fusion research and unlocking its commercialization potential. AI not only accelerates the research process but also attracts private investment, driving the adoption of fusion technology for sustainable energy solutions. In essence, AI's speed and adaptability are revolutionizing nuclear fusion research, bringing us closer to realizing the promise of clean and limitless energy.[24] The point is, without AI, the research was moving at a speed and cadence that was slow. AI gave the project greater momentum and attracted larger investment.

Using Speed and Cadence to Enhance the Competitive Landscape

In an AI transformation, leveraging cadence and speed effectively can enhance the competitive landscape and drive teams to contribute to the North Star strategy and metrics by aligning actions with strategic goals and enabling rapid adaptation to market dynamics.

In an AI transformation, the strategic use of cadence and speed can profoundly impact the competitive landscape within the education sector while guiding teams toward achieving overarching strategic objectives and metrics.

The education industry grapples with multifaceted challenges like student engagement, personalized learning, and streamlining administrative processes. Leveraging AI technologies presents a promising avenue for addressing these issues by automating mundane tasks, tailoring learning experiences, and enhancing overall educational outcomes. Through consistent cadence and swift execution, educational institutions can effectively harness the potential of AI in various areas.

For instance, automated administrative processes can be streamlined through regular data updates and workflow automation, ensuring efficient handling of student registrations, attendance tracking, and grading. Similarly, personalized learning experiences can be optimized by regularly analyzing student performance data and swiftly adapting learning paths to cater to individual needs. Predictive analytics powered by AI enable institutions to proactively identify at-risk students and implement timely interventions to improve retention rates.

---

24   Department of Energy, "Department of Energy to Provide $21 million for Artificial Intelligence and Machine Learning Research on Fusion Energy," Energy.gov, August 19, 2020, https://www.energy.gov/articles/department-energy-provide-21-million-artificial-intelligence-and-machine-learning-research; Colton Poore, "Using AI to Wrangle Fusion Energy," Princeton University, May 10, 2024, https://engineering.princeton.edu/news/2024/05/10/using-ai-wrangle-fusion-energy.

Additionally, the availability of virtual teaching assistants ensures immediate support and guidance for students around the clock, enhancing overall satisfaction and support. To drive organizational departments toward the North Star strategy and metrics, institutions must foster alignment with educational objectives, promote data-driven decision-making, facilitate agile iterations, and encourage collaboration among cross-functional teams. By embracing a data-driven approach and capitalizing on AI speed, educational institutions can not only enhance their competitiveness but also advance strategic goals and ultimately elevate student success.

Using Speed and Cadence to Enhance Organizational Redesign

Cadence and speed are crucial factors in redesigning an organization to adopt and internalize AI effectively. In the context of AI integration, speed is essential because the technological landscape is evolving rapidly, and organizations need to adapt quickly to stay competitive. The pace at which decisions are made, strategies are implemented, and AI technologies are adopted directly impacts an organization's ability to seize opportunities and address challenges presented by AI-driven disruption.

Furthermore, cadence is equally important, as it ensures that the adoption of AI is not just a one-time event but rather a continuous and structured process. By establishing regular intervals for assessment, refinement, and optimization, cadence enables organizations to maintain momentum and sustain progress in their AI transformation journey. It provides the framework for systematic execution, allowing teams to iterate, learn from experiences, and make iterative improvements over time.

In combination, speed and cadence create a dynamic approach to organizational redesign for AI adoption. Speed ensures that organizations can keep pace with the rapid changes brought about by AI, while cadence ensures that this transformation is managed effectively over time, avoiding burnout and ensuring sustained progress. Together, they enable organizations to embrace AI as a fundamental part of their operations, driving innovation, efficiency, and competitive advantage in an increasingly AI-driven world.

Finding Your Coordinates: Altitude, Longitude, and Latitude

To leverage speed and cadence effectively in an AI transformation, a comprehensive reorganization of the company's organizational design is essential across hierarchy (altitude), business units (longitude), and functions (latitude). Beginning with altitude, flattening the hierarchical structure is crucial to facilitate quicker decision-making and enhance agility. This involves reducing management layers and empowering teams at lower levels to make autonomous decisions, fostering agile leadership practices, and establishing clear communication channels throughout the organization. In terms of longitude, promoting collaboration and integration among business units is paramount to breaking down silos and fostering cross-functional synergy. Creating interdisciplinary teams and aligning business units around common AI goals ensures that each unit contributes to the overall AI strategy, with centralized AI centers of excellence or innovation labs serving as hubs for driving strategy and knowledge sharing. Regarding latitude, integrating AI capabilities into core functions and processes is imperative, embedding AI expertise within functional teams and fostering cross-functional collaboration through AI task forces or working groups. Additionally, providing training and development opportunities to upskill employees across different functions in AI-related competencies fosters a culture of continuous learning and experimentation. By reorganizing the organizational design to address these structures, organizations can harness speed and cadence more effectively in their AI transformation, promoting agility, collaboration, and innovation across the board.

Empowering Employees to Use Speed and Cadence in Their Own Personal Transformations

Empowering employees to leverage speed and cadence in their own personal transformations during an AI transformation involves fostering a culture of continuous learning, agility, and self-improvement. There are several strategies to achieve this:

- **Provide training and development opportunities:** Offer comprehensive training programs and resources to help employees develop the skills and competencies needed to adapt to the AI transformation. This includes technical training on AI tools and technologies as well as soft skills training on agility, adaptability, and resilience.

- **Encourage experimentation and innovation:** Create a safe and supportive environment where employees feel empowered to experiment with new ideas, technologies, and approaches. Encourage them to take calculated risks, learn from failures, and iterate on their ideas to drive innovation and personal growth.

- **Set clear goals and expectations:** Clearly define individual goals and expectations aligned with the organization's AI transformation objectives. Provide employees with a roadmap for their personal transformations, outlining key milestones and timelines to guide their progress.

- **Promote continuous feedback and reflection:** Foster a culture of continuous feedback and reflection where employees regularly assess their progress, seek input from peers and mentors, and adjust their strategies as needed. Encourage managers to provide constructive feedback and support to help employees overcome challenges and achieve their goals.

- **Recognize and reward progress:** Recognize and reward employees who demonstrate agility, adaptability, and a willingness to embrace personal transformation. Celebrate successes and milestones, whether they involve mastering new skills, achieving professional growth, or driving positive outcomes for the organization.

- **Lead by example:** Leadership plays a crucial role in modeling the behaviors and attitudes associated with personal transformation. Leaders should demonstrate their commitment to continuous learning and improvement, actively seek out opportunities for growth, and encourage their teams to do the same.

- **Provide resources and support:** Ensure that employees have access to the resources, tools, and support they need to succeed in their personal transformations. This may include access to online learning platforms, mentorship programs, coaching sessions, and peer support networks.

Research conducted by the *Harvard Business Review* emphasizes the psychological impact of speed and cadence in organizational transformations, including those involving AI. According to the study, a structured approach to change management, characterized by a consistent cadence of activities and rapid decision-making, can significantly influence employee attitudes and behaviors. When organizations maintain a steady rhythm of communication, feedback, and iteration, employees are more likely to feel a sense of progress, ownership, and empowerment, leading to higher levels of engagement and performance. Furthermore, the study highlights the importance of balancing speed with careful planning and execution to avoid overwhelming employees and causing burnout. By leveraging speed and cadence effectively, organizations can create a supportive environment where employees feel motivated, adaptable, and resilient in the face of organizational transformation.[25]

Aligning Communication and Collaboration to Help Teams Embrace Cultural Shift

Cadence and speed are paramount when considering communication, collaboration, and cultural shifts across lines of business and silos within an organization, particularly concerning AI adoption.

Establishing a regular cadence of communication ensures that updates, progress reports, and insights related to AI adoption are consistently shared across departments and hierarchical levels. Speed in communication enables swift dissemination of crucial information, allowing stakeholders to stay informed, aligned, and engaged. Clear and timely communication fosters transparency, reduces uncertainty, and builds trust among employees, facilitating smoother AI adoption processes.

---

[25] Andrew White, Michael Smets, and Adam Canwell, "Organizational Transformation Is an Emotional Journey," Harvard Business Review, July 18, 2022, https://hbr.org/2022/07/organizational-transformation-is-an-emotional-journey; Ron Carucci, "Balancing the Company's Needs and Employee Satisfaction," November 1, 2019, https://hbr.org/2019/11/balancing-the-companys-needs-and-employee-satisfaction.

Speed is essential for fostering agile collaboration among teams working on AI initiatives. Rapid decision-making and execution enable cross-functional teams to respond promptly to challenges, iterate on ideas, and capitalize on emerging opportunities. A structured cadence of collaboration activities, such as regular meetings, workshops, and brainstorming sessions, facilitates the exchange of knowledge, expertise, and best practices, driving innovation and accelerating AI adoption across the organization.

Cadence and speed play crucial roles in driving cultural change within the organization to embrace AI. Regular communication and collaboration activities create momentum and reinforce the organization's commitment to innovation and digital transformation. Swift execution of AI projects demonstrates tangible progress and success, motivating employees to embrace new technologies and ways of working. Consistent reinforcement of AI-related values and behaviors through ongoing communication, training, and recognition initiatives helps embed a culture of continuous learning, adaptability, and experimentation, which is essential for successful AI adoption.

Additionally, speed and cadence are equally important for ensuring alignment and collaboration across diverse business units and silos within the organization. Rapid communication and decision-making enable quick responses to changing market conditions and customer needs, driving agility and competitiveness. A structured cadence of cross-functional collaboration activities encourages knowledge sharing, breaks down silos, and promotes a shared understanding of AI's potential impact and benefits across the organization. By prioritizing both speed and cadence in communication, collaboration, and cultural shift efforts, organizations can accelerate AI adoption, foster collaboration and innovation, and cultivate a culture that embraces change and drives sustainable growth in the AI-driven digital era.

Slowing Down

Slowing down an AI organizational transformation initially might seem counterintuitive, but it can ultimately accelerate the process and yield more sustainable results. One critical aspect of slowing down is the value it brings to retraining resources.

- **Quality over speed:** By slowing down, organizations can focus on the quality of their AI transformation efforts rather than rushing through them. This approach allows for more thorough planning, evaluation, and implementation of AI initiatives, reducing the likelihood of costly mistakes or setbacks in the long run. It provides the opportunity to assess the organization's readiness for AI adoption, identify potential barriers or challenges, and develop targeted strategies to address them effectively.

- **Retraining resources:** Slowing down enables organizations to allocate sufficient time and resources to retrain employees for the AI-driven future. Investing in comprehensive training programs and upskilling initiatives ensures that employees have the necessary knowledge, skills, and capabilities to leverage AI technologies effectively in their roles. By prioritizing retraining resources, organizations can mitigate resistance to change, increase employee buy-in and confidence, and foster a culture of continuous learning and innovation, which are essential for long-term success in the AI era.

- **Avoiding burnout:** Rapid transformations can often lead to employee burnout and disengagement, undermining the effectiveness of AI initiatives. Slowing down allows employees to adapt to changes at a manageable pace, reducing stress and fatigue associated with rapid change. It also provides opportunities for regular feedback, support, and course corrections, ensuring that employees feel supported throughout the transformation process and remain motivated to contribute to its success.

- **Ensuring alignment:** Slowing down allows organizations to ensure alignment between AI transformation efforts and broader business objectives, strategies, and values. It provides the opportunity to engage stakeholders across the organization, gather feedback, and make necessary adjustments to ensure that AI initiatives are aligned with organizational priorities and contribute to the achievement of strategic goals. This alignment is essential for driving sustainable growth and maximizing the value generated by AI technologies.

So What?

This chapter underscores the crucial role of speed, cadence, and momentum in AI transformation. These elements are key for maintaining competitiveness, aligning strategy, and fostering a dynamic organizational culture. In the AI-driven world, quick adaptation to technological advancements and market changes is essential. Speed enables rapid decision-making and implementation, cadence ensures structured and consistent efforts, and momentum drives ongoing progress.

By mastering speed, cadence, and momentum, organizations can effectively navigate AI complexities, spark innovation, and cultivate a culture of continuous improvement. Moreover, these factors boost employee morale by creating a sense of urgency and purpose. Without them, frustration and disengagement can set in, damaging productivity. Prioritizing these elements not only enhances strategic success but also creates a positive, empowering work environment that fuels employee satisfaction and well-being.

Now What?

To capitalize on the insights provided, organizations embarking on AI transformations should prioritize the integration of speed, cadence, and momentum into their strategic planning and execution processes.

Going slow will guarantee success for your competition. Going fast in one area and not the other will create frustrations in delivery teams. Going at the right speed by leveraging methodical cadence and maximizing momentum, leaders can achieve the highest value realization from AI.

Additionally, organizations should invest in training and development programs to equip employees with the skills and competencies needed to thrive in the AI-driven landscape. By empowering employees to embrace personal transformations and providing them with the necessary resources and support, organizations can create a workforce that is resilient, agile, and capable of driving success in the AI era.

As an employee, you need to embrace cadence in your own personal transformation. Time to own your future. Make your commitment below. How long will it take you to be where you want to be? What is your next iteration as you scale with AI?

My Cadence to the next role

Play
Months to Learn

_____

_____

Grow
Months to Practice

_____

_____

Date to start looking for a new role

Day: _____ Month: _____ Year: _____

Figure 10.2. Personal cadence.

EPILOGUE

CONGRATULATIONS ON FINISHING our book! Through the course of our careers we have been active participants in the enterprise technology evolution. It was one of the motivators for writing this book. We don't want to sit on the sidelines as big changes happen. We have also learned that the evolution of technology often comes with more unknowns than knowns. This book aims to clarify those unknowns for us and to enable us to share our insights with you. As AI continues to emerge as a driving force and AI adoption becomes more prevalent, we hope our book will help you learn and lead.

For us, success means that the essential ideas woven throughout this book resonate with you, including:

1. **AI for All:** This mindset acknowledges that AI will permeate every aspect of our lives, creating an ecosystem that nurtures learning, growth, and transformation.

2. **Humanity Drives Technology:** We believe that humans are the heart of AI. By actively engaging with AI, we can enhance our intelligence, shifting our mindset from fear to curiosity and from resistance to creativity.

3. **Scale Human Intelligence with AI:** Embracing AI empowers us to improve our decision-making and problem-solving abilities, opening doors to innovation. This transformation helps us lead change and seize growth opportunities within our communities and organizations.

4. **Own Your Future:** The time to act is now! With 300 million to 800 million jobs expected to change in the next five years, it's crucial not to get left behind. Only you can shape your future,

and we are here to support you on your journey into the world of AI!

We wrote this book to demystify, educate, and even entertain you about AI and its role in the world of humans and organizations. As we wrap up, we invite you to reflect on three important questions:

- Do I know about AI?
- Do I understand how AI will impact my life?
- Do I know how to turn AI into an opportunity?

Think about how your answers have evolved through the pages of *Own Your Future - AI for All.*

We hope you've experienced your own "aha" moments—those sparks of understanding that make everything click. Maybe it struck you when we explored AI's fascinating history and how far we've come. Perhaps it was during our deep dive into AI's building blocks that helped you grasp how those complex algorithms function. Or maybe it was the insights into measurements and metrics that illuminated just how crucial they are for assessing AI's effectiveness. These moments of clarity not only inform you but also empower you on your journey through the AI landscape.

As you navigate this world, consider the paths available to you. Are you leaning towards role transformation or personal growth? We see you as lifelong learners at different stages of your leadership journey.

For the **Learner** in you:

- What did our *Touchstone* chapter spark within you?
- Did AI become less daunting?
- Do you feel motivated to dive into AI now?
- As you read *Play with AI*, did a particular approach resonate with you? What's the first step you'll take?

For the **Leader** in you:

- How did our *PACT* framework influence your thinking?
- Do you see the potential to disrupt with AI in your organization?

- Are you starting to connect the dots between monetization and strategic pivots?
- Have you recognized the importance of aligning internal and external stakeholders?
- And most importantly, do you now appreciate that culture truly matters?
- When the time comes to transform, do you know who to reach out to?

And for **Everyone**:

- What's happening with your role and organization in this evolving landscape?
- Have you identified your coordinates?
- How quickly is your organization progressing along its AI journey? Are you keeping pace with the marketplace, or do you need to catch up?

As we did throughout the book, we will say our goodbyes with our most favorite "So What" and "Now What" commentary. We love using this construct, because it helps us reflect on our experiences and distill what we've learned into actionable insights. It's our go-to framework for turning moments of understanding into meaningful steps forward, ensuring we're always growing and adapting together.

So What?

For learners and leaders alike, now is the moment to assess your current position on your AI journey, align your goals with AI's potential, and prioritize where to invest your efforts. This is your chance to embrace innovation, stay competitive, and drive lasting growth in an AI-powered future.

Learners:

- **AI for Personal Growth:** Understanding AI helps you redefine your role and ambitions, making you more valuable in today's job market.

- **Personal Accountability:** Embracing AI encourages you to take charge and engage with new technologies proactively.

Leaders:

- **AI as a Competitive Edge:** Understanding AI helps you make better decisions on its adoption, setting your organization ahead of competitors for success.
- **Vision for AI Transformation:** A "North Star" optimized with AI accelerators, sets the direction and investment from the top, making it a true magnetic north for the company and its customers.

For Antara and Winnie, writing this book gave a new perspective.

Antara's So What: Her "Aha", is the awareness that augmentation is different from the automation driven initiatives she has experienced throughout most of her career. Automation refers to using technology to perform tasks without human intervention, streamlining processes and eliminating repetitive work. Augmentation, on the other hand, enhances human capabilities by leveraging AI to assist with decision-making, creativity, and problem-solving, allowing people to focus on higher-value tasks. For Antara, the opportunity in harvesting the power of augmentation, lies in using AI not just to replace tasks but to empower individuals and teams. By combining human intuition with AI's predictive, cognitive, and generative strengths, leaders can foster innovation, drive better decisions, and unlock new growth possibilities.

Winnie's So What: As Winnie reflects on this journey, she realizes how profoundly it has reinforced her belief in the limitless potential to learn, grow, and make a meaningful difference. This book symbolizes her commitment not only to AI, but to empowering others by sharing her evolving knowledge, insights, and personal experiences.

What truly stands out to Winnie is the realization that AI, as a technology, is not inherently difficult to understand. She reinforced this belief by completing the Designing AI Products and Services certificate at MIT after writing this book. Her true "aha" moment lies in recognizing that combining AI's potential with her deep experiences in operations, technology, and business processes opens doors to new transformation possibilities for herself and others. This blend of knowledge enables her to take bold steps forward on her transformation journey and lead organizations to maximize the potential of AI.

Now What?

It's time to take action based on your understanding of AI and your Willingness, Awareness and Readiness. Here's how:

For Individuals:

- **Define Your AI Touchstone:** Identify your personal connection to AI and how it affects your role.
- **Anticipate Changes:** Predict how your role may evolve and help others recognize how their role may change.
- **Choose Your Path:** Decide whether to play, grow, or disrupt.
- **Find Your Coordinates:** Identify where you fit in the AI landscape.

For Technologists:

- **Communicate Effectively:** Use this framework to explain AI concepts, focusing on monetization and user experience.
- **Build It Right:** Remember that just because you create something, it doesn't mean people will adopt it.

For Non-Techies:

- **Engage with AI:** Use these concepts to understand and discuss AI's impact on your organization, especially where there are opportunities for improvement.
- **Collaborate with Tech Partners:** Work together to harness the potential of new AI capabilities.
- **Know Your Customers:** Understand your customers' needs to identify monetization opportunities and improve experiences.

For Organizational Leaders:

AI offers countless choices, and with limited time and resources, it's essential to sequence your strategies, actions, and resources in a synchronized manner. To effectively navigate your next steps, consider the following framework, which integrates predictive, cognitive, and generative AI accelerators with strategic methods:

- **North Star:** Evaluate your North Star with an AI lens and embed the power of AI.
- **Choice Architecture:** Evaluate your options and design your decisions to choose the path forward.
- **PACT (Pivot-Align-Culture-Transform):** Apply our framework to ensure that your strategies align AI capabilities cohesively.
- **Coordinates:** Assess the collection of functions, departments, lines of business, and geographic locations to maximize the potential of AI for your organization.
- **Mastering Motion:** Optimize your speed to market while balancing cadence and momentum.

By aligning these methods, you can create a synchronized roadmap for leveraging AI effectively, driving innovation, and achieving sustainable growth.

The key message is clear: **Do something!**

Antara's Now What:

Antara's "Now What" will focus on empowering leaders of non-profits, small businesses, startups, and corporations to unlock the transformative potential of AI. She will help them embed AI into their strategic vision and guide C-suite leaders in maximizing monetization potential with speed and precision. Through consulting, mentoring, and coaching, she will illustrate how to leverage Predictive AI for smarter decisions, Cognitive AI to stay ahead of market shifts, and Generative AI to foster faster, more creative, innovation. By embracing these capabilities, they will unlock new opportunities, drive meaningful change, and future-proof their organizations for lasting success.

Her magnetic North - Make AI accessible to ALL.

Winnie's Now What:

Having laid the foundation with this book, Winnie's next step is to fully immerse herself in the AI-driven future and practice what she preaches. Committed to bringing others along on this journey, she aims to ensure that no one, whether individuals, small or large businesses, are left behind in the AI revolution. Winnie will use the strategies such as choice architecture and PACT and bring AI to life for all classes of organizations. These will help businesses know when and how to integrate AI into their operations, freeing up capacity to focus on growth-driving priorities. Her focus is helping businesses understand AI and strategically prioritize and incorporate it to enhance customer experiences and drive competitive success.

Winnie plans to stay current with advancements in AI through her own continuous learning, enabling her to apply this expertise in customized workshops and training programs. By sharing her knowledge and experiences, she hopes to inspire others to take bold steps in their own AI journeys. This phase goes beyond teaching AI concepts; it's about helping people create AI-driven solutions that align with their personal transformation goals. Winnie's mission is to make AI accessible and essential for future success, driving real impact and inspiring others to shape their AI path.

Her mantra is: Humanity drives technology. Now, let's make it happen.

Collectively, Antara and Winnie will work together to offer AI for All focused services to communities, academia, and businesses of all sizes. Workbooks, workshops and books are all in development. They are dedicated to helping organizations use AI to improve decision-making, streamline processes, and spark innovation. Their call to action is to continue demystifying AI, fostering curiosity and experimentation within teams across industries globally. By combining their expertise, they will create resources that help participants define their AI touchstones, engage with technological advancements, and implement and refine strategic frameworks such as choice architecture, North Star evaluations, and PACT integration. This approach ensures that everyone including techies, non-techies and executive leaders, can effectively and confidently harness the potential of AI.

Conclusion

As we wrap up, we hope this book has sparked your curiosity, deepened your understanding, and inspired you to take action. The journey with AI is just beginning, and whether you're leading an organization, growing a small business, or exploring new opportunities, the future is yours to shape. Stay curious, embrace change, and continue to push boundaries—because the world of AI is evolving, and so can you. We're excited to see where your journey takes you!

Connect with us!
https://www.linkedin.com/in/antaradutta/
https://www.linkedin.com/in/winniekroculick/

ABOUT THE AUTHOR

Antara

ANTARA DUTTA IS a prominent leader in the financial services sector, celebrated for her strategic foresight and transformative influence. At renowned institutions such as PayPal, Barclays, and JP Morgan Chase, she has led initiatives that have reshaped core banking platforms, enhanced client experiences, and drove innovation at scale resulting in substantial revenue growth and profitability.

As the founder of Ayuvia, Antara has made significant strides in healthcare by leveraging technology to improve access, efficiency, and care quality. Her vision for Ayuvia is centered on creating an inclusive healthcare system that offers equitable access to care for everyone, regardless of socioeconomic status or location.

Antara holds a Bachelor's degree in Computer Science from Texas A&M University, which underpins her technical expertise and strategic acumen. Her ongoing dedication to innovation and societal betterment continues to drive positive change in both the financial and healthcare sectors.

In addition to her corporate success, Antara is fiercely dedicated to social responsibility and advocacy. She actively mentors and supports women leaders and small business owners through programs like SCORE and Think MainStreet/WEThink. As President of SCORE, she has provided invaluable guidance to aspiring entrepreneurs, fostering an environment of empowerment and growth. Her advocacy for digital empowerment of small and medium-sized businesses highlights her belief in technology's transformative impact.

Antara is married to her soulmate Sam, a fellow first generation immigrant, who travel the world together every spare moment they find from their corporate lives in fintech.

https://www.linkedin.com/in/antaradutta/

Winnie

WINNIE KROCULICK IS a versatile transformation program and product leader, with over two decades of profound experience in steering outcomes within digital marketing, payments, acquisitions and servicing domains for Fortune 100 Financial Services Companies. Her narrative is characterized by a steadfast focus on strategic planning, seamless stakeholder communication, and the art of crafting compelling business cases, all of which have left their mark on the digital trajectories of major financial institutions.

She has occupied pivotal roles at large scale financial institutions including, Capital One, TD Bank, Citi and JP Morgan Chase where she led digital transformative efforts driving innovations focused on making the customer experience crisper, clearer and streamlined while erecting agile practices and frameworks designed to open throughput and bring more features and capabilities to market for consumers. Her contributions have ushered in a new era of operational efficiency and galvanized strategic alignment across multifarious teams and endeavors.

Winnie's purview extends beyond the confines of conventional program management and encompasses the delivery of strategic technology initiatives, test automation, and the orchestration of data and analytics solutions. Her ascendancy has been punctuated by a slew of prestigious accolades, including the esteemed Citi Leaders in Excellence award and the illustrious TD WOW award.

In her ongoing quest for excellence, Winnie remains deeply enmeshed in the fabric of organizational change leadership and mentoring initiatives, where her expertise serves as a guide for the advancement of women in project management. With an unwavering zeal for continuous learning and a keen eye for innovation, she remains at the vanguard of emerging technologies.

Winnie has her M.B.A. from Temple University and holds both a B.S. in Business Administration & Management and a B.A. in Speech Communications with a minor in Spanish from Kutztown University. She is a Certified Project Management Professional (PMP), holds a SAFe Agilist and SAFe Product Owner/Product Manager certifications. She also boosts a certification in Designing AI Products and Services from MIT. Her quest to learn and grow is never over.

She embraces a number of interests and hobbies outside of her professional passions, including hiking, mountain biking and skiing. Winnie is the proud mom to three young adults, whose journey to realizing their full potential is inspired by the boundless dedication and unwavering support of their mother. At home, she is supported by her husband, Michael, and their loving Goldendoodle, Giuseppe, who bring joy and warmth to their everyday lives.

https://www.linkedin.com/in/winniekroculick/

Together

ANTARA AND WINNIE met as colleagues and have built a relationship that extends beyond co-workers. They have been friends for over 20 years, sharing a profound passion for transformative change and its profound impact on both business and society. Recognizing the power of their shared vision, they have joined forces to bring their insights to readers through the groundbreaking book, "Own Your Future - AI for ALL". This collaboration represents the authors willingness to debate, research, grow and learn as technological and societal advancements move at a rapid pace. This collaboration represents not only their professional synergy but also their shared commitment to dispel the myth that AI is for technologists only. This collaboration truly represents the deep rooted desire to democratize AI for All.

GLOSSARY

A

- **Accountability**: The obligation of an individual or organization to account for its activities, accept responsibility, and disclose results in a transparent manner.
- **Accuracy**: The degree to which the result of a measurement, calculation, or specification conforms to the correct value or a standard.
- **Adapt**: The ability to adjust to new conditions or changes in the environment.
- **Agile**: A methodology in project management and software development that promotes continuous iteration, collaboration, and flexibility.
- **Aha**: A moment of sudden insight or discovery.
- **AI:** (Artificial Intelligence): The development of computer systems that can perform tasks typically requiring human intelligence, such as learning, problem-solving, language understanding, and decision-making.
- **Alexa**: Amazon's virtual assistant AI technology, used in various devices for voice interaction, music playback, making to-do lists, and more.
- **Align**: To arrange in a straight line or in correct relative positions; to bring into agreement or cooperation.
- **Altitude 1**: The height of an object or point in relation to sea level or ground level.
- **Altitude 2**: In the book, altitudes refer to an individual's level of expertise and influence within an organization. This concept

illustrates their role in leadership, innovation, and adaptability, showing how they contribute to the organization's goals at various levels.

- **Amplify1**: To increase or enhance the impact, importance, or effectiveness of something. In a business context, it often refers to boosting communication, influence, or performance to achieve greater results.
- **Amplify2**:In the book, "amplify" means enhancing organizational structures and practices to maximize the benefits of artificial intelligence. By coordinating efforts and adapting effectively, individuals and organizations can improve their effectiveness and resilience in the evolving AI landscape.
- **Analytics**: The systematic computational analysis of data or statistics to discover patterns, correlations, and insights.
- **API** (Application Programming Interface): A set of rules and protocols for building and interacting with software applications, allowing different systems to communicate.
- **Assess**: To evaluate or estimate the nature, ability, or quality of something.
- **Augmentation**: The process of making something greater by adding to it; in technology, it often refers to enhancing human capabilities with digital tools.
- **Automation**: The use of technology to perform tasks without human intervention, increasing efficiency and reducing errors.
- **Awareness**: The knowledge or perception of a situation or fact.
- **Axis 1**: An imaginary line about which a body rotates, or a fixed reference line for the measurement of coordinates.
- **Axis 2**: Axis: In the book, "axis" refers to foundational chapters that guide readers in understanding and using artificial intelligence (AI).

B

- **Behavioral Science**: The study of human behavior through systematic analysis and investigation.
- **Boundaries**: Limits that define acceptable behavior, responsibilities, and roles within relationships or organizations.

- **Broadcast Media**: Channels of communication, such as television and radio, that disseminate information to a wide audience.
- **Budget**: An estimate of income and expenditure for a set period of time.

C

- **Cadence**: The rhythm or flow of a sequence of actions or steps, often used in project management to describe the regular intervals at which tasks are completed.
- **CADIAG-IV:** A clinical decision support system designed to assist doctors in diagnosing diseases by analyzing medical data. It uses logical reasoning and probabilistic methods to suggest possible diagnoses based on patient symptoms, test results, and medical history.
- **Choice Quads**: A decision-making framework that involves evaluating options based on four key criteria or quadrants.
- **CICD (Continuous Integration/Continuous Deployment)**: A method in software development where code changes are automatically tested and deployed to production, ensuring rapid and reliable updates.
- **Cognitive**: Relating to mental processes such as thinking, learning, memory, and perception.
- **Collaboration**: The act of working together with one or more people to achieve a common goal, often involving sharing ideas and resources.
- **Comfort Zone**: A psychological state where a person feels at ease and in control, often leading to a lack of risk-taking and new experiences.
- **Communication**: The process of exchanging information, ideas, or feelings between individuals or groups through speaking, writing, or other mediums.
- **Community**: A group of people with common interests, values, or goals, often living in the same area or connected through shared activities.

- **Company**: A business organization that sells goods or services in exchange for money, typically structured as a corporation, partnership, or sole proprietorship.
- **Competitive Landscape**: The dynamic environment in which businesses operate, including the analysis of competitors, market trends, and strategic positioning.
- **Computer Vision**: A field of artificial intelligence that enables computers to interpret and process visual information from the world, similar to human vision.
- **Consumer**: An individual who purchases goods or services for personal use.
- **Coordinates -1**: Numerical values that define a specific point in space, often used in mapping and navigation.
- **Coordinates -2**: In the book, "coordinates" refer to a framework for understanding organizational design and scale factors, highlighting patterns in structures and the importance of knowing one's position as organizations adapt with artificial intelligence (AI).
- **Creativity**: The ability to generate new, original ideas or solutions by thinking outside traditional frameworks and approaches.
- **Crowdfunding**: A way to raise money from many people online to fund a project, business, or cause.
- **CSF**: Critical Success Factors, essential elements necessary for an organization to achieve its mission.
- **Culture**: The shared values, beliefs, behaviors, and practices of a group of people, often influencing their social interactions and way of life.
- **Curiosity**: A strong desire to explore, learn, and understand new concepts, often driving innovation and discovery.
- **Customer**: An individual or organization that purchases goods or services from a business.
- **Customer Experience**: The overall perception and satisfaction a customer has with a company's products, services, and interactions.

- **Customer Journey**: The complete experience a customer goes through when interacting with a company, from initial awareness to post-purchase support.
- **Customer Satisfaction**: A measure of how well a company's products or services meet or exceed customer expectations.

D

- **Demand**: The desire for a particular good or service backed by the ability to pay for it.
- **Department**: A distinct part of an organization with specific responsibilities.
- **DevOps**: A set of practices that combine software development (Dev) and IT operations (Ops) to shorten the development lifecycle.
- **Disruption:** A major change that shakes up existing processes or industries, often by introducing new technologies, business models, or ideas that transform how things are done.
- **Division**: A large and distinct unit within an organization.
- **Domain**: An area of knowledge or activity; in computing, a distinct subset of the internet with a common address suffix.
- **DVD**: Digital Versatile Disc, a type of optical storage media.

E

- **Economics**: The study of how societies use resources to produce goods and services and distribute them among individuals.
- **Effectivity**: The ability to produce a desired result.
- **Efficacy**: The ability to produce a desired or intended result.
- **Efficiency**: The ability to accomplish a task with minimal waste of time and resources.
- **Errors**: Mistakes or inaccuracies in data or processes.
- **Exponential**: Increasing rapidly by a constant proportion at each step.

F

- **Failures**: Instances where a process or system does not achieve its intended outcome.
- **FDD**: Feature-Driven Development, an iterative and incremental software development methodology.
- **FPGA**: Field-Programmable Gate Array, an integrated circuit that can be configured by the customer after manufacturing.
- **Framework**: A basic structure underlying a system, concept, or text.
- **Function**: A specific task or activity performed by a system or component.

G

- **Generative**: Relating to the production of new content or ideas, often used in the context of AI.
- **Goals**: Desired outcomes or targets that individuals or organizations aim to achieve.
- **Google Glass:** A wearable smart device developed by Google with a small display near the user's eye. It allows hands-free access to the internet, taking photos, recording videos, and using apps through voice commands and gestures.
- **Google's knowledge graph:** A large database used by Google to enhance search results by connecting information about people, places, and things. It helps provide quick, accurate answers and shows related facts based on these connections.
- **GPU**: Graphics Processing Unit, a specialized processor designed to accelerate graphics rendering.
- **Growth**: The process of increasing in size, number, value, or strength.

H

- **Hypothesis**: A proposed explanation for a phenomenon, to be tested through experimentation.

I

- **IaC**: Infrastructure as Code, the management of infrastructure through code rather than manual processes.
- **Image Recognition:** A technology that enables computers to identify and process images, recognizing objects, patterns, or features within them, often used in AI for tasks like photo tagging or facial recognition.
- **Income**: Money received, especially on a regular basis, for work or through investments.
- **Incremental**: Relating to small, gradual changes or additions.
- **Industry**: A group of businesses that produce similar products or services.
- **Insights**: Deep understanding of a situation or problem.
- **Integration**: The process of combining different systems or components to work together.
- **Intelligence**: The ability to acquire and apply knowledge and skills.
- **Interface**: A point where two systems, subjects, organizations, etc., meet and interact.

K

- **KPI**: (Key Performance Indicator): A measurable value used to assess how effectively a person, team, or organization is achieving specific goals. KPIs help track progress and performance in areas like business growth, customer satisfaction, or operational efficiency.

L

- **Latitude 1**: The angular distance of a place north or south of the earth's equator.
- **Latitude 2**: In the book, latitudes refer to leaders of functions within an organization, such as finance and marketing. They manage their areas and encourage collaboration to achieve organizational goals.

- **Leverage**: The use of various financial instruments or borrowed capital to increase the potential return of an investment.
- **Library**: A collection of resources, such as books or software, that are available for use.
- **Longitudes 1**: The angular distance of a place east or west of the prime meridian.
- **Longitudes 2**: In the book, longitudes represent leaders of specific business units within an organization, focused on managing products, services, or markets with independence while aligning with overall company goals.

M

- **Machine Learning**: A subset of AI that involves the development of algorithms that allow computers to learn from and make predictions based on data.
- **Margin**: The difference between the cost of producing something and its selling price.
- **Market**: A place or system in which commercial dealings are conducted.
- **Maturity**: The state of being fully developed or grown.
- **MBR**: Monthly Business Review, a regular meeting to review business performance.
- **Measurements**: The size, length, or amount of something, typically ascertained by comparing it with a standard.
- **Method**: A particular procedure for accomplishing or approaching something.
- **Metrics**: Standards of measurement by which efficiency, performance, progress, or quality of a plan, process, or product can be assessed.
- **Mission**: A specific task or goal assigned to a person or group.
- **Momentum**: The impetus gained by a moving object or process.
- **Monetization**: The process of earning revenue from an asset, business, or service.
- **Monitor**: To observe and check the progress or quality of something over a period of time.
- **Monopoly**: The exclusive possession or control of the supply or trade in a commodity or service.

- **MYCIN:** A 1970s expert system designed to help doctors diagnose and treat bacterial infections. It used patient data and rules to suggest treatments and influenced the development of medical AI.

N

- **NLTK**: Natural Language Toolkit, a suite of libraries and programs for symbolic and statistical natural language processing.
- **NLU**: Natural Language Understanding, a subfield of AI that focuses on machine reading comprehension.
- **North Star**: A guiding principle or goal that directs the course of an organization or individual.

O

- **Object Recognition:** A subset of image recognition, focusing on identifying and classifying specific objects within an image, such as cars, animals, or faces, used in AI applications like autonomous vehicles and security systems.
- **Opt-In Opt-Out**: A system where users can choose to participate (opt-in) or not participate (opt-out) in a service or program.
- **Organization Location**: The physical or virtual place where an organization operates.

P

- **PACT**: An agreement or treaty between two or more parties.
- **Personal**: Relating to an individual's private life and relationships.
- **Personalization**: The process of tailoring products, services, or experiences to individual users.
- **Pivot**: A fundamental change in strategy or approach.
- **Plan**: A detailed proposal for achieving something.
- **Polaroid**: A type of instant camera and film that produces a photograph shortly after taking the picture.
- **Precision**: The quality of being exact and accurate.

- **Predictive**: Relating to the ability to predict future events or trends.
- **Productivity**: The efficiency with which goods or services are produced.
- **Professional**: Relating to or connected with a profession.
- **Profit**: The financial gain made in a transaction or operation.
- **Prompt Engineering**: The process of designing and refining prompts to elicit desired responses from AI models.

Q

- **QBR**: Quarterly Business Review, a meeting held every quarter to review business performance and strategy.

R

- **Readiness**: The state of being fully prepared for something.
- **Revenue**: The income generated from normal business operations.
- **Risk - Reward**: The potential for loss or gain in an investment or decision.
- **Roadmap**: A plan or strategy intended to achieve a particular goal.
- **Robotics**: The branch of technology that deals with the design, construction, operation, and application of robots.
- **ROI**: Return on Investment, a measure of the profitability of an investment.

S

- **Scale**: The size or level of something, especially in comparison to something else.
- **Shareholder**: An individual or institution that owns shares in a company.
- **Siri**: Apple's virtual assistant AI technology
- **SpaCy**: An open-source software library built for advanced natural language processing (NLP) tasks. Written in Python and

Cython, it enables high-speed processing of large text datasets, making it ideal for developing models and deploying production applications such as document analysis, chatbots, and other NLP-based solutions.

- **Span of Control**: The number of subordinates or teams a manager directly oversees. It determines how many employees report to one manager, influencing organizational structure and decision-making.

Z

- **ZBB**: Zero-Based Budgeting - A budgeting method where every expense must be justified from scratch for each new period, rather than adjusting based on the previous year's budget. Each department starts with a "zero base" and builds a budget by justifying needs and costs.

CITATIONS

#	Citation	Page
1	Michelle Toh, "300 Million Jobs Could Be Affected by Latest Wave of AI," CNN, March 29, 2023, https://www.cnn.com/2023/03/29/tech/chatgpt-ai-automation-jobs-impact-intl-hnk/index.html	vi
2	Kweilin Ellingrud, Saurabh Sanghvi, Gurneet Singh Dandona, Anu Madgavcar, Michael Chui, Olivia White, and Paige Hasebe, "Generative AI and the Future of Work in America," McKinsey Global Institute, July 26, 2023, https://www.mckinsey.com/mgi/our-research/generative-ai-and-the-future-of-work-in-america	vi
3	B. J. Copeland, "Artificial Intelligence," Britannica, last updated March 25, 2024, https://www.britannica.com/technology/artificial-intelligence	4
4	"What is AI?," IBM, accessed March 27, 2024, https://www.ibm.com/topics/artificial-intelligence	4
5	Daniel Klein, "Mighty Mouse," MIT Technology Review, December 19, 2018, https://www.technologyreview.com/2018/12/19/138508/mighty-mouse/	5

6	Coursera staff, "The History of AI: A Timeline of Artificial Intelligence," Coursera, May 16, 2024, https://www.coursera.org/articles/history-of-ai	6
7	Radhika Wijendra, "AI Winter: Past, Present and Future," Medium, August 11, 2021, https://medium.com/@radhika_wijendra/ai-winter-955874b1f18c	7
8	Deborah Yao, "25 Years Ago Today: How Deep Blue vs. Kasparov Changed AI Forever," AI Business, May 11, 2022, https://aibusiness.com/ml/25-years-ago-today-how-deep-blue-vs-kasparov-changed-ai-forever	8
9	Javier Canales Luna, "What Is BERT? An Introduction to BERT Models," DataCamp, Radar AI Edition, November 2023, https://www.datacamp.com/blog/what-is-bert-an-intro-to-bert-models	10
10	Sydney Butler, "ChatGPT vs. GPT-3: What's the Difference?" How-to Geek, July 10, 2023, https://www.howtogeek.com/897570/chatgpt-vs.-gpt-3-whats-the-difference/	16
11	Stuart Brameld, "The North Star Metric & Framework," Grow the Method, February 2023, https://growthmethod.com/the-north-star-metric/	29
12	Petroc Taylor, "Annual Mobile Data Usage Worldwide from 2020 to 2027, By Device," Statista, April 27, 2023, https://www.statista.com/statistics/1370201/global-mobile-data-usage/; Kateryna Hanko, "35+ Must-Know Phone Usage Statistics for 2022," Clario, April 8, 2022, https://clario.co/blog/phone-usage-statistics/	33

13	Daniel Pereira, "Netflix Mission and Vision Statement," Business Model Analyst, June 22, 2023, https://businessmodelanalyst.com/netflix-mission-and-vision-statement/	35
14	"Netflix History: From DVD Rentals to Streaming Success," BBC, January 23, 2018, https://businessmodelanalyst.com/netflix-mission-and-vision-statement/; Roland Wijnen, "Netflix: How a DVD Rental Company Changed the Way We Spend Our Free Time," Business Models Inc. (blog post), accessed March 22, 2024, https://www.businessmodelsinc.com/en/inspiration/blogs/netflix-how-a-dvd-rental-company-changed-the-way-we-spend-our-free-time	35
15	Shruti Mishra, "Metric That Fueled Netflix's Ability to Become a Media Giant of 150 Billion USD," Medium, November 19, 2022, https://medium.com/@heyshrutimishra/metric-that-fueled-netflixs-ability-to-become-a-media-giant-of-150-billion-usd-7c719755ab65	36
16	Brian Dean, "Netflix Subscriber and Growth Statistics: How Many People Watch Netflix in 2023," Blacklinko, March 27, 2023, https://backlinko.com/netflix-users	36
17	Julia Stoll, "Quarterly Netflix Subscribers Count Worldwide 2013–2023," Statista, January 31, 2024, https://www.statista.com/statistics/250934/quarterly-number-of-netflix-streaming-subscribers-worldwide/	37
18	"Netflix Revenue 2010–2024 NFLX," Macrotrends, accessed June 7, 2024, https://www.macrotrends.net/stocks/charts/NFLX/netflix/revenue	37

19	Human Kinetics, "Definitions of Leisure, Play, and Recreation," accessed June 23, 2024, https://us.humankinetics.com/blogs/excerpt/definitions-of-leisure-play-and-recreation	122
20	Interaction Design Foundation, "What Are the Gestalt Principles?" accessed June 26, 2024, https://www.interaction-design.org/literature/topics/gestalt-principles	158
21	Wendy Whitman Cobb, "How Elon Musk's SpaceX Lowered Costs and Reduced Barriers to Space," The Wire Science, February 3, 2019, https://science.thewire.in/aerospace/how-elon-musks-spacex-lowered-costs-and-reduced-barriers-to-space/	177
22	Joseph Schumpeter, Capitalism, Socialism, and Democracy (New York: Harper and Brothers, 1942)	179
23	Nina Bai, "Going Beyond 'How Often Do You Feel Blue?'" Stanford Medicine Magazine 1 (April 29, 2024), https://stanmed.stanford.edu/ai-mental-crisis-prediction-intervention/	184
24	Department of Energy, "Department of Energy to Provide $21 million for Artificial Intelligence and Machine Learning Research on Fusion Energy," Energy.gov, August 19, 2020, https://www.energy.gov/articles/department-energy-provide-21-million-artificial-intelligence-and-machine-learning-research; Colton Poore, "Using AI to Wrangle Fusion Energy," Princeton University, May 10, 2024, https://engineering.princeton.edu/news/2024/05/10/using-ai-wrangle-fusion-energy	232

| 25 | Andrew White, Michael Smets, and Adam Canwell, "Organizational Transformation Is an Emotional Journey," Harvard Business Review, July 18, 2022, https://hbr.org/2022/07/organizational-transformation-is-an-emotional-journey; Ron Carucci, "Balancing the Company's Needs and Employee Satisfaction," November 1, 2019, https://hbr.org/2019/11/balancing-the-companys-needs-and-employee-satisfaction | 236 |